Conversation
Analysis and
Discourse Analysis

Conversation Analysis and Discourse Analysis

A Comparative and Critical Introduction

Robin Wooffitt

SAGE Publications

London ● Thousand Oaks ● New Delhi

First published 2005

Reprinted 2006

SAGE Publications Ltd
1 Oliver's Yard
55 City Road
London EC1Y 1SP

SAGE Publications Inc.
2455 Teller Road
Thousand Oaks, California 91320

SAGE Publications India Pvt Ltd
B-42, Panchsheel Enclave
Post Box 4109
New Delhi 110 017

British Library Cataloguing in Publication data

A catalogue record for this book is available from the British Library

ISBN-10 0-7619-7425-3   ISBN-13 978-0-7619-7425-3
ISBN-10 0-7619-7426-1 (pbk)   ISBN-13 978-0-7619-7426-0 (pbk)

Library of Congress Control Number 2004099541

Typeset by C&M Digitals (P) Ltd., Chennai, India
Printed on paper from sustainable resources
Printed in Great Britain by TJ International, Padstow, Cornwall

For Wendy

Contents

Acknowledgements

I would like to thank my commissioning editor at Sage, Michael Carmichael. Throughout the period of writing this book, he has been extremely helpful and supportive; we had numerous meetings at which we discussed the (occasionally slow) progress of the manuscript, and he always exuded a quiet confidence in the project, which invariably fired my enthusiasm. He's an excellent editor, and it has been a pleasure working with him. (He is also largely responsible for this book, probably much more so than most editors, for it was he who adroitly sidestepped my initial proposal to write a book on an entirely different topic, and gently suggested that I might like to consider writing something about the relationship between CA and DA. So it's his fault, really.)

There is a community of scholars whose work has had an important influence on my own, and their research figures prominently in the pages which follow; and whose company at various conferences around the world has been great fun. You know who you are. To all of you, for providing such a supportive intellectual and (extended) social environment, I thank you.

Derek Edwards and Jonathan Potter deserve a special mention. They read an earlier version of the manuscript and made numerous suggestions, all of which have made this a better piece of work.

Finally, my debt to Wendy Tunnicliffe is enormous. For too long, I've been a peripheral presence at weekends and in the evenings, and she has put up with that without complaint. The dedication of this book to her in no way settles the debt, but it's a start.

Introduction

This book has three objectives. First, it sets out to introduce conversation analysis (CA) and discourse analysis (DA) as methodological approaches to the study of talk, both of which have far-reaching implications for our understanding of social interaction and the role of discourse and communication in everyday life.

Conversation analysis is one of the key methodological approaches to the study of verbal interaction, and this is one of the reasons that it is given so much prominence in this book. But there are other approaches to the study of discourse and communication which can be applied to face-to-face or telephone interaction: of course there is discourse analysis; but there is also discursive psychology, rhetorical psychology, speech act theory, critical discourse analysis and Foucauldian forms of discourse analysis, or the analysis of discourses. This burgeoning range of empirical methodologies, not unsurprisingly, can be confusing to the student new to the field: In what ways do discourse analysis and conversation analysis differ? Is critical discourse analysis the same as Foucauldian discourse analysis? Do these varied approaches simply study the same things, but in different ways? Or do their theoretical assumptions ensure that the substantive topics of their enquiries are formulated in radically different ways? The second objective of the book, then, is to outline the distinctive characteristics of each approach – to explain for each, what is studied, why it is studied and how it is studied – and chart some of the complex relationships between them.

The third and final objective of the book is to make a case for the power and scope of conversation analysis.

There are now a number of texts which either focus on or contain introductions to discourse analysis (in its broadest sense) which offer an account of the various ways in which social scientists analyse talk and texts, or which illustrate specific methodological approaches (for example, Antaki, 1988; Banister *et al*, 1994; Burman and Parker, 1993a; Hayes, 1997; Phillips and Jørgensen, 2002; Richardson, 1996; Schiffrin, 1994; Smith, 2003; Willig, 1999, 2001a, 2001b; Wood and Kroeger, 2000), or which illustrate traditions of work in discourse and interaction (Jaworski and Coupland, 1999; Wetherell *et al*, 2001a, 2001b). These texts are extremely helpful and practical guides to issues in studies of discourse. However, while many of them acknowledge the empirical and theoretical variations in approaches to the study of discourse, few systematically focus on the tensions in the field, or argue for the value of one approach over others. And it is in this sense that this book departs from more conventional introductions. As will become apparent in later chapters, the argument is not impartial, but increasingly makes a case for the greater value of conversation analysis over alternative methodological approaches (a value which is reflected by its increasing influence in forms of discourse analysis). This is not because I believe other approaches have little or no value; on the contrary, a cursory examination of the literature in critical discourse analysis or Foucauldian discourse reveals committed, creative and thought-provoking research. And I am convinced that a researcher's conceptual sophistication and analytic skills can be increased by serious and sustained engagement with alternative positions and methods. But what remains as the fundamental issue – for me at least – is this question: analytically, what is the best way to understand everyday communicative activities? And for reasons which will become clear, I believe conversation analysis offers the most sophisticated and robust account of language in action.

There are tensions in writing a book which tries to outline in an objective and impartial way the similarities and differences between different methodologies, while at the same time crafting an argument which reflects a methodological preference. Throughout, I have tried to make the argument for conversation analysis by showing that it offers extremely valuable accounts of the organisation of verbal interaction, but also that it can make a significant contribution to research issues which are associated with scholars in other traditions. Only in one chapter (Chapter 8) is the argument for conversation analysis forged out of a direct engagement with the writings and empirical practices of other perspectives. But even here, I believe the argument is primarily responsive, in that it attempts to interrogate the adequacy of those methodological practices by comparison to which CA's own empirical stances are often held to be deficient. Here, as in the rest of the book, I have tried to be fair in my accounts of those perspectives about which I have some reservations; and at least the reader knows where I stand as they read what follows. But I sincerely hope that colleagues who work in other traditions, and who will no doubt disagree with me, find that my accounts fairly convey their research practices and objectives.

Overview of the book

The book is organised into three parts. Assuming no prior knowledge, the first four chapters introduce students to the way in which conversation analysis has transformed our understanding of how people interact together when they are talking. There will be a historical account of how Sacks' first came to study conversational interaction and a brief description of the key developments within the field since then, focusing on the distinctive character of CA's methodological orientations. These chapters emphasise the dynamic and action-oriented nature of utterances, the highly patterned nature of inter-actional sequences, and the socially organised communicative competencies which inform the way we conduct interaction.

These chapters also chart the historical emergence of the kind of work now known commonly as discourse analysis. The use of the term 'discourse analysis' will be traced back to Gilbert and Mulkay's studies in the sociology of scientific knowledge, the ethnomethodologically informed critique of cognitive psychology of Derek Edwards, and the adoption of DA by Mulkay's students, particularly Jonathan Potter in his work in psychology. We discuss Potter and Wetherell's key text, *Discourse and Social Psychology* (1987), showing how the method became more formalised and focused in their critique of broadly cog-nitivist approaches in social psychology. These chapters show how, even from its earliest days, conversation analytic findings and approaches were beginning to inform the focus of discourse analytic studies. The discussion will also highlight the interdisciplinary roots of the method, and consider some of the reasons why it has been less successful in sociology, ostensibly its 'host' discipline.

A feature of the book is that I have tried to trace the emergence and develop-ment of CA and DA comparatively: thus in each of the first four chapters there are discussions of aspects of both perspectives. This allows me to high-light that in the context of traditional social sciences, each approach can be seen as a fairly radical development. Moreover, it allows me to ground later arguments that there are significant differences between CA and DA. An assessment of points of convergence and divergence is offered in Chapter 4.

These first four chapters are designed for undergraduates with no prior knowledge of conversation or discourse analysis. To make these chapters more effective pedagogically, I focus on a smaller range of important points. This necessarily means that some important topics are excluded from the text. Consequently, at the end of each of these first four chapters, there are recom-mendations for further reading to allow interested readers to develop a wider understanding of CA and DA. The subsequent chapters build on the earlier ones and assume a more knowledgeable reader, and a wider range of issues are included in the text (along with relevant references), so no further readings are provided.

Chapters 5 and 6 outline two foci for discourse analytic research since its emergence in social psychology: the way that language can be used to produce factual or authoritative accounts; and discursive psychology, which investi-gates the use of a psychological vocabulary, and the invocations of mental or cognitive properties or attributes, as socially organised and interactionally oriented discursive activities. Chapter 7 departs from discourse analysis to cover critical discourse analysis and Foucauldian discourse analysis. However, I try to show the links between more Foucauldian DA and some of the goals of discourse analysis as it was developed in Potter and Wetherell's (1987) account. One of the features of this chapter is that I try to show the clear differences between conversation analytic research and the assumptions and methods of more critical discourse studies. This discussion allows me to sketch some of the main criticisms of CA's perspective on social interaction and its methodology.

In Chapters 8 and 9, I assess the strength of two related criticisms of conversation analysis: that its methodological practices are unnecessarily restrictive, and need to be supplemented by reference to post-structuralist writings on 'subject positions' in 'discourses'; and second, that CA is unable to address issues which motivate more traditional social sciences, such as the operation of power and injustices in social relationships. In Chapter 8, I argue that the preferred methodological practices of CA's critics are themselves unsatisfactory, and offer no obvious benefit. And in Chapter 9, I show that conversation analysts are perfectly capable of addressing issues such as power; and that its methodological resources have proved attractive to researchers outside CA for whom matters of power and oppression are a fundamental concern.

1
Origins and Orientations

In this chapter we will first examine the broader intellectual contexts in which conversation analysis (CA) and discourse analysis (DA) emerged. This provides some historical background, and allows us to identify just how novel and radical these developments were: they offered new ways of doing sociology, and placed the empirical study of communication at the heart of the social science enterprise. We start with conversation analysis.

Conversation analysis

The mode of analysis which subsequently grew into CA began with a puzzle.

The style of work which has come to be known as conversation analysis is associated with the pioneering research of Harvey Sacks. As Schegloff reports in his introduction to the published collection of Sacks' lectures (Schegloff, 1992a), Sacks had been examining a corpus of recorded telephone calls to the Los Angeles Suicide Prevention Center. One of the tasks of the Center's staff was to try to obtain the caller's name; and on many occasions, if they gave their name, they found that the callers would then identify themselves in reply. In many cases, however, the Center's staff had difficulty getting callers to state who they were: either callers would not say their name after the Center's staff had introduced themselves; or later, when explicitly asked for their name, they would refuse to disclose it. For the Center, then, the problem was getting callers to reveal their names.

Schegloff notes that for Sacks, however, a different issue became pressing. Displaying the original and distinctive approach that came to characterise his work, Sacks began to wonder 'where, in the course of the conversation could you tell that somebody would not give their name' (1992, vol. I: 3). With this puzzle in mind, Sacks became interested in the following opening section from one of the calls, in which the caller (B) seemed to be having trouble with the agent's name.

(1.1)   (Sacks, 1992, vol. I: 3)

> A: this is Mr. Smith, may I help you
> B: I can't hear you
> A: This is Mr <u>Smith</u>
> B: Smith

(You will notice that in A's second turn, the word 'Smith' is underlined. This indicates that the speaker has emphasised or stressed this word. In conversation analysis, transcripts try to capture not only what was said, but also the way it was said. Consequently, a series of symbols, such as underlining, have been used to capture, amongst other things, the way words are pronounced. We will discuss the rationale behind CA's distinctive approach to transcription later in this chapter; but at this point, it is advisable that readers consult the Appendix, in which CA transcription symbols are explained.)

Sacks began to examine the caller's utterance 'I can't hear you'. Instead of treating it as a straightforward report of a communication problem, he examined it to reveal what it might be doing. In particular, he wondered if this utterance was produced so as to allow the caller to avoid giving his name, while not explicitly having to refuse to do so. With this question, Sacks raised the possibility of investigating utterances as objects which speakers use to get things done in the course of their interactions with others.

Sacks observes that there are norms concerning where in conversation certain kinds of activities should happen; and in conversation between strangers names tend to be exchanged in initial turns. Developing this, Sacks argues that the caller is using the utterance 'I can't hear you' to fill the slot in the conversation where it would be expected that he return his name. However, he has not had to refuse to give his name: instead he has used that slot to initiate what is called a repair sequence, which is a short series of turns in which some 'trouble' (in this case, 'not hearing') is resolved. By doing 'not hearing', the caller has been able to move the conversation on from that point at which he might be expected to give his name. In this case, then, the caller's expression of an apparent hearing difficulty is a method by which he could accomplish the activity of 'not giving a name' without explicitly refusing to do so.

Sacks was not claiming that on every occasion when someone says 'I can't hear you' they are avoiding giving their name; nor was he saying that doing 'not hearing' was the only method of avoiding giving a name. He was simply noting that it was possible to analyse how, in this instance, this particular utterance performed this particular activity in this particular slot, or place in the interaction.

It is important to focus on the idea that there are slots in interaction where specific kinds of actions are appropriate, or expected. This is because it allows us to grasp the idea that verbal interaction has a structure, an architecture, which can be formally described by reference to the relationship between the actions our utterances perform. To illustrate this further, think of the number of utterance activities that seem to occur in pairs. As Sacks notes in his very first lecture, there are paired units such as greetings ('hi' – 'hi'); questions and answers; invitations and responses, and so on. We will discuss these paired units more formally in a later chapter, but the point to remember is that these paired actions seem to go together: answers seem appropriate responses to questions and so on. So much so that if a question has been asked and an answer is not offered, there seems to have been a minor breakdown in expectations which underpin interpersonal interaction. Look at the following data fragment which comes from a corpus of calls to the British Airways flight information service:

(1.2)   (From Woolffitt *et al*, 1997: 80. 'A' is the (female) British Airways agent, 'C' is the (male) caller, a member of the public. Modified transcript.)

```
 1  A:   British Airways flight information
 2          can I help you
 3          (1.3)
 4  A:   hel↑lo
 5  C:   hello
 6  A:   can I help you at al⌐l sir?
 7  C:                        ⌊oh yes (.) erm: I've got
 8          a note here to sort of find out about ehm:
 9          (1)
10          a flight from Gatwick
```

The BA agent has offered a service ('can I help you?') and the response is an acceptance or refusal; and as the caller has called the flight information service one can presume that he or she requires some kind of service. But there is no immediate response. Instead, after a delay of 1.3 seconds, the agent speaks again, saying 'hello' with a rising intonation.

This 'hello' is an economical utterance, as it performs two actions. First, it acts as a check if the line is still live (as in 'hello – is there anybody there?'). But it also addresses the possibility that the line is live but the caller is momentarily distracted and has not realised they have been connected (as in 'hello – I'm here'). The subsequent exchanges suggest that the caller had not realised he had been connected: he responds with another 'hello' and then the agent reissues the offer of a service and the caller then produces the request for information.

This reveals a lot about the architecture of interaction, and the attendant expectations. The agent has performed the action of offering a service, and the expected next action is an acceptance of the offer: in this case, a request for information. But this response is not forthcoming. The agent does not, however, simply connect to another call, but actively seeks a response: her 'hello' is designed to check that the line is still working, or perhaps to signal to a distracted caller that they have got through. The agent's action demonstrates her assumption that her turn created a slot in the world for a particular kind of next action from the caller; and that its absence is a noticeable and accountable matter: something which requires investigation and resolving.

When we talk, we produce utterances which perform actions, which in turn invite particular next kinds of actions (or which at least limit the range of actions which can come next without seeming unusual). In this sense, verbal interaction exhibits a structure: the shape and form of the ways in which contributions to interaction form a connected series of actions. And one of the tasks of conversation analysis is to discover and describe the architecture of this structure: the properties of the ways in which interaction proceeds through activities produced through successive turns.

Now compare this to a 'common sense' model of language and communication (and one that held sway in academic research for many decades): that it is simply a medium through which we pass thoughts (ideas, intentions, directions, information) between each other. In this model, language is simply a mechanism which transports cognitive 'stuff' between individual brains, and which is therefore a relatively unimportant feature of this process. And this is why Sacks' insights were so extraordinary: his preliminary observations on activities conducted in the opening exchanges in the call to the Suicide Prevention Center indicated that language in interaction had a *social* organisation with formal properties which were independent of whatever information might be in transit between the brains of the participants.

Sacks' initial observations on interaction were drawn from his analysis of the calls to the Suicide Prevention Center and recordings of therapy sessions with juvenile offenders. However, he and his colleagues, Emanuel Schegloff and Gail Jefferson, soon began to examine recordings of what might be termed mundane conversation. Their work began with the assumption that turns – lengthy utterances, phrases, clauses, or even single words – were systematically designed objects which performed some activities in interaction. The goal of analysis, then, was to investigate the nature of these objects – how they were designed, what they did, where in interaction they occurred, how they were connected to prior turns, and their implications for subsequent turns – and to describe the underlying organisation of the way interaction unfolded on a turn-by-turn basis.

The interest in how turns connected to each other led to a focus on *sequences* in interaction: regularities in the patterns of activities. To illustrate briefly we will examine the sequential organisation of two related kinds of events: starting and ending telephone conversations.

(It should be noted that what follows is taken from analyses of conversations on static or land line telephones, where the called party does not know who is calling. Some of the following observation, therefore, would not apply to interaction on mobile or cell phones, in which the handset identifies the caller by name or number.)

The following extract is taken from Schegloff's (1986) study of the stages in the openings of telephone interaction, and comes from a call between two friends.

(1.3) (From Schegloff, 1986: 114)

```
 1  (Telephone ringing)
 2  Nancy:  H'llo?
 3  Hyla:   Hi:,
 4  Nancy:  Hi::.
 5  Hyla:   How are yuhh=
 6  Nancy:  =Fi:ne how er you,
 7  Hyla:   Oka:┌y,
 8  Nancy:      └Goo:d,
 9          (0.4)
10  Hyla:   .mkhhh  ┌hh
11  Nancy:          └What's doin',
```

This extract illustrates what Schegloff (1986) calls 'core' phases of openings in telephone calls, each of which is organised around pairs of activities. First there is a summons–answer sequence (lines 1 and 2): the telephone acts as a summons and the called party responds accordingly. Then there is an identification–recognition sequence (lines 3 and 4), in this case achieved by voice recognition of the two 'Hi' components, thus obviating the need to state or check identities; and then there follows a sequence of reciprocated 'howareyous', at which point the caller moves to the first topic of the conversation: 'What's doin','. Schegloff shows how these paired units allow participants to deal with a range of business prior to moving into substantive topics. Moreover, he points out that this organisation provides an interpretative framework by which ostensible departures from these sequences can be accommodated by the participants.

Core sequences also inform the ways in which we negotiate an exit from telephone interaction (Button, 1987; Schegloff and Sacks, 1973). There is a pre-closing stage, in which participants each use items such as 'okay' in slots in which they could continue to talk (for example, by introducing another topic, or returning to an earlier topic), thus displaying they are passing on the opportunity for further contributions. Only when both participants have gone through pre-closing, do they move to terminal exchanges: reciprocated farewells.

(1.4) (From Button, 1987: 101–2)

```
P:  hhOh    ┌well than:ks ┌any way
V:           └I:'m so      └rry Pa:m
            (.)
P:  Okay,=                       pre-closing 1
V:  =Okay=                       pre-closing 2
P:  =Bye:                            terminal exchange 1
V:  =Bye.                            terminal exchange 2
    End of call
```

The sequences illustrated by these data fragments are not unique to these calls, or to these particular participants. They are regular practices through which we negotiate a specific range of activities: entry to and exit from telephone interaction.

Sacks was not the only one who was interested in the actions performed by language. At the University of Oxford, the British philosopher J.L. Austin was developing his Theory of Speech Acts at roughly the same time (although there is no indication that either was aware of the other's work). Austin focused on instances of specific types of sentences. He began by distinguishing between two types of utterances: constative utterances, which report some aspect of the world; and performative utterances, which perform a specific action. An example of a performative is 'I suggest you open the window', where saying these words is to perform the action of suggesting. Other examples are promises, warnings, declarations, and so on. He termed such utterances, speech acts. However, Austin made the distinction between performative and constative sentences only to allow him to show that it was untenable, which in turn allowed him to make the more substantial claim that there was a performative element to all spoken sentences. He then set about trying to describe the preconditions which would be required for a sentence to be said to have legitimately performed a certain kind of action (Austin, 1962).

Initially, it might seem that Austin and Sacks were developing much the same kinds of analytic concerns. However, there are significant differences. Scholars who built on Austin's Speech Act Theory tended to base their analysis on artificially constructed examples of sentences, whereas Sacks insisted on working on utterances (which may depart radically from properly formed grammatical sentences) taken from recordings of real-life interaction. But what was really distinctive about Sacks' work was that he was able to show the critical relationship between the kind of activity an utterance might be performing and its positioning in the flow of interaction. So, for example, Sacks' analysis of 'I can't hear you' was informed by an analysis of the normative expectation that, in conversations between strangers, especially in service encounters between representatives of a business or an agency and members of the public, names tend to be exchanged at the start. In that instance, 'I can't hear you' performed the activity of 'not giving a name' partly by virtue of its placement in a slot where reciprocal name exchange would be expected.

Sacks argued that intuition does not equip the researcher to anticipate the range of sequential contexts in which utterances might be produced. It was necessary, then, to study only naturally occurring data; and to examine the activities people perform with their utterances in the real-life situations. Audio-recording technology made collection of naturally occurring interaction relatively simple. Everyday speech, though, does not resemble fictional depictions of talk. It is not grammatically neat and tidy, but appears on the surface to be disorganised and messy. However, it was felt that it would be premature to decide prior to analysis which contributions were significant and

which could be excluded from analysis. All aspects of interaction – even those that seem on first inspection to be routine, 'accidental', or ungrammatical – had to be considered. This methodological principle transpired to be profoundly important: subsequent studies discovered that even the most minor or apparently irrelevant speech events may be interactionally significant, and exhibit a previously unimagined orderliness. However, it placed a burden on the transcription of data as it entailed not only transcribing the spoken words, but also those dysfluencies and non-lexical contributions which might normally be filtered out in some form of 'tidying up' process. This does mean that CA transcriptions may seem daunting to the untrained eye, but they are extraordinarily valuable resources in the analysis of audio data because they capture details which might be interactionally significant, but which would be omitted from more traditional transcriptions which merely focus on the spoken word.

Gail Jefferson devised a system of transcribing which uses symbols available on conventional typewriter and computer keyboards. It is particularly useful for capturing aspects of speech production and the temporal positioning of utterances relative to each other. The system focuses on, first, the properties of turn-taking, such as the onset of simultaneous speech and the timing of gaps within and between turns; and second, it captures features of the production of talk, such as emphasis, volume, the speed of delivery and the sound stretching.

To illustrate why a detailed transcript is so important, consider the two following extracts (1.5a and 1.5b). These come from a study of verbal interaction in laboratory based ESP (extra-sensory perception) parapsychology experiments (Wooffitt, 2003). During an earlier phase of the experiment, the subject had to describe the images and impressions which appeared in her consciousness during a set period of time. In the phase of the experiment from which this fragment is taken, the experimenter is reviewing the images the subject had reported earlier.

They are two different transcriptions of the same section of the experiment. The first is a conventional transcript which merely records the words spoken; the second comes from a retranscription using conversation analytic conventions.

(1.5a)   (From Wooffitt, 2003: 309. 'E' is the experimenter, 'S' is the subject.)

E: Something red, looks like it might be a porcupine with lots of spines standing up. And then a frog, a frog's face peering over something. A ghost coming out of a door or a chair like a mirror in a funny house. Shapes in this funny house and shapes look like bunny rabbits with weird ears. Then you said sheep lots of sheep.
S: I didn't know what it was
E: Okay. Something in the ceiling
      ((Continues))

(1.5b)

```
 1   E:   hh something re:d. ehrm:: i- looks like it might be a
 2        porcupine with lots of spines standing hhh standing up
 3   S:   yeah ˙hh
 4   E:   and then a frog=a frog's face peering over something
 5        (0.8)
 6   E:   hh a ghost? coming out of a door: or a chai:r (0.5) like a mirror. (.)
 7        in a funny house,
 8   S:   yeah=
 9   E:   =hh shapes (0.3) ahr:: are in this funny house
10        and shapes look like ehm ↑bunny rabbits with weird ears
11   S:   yeah (ch)hhuh huh ˙hhhh
12   E:   then you said sheep lots of sheep
13   S:   ˙hhhh (g)oads of sheep (pf)ah didn't know what
14        it was (hi-) ˙h⌐hhh (k)huh uh        ((smiley voice))
15   E:                 ⌊ok(h)a(h)y            ((smiley voice))
16        (0.5)
17   E:   huh
18        (3.5)
19   E:   okay ˙hh something in the ceiling
          ((continues))
```

The CA transcript captures a range of detail missed by the more conventional transcript. For example, the subject's turns in lines 3, 8 and 11 are included. These kinds of ostensibly 'minor' contributions and non-lexical items may be interactionally significant: even a minimal turn consisting only of one word can signal the speaker's understanding of the on-going interaction, and thereby facilitate or constrain the range of possible next turns other speakers may produce. The transcript also includes records of audible breathing. These are important because a sharp intake of breath can be heard as indicating that the speaker is about to start talking. The transcript records non-lexical items such as 'er', 'erm' and their variations. Again, research has shown that these kinds of items can perform delicate interactional tasks: for example, they display that the current turn might be on-going, thus establishing continued speakership rights (Jefferson, 1984a; Schegloff, 1981). The CA transcript indicates the way in which words are delivered. This has clear interactional consequences. For example, consider how the experimenter says 'bunny rabbits': '↑bunny rabbits'. The first part of 'bunny' is emphasised and the onset of the word is marked by a clear rising or 'punched up' intonation. Its unusual delivery marks it out as something for the recipient's attention. The transcript attempts to capture laughter and words which are produced in conjunction with breathy bubbles of laughter. It also seeks to identify those words that sound like they have been delivered through a mouth forming a smile, as indicated by the 'smiley voice' characterisation. Finally, conversation analysts take great care in transcribing sections of overlapping talk: moments when more than one participant is speaking at the same time. Although there is no instance of this in the fragment, there is overlapping activity. In line 14 the subject laughs at the oddness of the image she has reported. During this brief burst of laughter, the experimenter says 'okay', pronounced with a slight roll of breathy plosives: she is laughing at the same time. The use of the overlap bracket allows us to see that the onset of the experimenter's laughter begins just after the first contracted bubble of laughter in the subject's on-going turn. It is thus timed to coincide with the subject's laughter, and thus acts as a form of alignment and affiliation with the speaker's on-going talk (Jefferson *et al*, 1987).

There are many other features of the revised transcript which could be discussed: the importance of timing periods of absence of talk; the significance of elongated or stressed words, and so on. But it should be clear that careful transcription of the detail of what actually happens in interaction is an important methodological procedure. It is important to keep in mind, though, that CA is not simply the study of transcripts: it seeks to make sense of those events of which the transcription is a representation. The transcript is merely an aid (albeit a valuable one) in the analysis of the events recorded on tape.

Sacks' work was disseminated primarily through transcripts of his lectures at the universities of Irvine and Berkeley, which were distributed to scholars interested in his ideas. Although he did formally publish some of his work, his untimely death in 1975 meant that many of his ideas were only available from the lectures. Many of his lectures were prepared for formal publication by Gail Jefferson. Eventually, however, the lectures were published in their entirety (Sacks, 1992), and remain an invaluable resource for researchers.

Summary

- Conversation analysis developed from the work of Harvey Sacks.
- It examines language as social action.
- Talk-in-interaction is taken to be systematically organised and ordered.
- The primary data for research are audio (and, where necessary or appropriate, video) recordings of naturally occurring interaction. Transcripts assist the analysis of audio/video materials.
- The transcription system provides a detailed characterisation of 'messiness' of everyday interaction, focusing on speech production and turn-taking organisation.

Discourse analysis

The mode of analysis which subsequently grew into DA began with a problem.

Sociologists have had a long-standing interest in science and its relationship to wider society. They had studied a variety of topics: the organisation of the scientific community (Crane, 1972; Hagstrom, 1965); the norms of scientific practice (Merton, 1973); the relationship between science and public funding, and wider political developments (Sklair, 1973); and the processes which informed revolutionary developments in scientific knowledge (Kuhn, 1970).

Sociologists tended to adopt the view held in the scientific community that the content of scientific knowledge was a more or less accurate reflection of objective universal truths, and, therefore, unaffected by culture, context, the personalities or motivation of the scientists and so on. Thus sociologists did not try to analyse the reasons why scientists came to believe theories and findings which were taken to be true. It was assumed that failed or discredited scientific theories and findings did not reveal the objective properties of the universe; therefore, it followed that there must have been some other reasons why they were advanced or, indeed, initially supported. This is where the sociologists could be of use: they could discover the social factors which had led to scientists propounding unsound or false claims about the world.

During the 1970s, however, there was a radical development in the sociological study of science. Some sociologists began to argue that if they merely studied failed scientific endeavours, or rejected theories, then, inadvertently, they would merely be endorsing the scientific status quo, and not revealing how that status quo was established and maintained. Moreover, in the past scientific revolutions have occurred in which once-accepted paradigms are subsequently rejected; thus it seemed inappropriate and indeed hasty to accept the current state of scientific knowledge as the definitive account of the physical universe. Subsequently, many sociologists began to adopt a relativist position with respect to the factual status of the claims of the scientists. They wanted to explore the social dimensions which underpinned accepted or true scientific knowledge. This is not because as individuals they believed that, for example, claims about witchcraft and the laws of thermodynamics were equivalent. The relativist approach was *methodological* in that it allowed sociologists to study aspects of scientific work and knowledge production which had hitherto been regarded as beyond the scope of sociological investigation: everyday scientific practice, the production of scientific knowledge claims and their acceptance (or rejection) by the scientific community, and the ways in which scientific disputes were resolved (Collins, 1992; Collins and Pinch, 1982; Woolgar, 1988).

Although there were a variety of approaches within the sociology of scientific knowledge (SSK), what united them was a concern to reveal the underlying social processes through which knowledge claims were produced and validated by the scientific community. This, however, was tricky: once the scientific community reached a consensus about a particular theory or empirical claim, and it became accepted as part of the store of knowledge and found its way into textbooks, those processes were lost to sociological analysis. Consequently, sociologists became very interested in scientific disputes where a consensus had not yet emerged, because the social processes which underpinned knowledge production were still in operation, thereby making them available for sociological investigation.

Nigel Gilbert and Michael Mulkay were sociologists interested in one such scientific dispute. This was in an area of biochemistry concerned with the ways in which chemical and other kinds of energy are created, transported or stored within cell structures. In particular, the dispute was about a complex molecule called adenosine triphosphate (ATP), which animals, plants and bacteria use to store energy within the cell. Two theoretical positions had emerged regarding ATP. One theory suggested that its production required the presence of chemical intermediaries. The other position argued that chemical reactions in the cell wall were responsible for energy transfer. This was a significant dispute: eventually the latter theory prevailed, and its leading proponent was awarded a Nobel Prize. It also generated a substantial number of publications in scientific journals and presentations at academic conferences.

Gilbert and Mulkay collected various kinds of qualitative data. First, they tape recorded interviews with the leading researchers in the UK and the USA. They also collected approximately 400 articles from the research literature, plus the relevant sections of biochemistry textbooks. In addition to these formal materials, they also obtained a collection of private letters between the main figures working in the area.

At the outset of the project, they wanted to produce a single, definitive sociological account of the social processes which were at work in the way this community of scientists resolved this dispute. In the preface to the book they were subsequently to write, Gilbert and Mulkay described the genesis and original goals of their research.

> The research reported in this book was conceived when a scientist friend showed us a copy of a letter written by a biochemist which seemed to indicate by its tone that there was a raging, and, so we thought, sociologically interesting controversy going on in an area of biochemistry called 'oxidative phosphorylation'. Like other sociologists of science ... we assumed that part of the job of the sociologist was to strip away the formal side of the debate, and show what was *really* going on ... (Gilbert and Mulkay, 1984: vii; original italics)

But it was at this point that Gilbert and Mulkay recognised that they were facing a significant methodological problem: variability in the accounts. In their data, they observed that they had a variety of different versions of ostensibly the same things: different accounts of the importance of theoretical developments, and conflicting statements about the significance of experimental procedures and subsequent results. They also observed that there were different styles of accounts: some exhibited formal language and terminology, and emphasised the strict adherence to scientific procedure and its role in revealing an objective reality, while others employed a more informal tone, and focused on the relevance of such matters as scientists' biographies, personality and intellectual commitment. More significantly, it was not simply the case that different versions were produced by scientists in accordance with their membership of, or affiliation to, one side in the dispute: competing and conflicting accounts of social actions could be found in the discourse of the same scientists. Thus they found that

> ... chemiosmosis was both complex and simple. It was empirically grounded, yet based only on an aura of fact. Similarly, Gowan [a scientist involved in the dispute] was highly gifted scientifically yet incompetent in various respects, enormously industrious but also unwilling to make the necessary effort on a fundamental issue, putting forward criticisms of chemi-osmosis which clearly showed that he did not understand the hypothesis yet which required much further experimental exploration before the inadequacy could be demonstrated. (Gilbert and Mulkay, 1984: 73)

The very nature of their data, then, seemed to resist production of a single, harmonious sociological account.

Gilbert and Mulkay realised that the variability in interview accounts, and other kinds of textual or discursive materials, was not unique to their data, but was a feature of any sociological research which relied upon the use of accounts of action as an investigative resource. And indeed, even a cursory reflection will alert us to the extent of variability in everyday affairs. Our world is marked by dispute and disagreement: in courts, in television interviews, in political debate and in everyday social life. Mundane interaction is rife with arguments, accusa-tions, rebuttal, blamings, criticism and complaint. It is a perfectly normal feature of everyday life that we engage in arguments with other people. And of course, argumentative activity often revolves around disputes as to what the facts are: Did we arrange to meet at 7 o'clock or 8 o'clock? Is the rail service in the United Kingdom run down because of the actions of previous Conservative govern-ments or the policies of the present Labour government? Does the production of adenosine triphosphate require the presence of chemical intermediaries or not? And of course we are unable to resolve these kinds of disputes by reference to the facts of the matter because 'what the facts are' is precisely what is being disputed. The possibility of variation in and between versions of events is built into the fabric of everyday life. (See also Potter and Wetherell, 1987.)

So how do other qualitative studies which use discursive data yield coher-ent and definitive sociological accounts? Gilbert and Mulkay argued that a basic four-step procedure informs much qualitative sociological research and allows the analyst to overcome the problems posed by variability:

1 Obtain statements by interview or by observation in a natural setting.
2 Look for broad similarities between the statements.
3 If there are similarities which occur frequently, take these state-ments at face value, that is, as accurate accounts of what is really going on.
4 Construct a generalised version of participants' accounts of what is going on, and present this as one's own analytic conclusions.
  (Gilbert and Mulkay, 1984: 5)

Moreover, they note that analysts tend to perform three distinctive analytic procedures when organising the kinds of accounts which are found in interview data. First, people's own accounts are subsumed under more general concepts. For example, they cite a study by Blisset (1972) in which he claims that scientists' discourse which addresses 'manipulation, influence and manoeuvring' in scientific work constitute a form of *political* activity. Second, in qualitative sociological work there is a tendency to generalise; accounts about particular social actors or social actions are generalised to wider classes of actors or actions. Finally, and most crucially, it is assumed that analysts are able to identify which accounts in their data are more trustworthy, reliable or informative and, therefore, of greater analytic value. Putting it crudely, it was assumed that a 'real signal' of accurate or sociologically credible versions could be detected in, or would emerge from, the 'noise' of sociologically irrelevant distortion, and self-serving reports. This in turn rests upon the assumption that some accounts accurately represent an underlying social reality.

Gilbert and Mulkay were not convinced by these procedures. They identified several problems. First, they were uncomfortable with the assumption that the social scientist possesses sufficient expertise to distinguish the accurate or objective accounts from those which were partial or distorted. Moreover, this simply fostered a dependence upon the analysts' own interpretative efforts, the bases of which were often obscure or unstated.

Second, they rejected the idea which informs much sociological research that if a sufficient number of people say the same thing, then those accounts can be taken as unproblematically representing an objective state of affairs. Drawing from Halliday's (1978) work on the relationship between language and social context, they argued that it is necessary to acknowledge that any particular account or version of the world will be intimately related to the circumstances of its production. This has important implications. Regularities in participants' discourse may be due to similarities in the context of their production: for example, an interview arranged as part of a social science research project. And this in turn suggests that we should be cautious about treating regularities in discourse as literal descriptions of social action.

Third, Gilbert and Mulkay argued that conventional sociological research rests on a naive view of language in which it is assumed that any social event has one 'true' meaning. Alternatively they suggest that social activities are the 'repositories' of multiple meanings, by which they mean that the 'same' circumstances can be described in a variety of ways to emphasise different features. We can illustrate this important principle by considering Schegloff's discussion of some of the issues which inform how speakers in ordinary conversation formulate locations, or 'place'. He points out that any particular location may be described in a potentially inexhaustible variety of ways.

> Were I now to formulate where my notes are, it would be correct to say that they are: right in front of me, next to the telephone, on the desk, in my office, in the office, in Room 213, in Lewisohn Hall, on campus, at school,

> at Columbia, in Morningside Heights, on the upper West Side, in Manhattan, in New York City, in New York State, in the North east, on the Eastern seaboard, in the United States, etc. Each of these terms could in some sense be correct ... were its relevance provided for. (Schegloff, 1972b: 81)

This illustrates an important point: whenever we produce a description or refer to a place, object, event or state of affairs in the world, we invariably select from a range of possible words and phrases. In everyday interaction, this does not trouble us: we produce descriptions which are adequate for the practical purposes at hand. This further undermines sociological approaches which treat discourse as an unproblematic reflection of social or psychological reality. Descriptions, anecdotes, stories, comments, accounts – the kinds of linguistic events that occur in interview data – are constructions which not only depend upon the context in which they are produced, but will also reflect the functions they have been designed to perform. Consequently, 'it follows that discourse can never be taken as simply descriptive of the social action to which it refers, no matter how uniform particular segments of that discourse appear to be' (Gilbert and Mulkay, 1984: 7).

Gilbert and Mulkay argued that it was inappropriate that social scientists should ignore this feature of the social world just because it hampered the production of neat, coherent sociological stories. The complexities of accounting practices should themselves be addressed in sociological analysis, and not regarded as a problem to be resolved via various methodological practices. Indeed, they argued that it was necessary to give analytic prominence to variability in discourse, and the conditions which give rise to it, and to abandon the traditional social scientific goal of providing an account of 'what really happened'. Consequently, as an alternative to traditional sociological approaches which overlooked or obscured the variability and context dependence of accounts, Gilbert and Mulkay advocated discourse analysis: a method of analysis which focused entirely on participants' language.

Summary

- Discourse analysis emerged in the sociology of scientific knowledge.
- It established a departure from realist accounts of scientists' actions to a study of scientists' accounting practices.
- It proposes that language is used variably. Accounts are constructed from a range of descriptive possibilities, and are intimately tied to the context in which they are produced and the functions they perform.

Language use as topic: interdisciplinary implications

CA and DA suggest that the way we use language can be studied in its own right, but for different reasons. For Sacks, ordinary language can be analysed as a vehicle through which we perform interpersonal actions; moreover, these actions are organised socially: that is, they display regular patterns which emerge out of the contributions of different participants. For Gilbert and Mulkay, the focus on language was a consequence of their argument that accounts and descriptions cannot be treated as neutral representations of an objective social reality. In this section, I want to highlight the radical nature of these arguments by comparing them to the kinds of assumptions about language and communication which have had a powerful influence in linguistics, psychology and sociology.

Linguistics

A key strand of linguistic research developed from the writings of Noam Chomsky (Chomsky, 1965). He argued that there were two features to language. First, there is linguistic *competence*, a term he used to refer to the innate rules which inform the production of grammatically correct sentences. Second, there is linguistic *performance*: the actual use of our linguistic competencies. He argued that the goal of linguistics should be to study underlying linguistic competencies: the rules which inform the production of grammatical sentences. And the best way to do this was to rely on our own expert knowledge and intuition about language. This is because, first, we intuitively know that certain relationships between nouns, clauses, verbs, etc., are 'right', and others are 'wrong' or nonsensical; second, and more important, he argued that the performance of language – everyday speech – was chaotic and disorganised, and offered no insight to the underlying rules of language.

> Linguistic theory is concerned with an ideal speaker-hearer in a completely homogeneous speech-community, who knows its language perfectly and is unaffected by such grammatically irrelevant conditions as memory limitations, distractions, shifts of attention and interest, and errors (random or characteristic) in applying his knowledge of the language in actual performance. (Chomsky, 1965: 3)

For Chomsky, then, the focus was on the underlying structure of language; actual speech was viewed as disorderly, and therefore not worthy of serious study.

Sacks' key insight – and a clear finding from his studies and subsequent work in CA – is that ordinary mundane speech exhibits an extraordinary level of orderliness. Moreover, this orderliness is not determined by innate *cognitive* structures of language (although formal grammatical considerations clearly inform the design of utterances) but reflects a *socially organised* order of interpersonal action. Indeed, knowledge of underlying linguistic competence seems ill-equipped to allow us to understand the observable orderliness of everyday interaction.

Our linguistic competence clearly tells us that certain sequences of words do not belong to the English language: for example, the following data extracts come from Schegloff's (1987a) study of a phenomenon he identifies as 'recycled turn beginnings':

> 'I don't think they grow a I don' think they grow a culture to do a biopsy.'

> 'The school school book store doesn't carry anything anymore.'

> 'She teaches she teaches a course at City College in needlecrafts.'

In each case there is a short sequence in which a word or phrase is repeated: 'I don't think they grow a I don' think they grow a', 'school school', and 'she teaches she teaches'. Intuitively, we might assume that such instances are the product of some mistake or speech error – a corruption of our underlying speech competence. However, Schegloff's analysis shows that these recyclings are not random, nor errors of pronunciation. Rather, speakers produce these forms of partial repeats when a spate of someone else's talk overlaps with their own talk. The recycled component of the turn (the repeated word or phrase) invariably occurs just at the point at which the overlapping talk has stopped. For example, the first case comes from a conversation about the participants' sick friend.

(1.6)   (From Schegloff, 1987a: 75. Terminal overlap brackets added.)

```
R:  Well the uhm in fact they must have grown a culture, you know,
    they must've- I mean how long- he's been in the hospital
    for a few days, right? Takes a ⌜bout a week to grow a culture⌝
K:                                  ⌞I don't think they grow a    ⌟I don'
    think they grow a culture to do a biopsy.
```

So, these apparently ungrammatical features of language use do actually exhibit orderly properties. But the basis for this orderliness is not to be found at the level of language competence, but in language performance: in particular, the performance of language in specific interactional circumstances.

Psychology

In psychology, there are two broad approaches to language. Some psychologists study the social use of language. And, as we shall see in later chapters, this has become more common since the emergence of discourse analysis. But the dominant perspective in psychology mirrored the Chomskyian approach, in that it stressed the importance of cognition, particularly the study of physical structures in the brain which are associated with specific speech activities. So for example, in her excellent introductory textbook, Hayes (2000) illustrates psychological interest by discussing the cognitive operations which underpin an imaginary piece of social interaction:

> The operation of these language areas [in the brain] can be visualised by imagining what happens if you are reading a letter which you have just

received. A companion asks: 'Who's that from?' 'Oh, it's from Jane,' you reply, scanning the letter. 'She's moving house.' ... When you were reading the letter, the visual information from the page went to the visual cortex, and then to the angular gyrus and supramarginal gyrus for interpretation ... *From there it would go ... to Broca's area where you would formulate the speech plans and words which would express what you were wanting to say;* and then on to the motor cortex which would direct the muscular movements of your lips, tongue and larynx. (Hayes, 2000: 303; italics added)

Earlier in this chapter I contrasted Sacks' approach to language and interaction with a view which treats speech as a mere conduit for the exchange of information. This quote fleshes out some of the assumptions which inform this 'conduit' view of language use. For example, it suggests that spoken language works merely to deliver particles of information; moreover, it implies that these packages of information are preformed and complete before they are despatched via language into someone else's head. To paraphrase Schegloff (1989), language is assumed to have the same relationship to information or meaning that telephone cables have to the conversation conducted through them.

The problem with this view is that it diverts attention away from the subtle social activities which we conduct through talk, and indeed, for which our talk is designed. To illustrate this, let's return to Hayes' imaginary dialogue. It is important to state that both CA and DA strongly resist the analysis of artificial data, but in this case it allows us to focus on the differences between the psychological and social perspectives on language. So for this occasion only, we will pretend that the dialogue was a real exchange between real people.

We can reproduce the dialogue in the same way that naturally occurring data are written.

A: Who's that from?
B: Oh, it's from Jane. She's moving house.

In the psychological model, 'Oh, it's from Jane' is merely a vessel which acts as a carrier service for the information: 'Jane sent this letter'. But there is more to it than this. First, presumably Jane has a surname, and a title. These are equally relevant things which B could refer to when stating who the letter comes from: 'Oh, it's from Ms Smith' or 'Oh, it's from Jane Smith'. And we can presume that the sender and the recipient have some sort of relationship; so B's response could have been 'Oh it's from a friend' or 'from my friend Jane'. There is, then, variability in the kinds of ways even the most routine utterance could be constructed. But this raises an interesting question: what issues informed the design of B's utterance on this occasion? And to answer that we need to explore not the operations of neurons and blood flow in Broca's area, but the interactional tasks for which it has been designed.

Utterances are designed for a particular recipient, or group of recipients, in this case, A, B's 'companion'. B uses a single name reference to refer to the author of the letter. There is no further information to facilitate recognition: 'Jane from York', for example. Nor is there any indication that there might be lots of people called Jane who may have written the letter. This means that B's use of a single name presumes A will know who Jane is such that no further identification is needed other than 'Jane'. Moreover, it tells A that this person is someone s/he *should* be able to recognise from the single name referent. And this is a powerful method by which B can invoke and establish the nature of the relationship with A. By relying on a single word referent she can be seen to be invoking 'common knowledge' between them. So whatever the formal or legal status of the relationship is between B and A, this utterance invokes and thereby maintains a level of co-familiarity, and, therefore, intimacy.

Of course, this is not real interaction, but the point holds: the cognitive or neurological correlates of verbal interaction do not in themselves account for the form and shape of the utterances we use, and offer no insight as to the social context in which they are used, and the specific interactional tasks for which they are designed. Indeed, conversation analytic research suggests that the precise design of utterances is shaped by the requirements of the moment, rather than micro-neurological events in the head.

Sociology

Sociology is an empirical discipline concerned with the social organisation of individual and collective human action. One of the defining features of humans is that we possess sophisticated means of communication, of which the most important is the ability to talk. Our communicative competencies facilitate the intricate and complex interrelationships which sociologists seek to understand, whether these occur in the context of the family, at work, in education; or whether they concern class, gender or ethnic relations, and so on. Given the importance of communication, then, it might be expected that the study of language is at the heart of the sociological enterprise. But it is not, and never has been.

Despite being the disciplinary home of conversation analysis and discourse analysis, the sociological study of talk-in-interaction has not yet emerged as one of the central core topics of the discipline. Indeed, it would be fair to say that language has been largely invisible to the sociological eye. It is likely that 'people talking to each other' is so commonplace and taken-for-granted that its relationship to the 'self-evidently' important issues has not been explored. Indeed, language has often been treated as a canvas onto which are projected the effects of sociological factors, such as the participants' relationship, class, gender, status, and so on.

While language and communication have not been a *topic* of sociological research, it has been a central *resource* in the research process (an observation associated with the ethnomethodological critique of sociology; e.g., Zimmerman and Pollner, 1970). Sociologists routinely rely on verbal data for their studies: people's accounts and narratives are collected in semi-standard and informal interviews, and from focus group discussions; they are recalled and written down by ethnographers in the field; and discourse is culled from printed and written sources, such as newspapers, autobiographies and archives. And it is here that Gilbert and Mulkay's argument begins to bite. Put simply it is this: so much of what counts as sociological knowledge is produced from analysis of verbal and textual accounts. By and large, sociologists have treated these accounts as 'good enough' representations of either an external social reality, or an inner mental realm of attitudes and opinions. But if these accounts are not accurate indicators of the social world – indeed, if, as Gilbert and Mulkay claim, language is not a representational medium at all – we have to wonder about the status of sociology's knowledge claims. How can we trust a scientific endeavour that has misunderstood the nature of so much of its data?

Further readings

Texts on conversation analysis

Because this book is not exclusively focused on conversation analysis, it is not possible to discuss some key areas of CA research, such as preference organisation and repair; even those topics which we will consider, such as turn-taking and sequential organisation, can only be dealt with briefly. It is, therefore, advisable for readers to familiarise themselves with more in-depth introductions to CA. Good comprehensive accounts can be found in Hutchby and Wooffitt (1998) and ten Have (1999). Psathas (1995) offers a succinct guide. Short, sophisticated chapter-length introductions can be found in Drew (1994) and Heritage and Atkinson (1984). Heritage (1984a) offers an excellent introduction to CA in his superb account of ethnomethodology and its origins. An accessible introduction to Sacks' work can be found in Silverman (1998). A short but useful discussion of the relationship between CA, Goffman and Garfinkel can be found in Heritage (2001).

In this book we will not discuss in any detail the relationship between conversation analysis and ethnomethodological studies of sense-making practices. Those interested in the relationship between CA and ethnomethodology should first consult Garfinkel (1967) and Heritage (1984a); Clayman and Maynard (1995) offer a shorter account of the relationship.

Nor will we explore how the origins of CA were influenced by Goffman's studies of the moral and social order of everyday life. For those interested in Goffman, a key (early) text is Goffman (1959) which outlines his powerful use of dramaturgical metaphors in the study of mundane social life. Manning (1992) offers a very good oveview of Goffman's work. Hutchby and Wooffitt (1998) provide a brief introduction to the relationship between Goffman and CA; an extended and focused treatment can be found in Schegloff (1988a).

Texts on discourse analysis

The best argument for and overview of discourse analysis can be found in
Potter and Wetherell (1987). The following also offer useful introductions: Gill
(1996); Potter (1996b, 1997, 2003c); Willig (1999, 2001b) and Wood and Kroger
(2000). A more advanced account of DA, which is grounded in a critique of social
psychological studies of attributions, can be found in Edwards and Potter (1995). An
advanced account which traces its relevance in the sociology of scientific knowledge
can be found in Mulkay, Potter and Yearley (1982). The collection of papers in
Gilbert and Abell (1983) is a useful overview of the rationale for discourse analysis,
and indicates the range of critical responses to its arguments.

2
Two Key Studies

In this chapter we will consider two key studies to illustrate conversation analysis (CA) and discourse analysis (DA). The first is Sacks, Schegloff and Jefferson's (1974) study of the organisation of turn-taking in everyday inter-action, and the second is Gilbert and Mulkay's (1984) study of scientists' discourse about a dispute in biochemistry.

These two studies are not the only studies of their kind, nor were they the first of their kind to be published. Sacks' lectures on the organisation of conversation date back to 1964, and although they were not published col-lectively until 1992, they were available in mimiographed form during the 1960s. Moreover, Sacks and his colleagues were publishing the results of their studies during the late 1960s and early 1970s prior to the publication of their research on turn-taking. Similarly, Mulkay and his colleagues were developing discourse analysis as an approach in the sociological study of scientific knowl-edge in numerous publications during the early 1980s. But there are good reasons for choosing these studies to illustrate CA and DA.

Both studies have attained a distinctive prominence in their respective fields. Each study is regularly cited in contemporary research papers. This means that the value and influence of the research has not diminished since their original publication. More important, each study addresses many of the issues which have subsequently developed into core concerns for CA and DA, or which are closely associated with these approaches. So, Sacks et al's study has been chosen because it illustrates key methodological features of conver-sation analysis, such as the analysis of mundane verbal interaction as a sys-tematic and highly organised phenomenon, and close attention to the detail of naturally occurring activities. It also allows us to indicate some of the kinds of substantive issues which have been at the centre of conversation analytic research since Sacks' groundbreaking studies. Similarly, Gilbert and Mulkay's study of scientists' discourse enables us to outline key features of the DA approach: for example, the focus on the functional orientation of language use, the acknowledgement of variability in accounts, and the examination of broad regularities in the ways in which accounts are constructed. In this sense, these studies stand as excellent exemplars of conversation and discourse analysis. But they also stimulated and gave shape to subsequent research in their respective fields. This means that they allow us to draw more general observations about CA and DA.

Conversation analysis and the organisation of turn-taking

Turn-taking in ordinary conversation is a remarkable achievement. At the start of any period of interaction, neither party knows in advance how many turns they will take, what the topics will be or the order in which they will be addressed, how long each turn may be, whether or not someone else will join in, and if they do, how turns are to be allocated among the respective parties, and so on. Moreover, the length of a speaker's turn is not fixed at the start of the turn. Yet despite these and numerous other uncertainties, it is highly likely that turn transfer will be achieved in an orderly fashion: there will be very few periods where more than one party is talking, and these will be relatively short-lived, and successive turns will be built so as to minimise any gap or delay before the next speaker, indicating that there is an impressive degree of precision timing in the placement of turns in relation to each other. How is this degree of orderliness achieved?

Sacks, Schegloff and Jefferson described the kind of systematic procedures that participants were using to conduct turn transfer. The system they identified has turn construction components and a set of procedures for turn allocation.

Turn construction components

Turns at talk are built out of turn construction units (TCUs): these are syntactically bounded lexical, clausal, phrasal or sentential units. They are, loosely, the building blocks from which turns are constructed. In addition to grammatically complete sentences, turns can be built from single words, non-lexical utterances ('huh?'), single phrases and clauses. These latter three turn types are illustrated in the following three extracts. (Arrows indicate the relevant turn.)

(2.1)   *Single word turn* (From Sacks *et al*, 1974: 702, n. 12)

```
     Fern:  Well they're not comin'
 ->  Lana:  Who.
     Fern:  Uh Pam, unless the c'n find somebody.
```

(2.2)   *Single phrase turn* (From Sacks *et al*, 1974: 702, n. 12)

```
     Anna:  Was last night the first time you met Missiz Kelly?
            (1.0)
     Bea:   Met whom?
 ->  Anna:  Missiz Kelly.
     Bea:   Yes
```

(2.3) *Single clause turns* (From Sacks *et al*, 1974: 703, n. 12)

```
        A:  Uh you been down here before ┌havencha.
        B:                               └yeh.
->      A:  Where the sidewalk is?
        B:  Yeah,
```

These three extracts also illustrate a common feature of everyday interaction: the absence of any gaps between successive turns. With the exception of the one second gap in extract 2.2 (which arises because of a problem in the inter-action, namely Bea's failure to recognise the person named in the prior turn), there seems to be a remarkable degree of precision timing in the way consec-utive speakers initiate their turns.

How is this managed? How do next speakers know when it is appropriate to start their turn? A key factor in this achievement is our tacit, taken-for-granted knowledge about turn construction units. At the end of each turn construction unit there occurs a transition relevance place (TRP). A property of any turn con-struction unit is that, at its completion, another speaker may start: it is a place where turn-transfer may be initiated. We say that turn-transfer becomes relevant at the end of a turn construction unit to emphasise that it is not mandatory; rather, that if it is going to occur, this is where it is likely to happen. And as we shall see, speakers overwhelmingly try to initiate their turns at, or in close proximity to, transition relevance places. This demonstrates that we operate with a tacit understanding that initiating turn-transfer at these places is normatively appropriate. A second property of turn construction units is that once they are underway, we can can anticipate when they will end. Being able to project a forthcoming transition relevance place means that next speakers are able to time their turn initiations with some precision. This can result in multiple simultaneous starts by possible next speakers; for example:

(2.4) (From Sacks *et al*, 1974: 707)

```
    Mike:    I know who d' guy is =
    Vic:     = ┌He's ba::d,
    James:   = └You know the gu:y?
```

Procedures for turn allocation

The turn allocation procedures for conversation are distributed into two groups: those in which the current speaker selects the next speaker, and those in which the next speaker is self-selected. So, at the initial transition relevance place of a turn, the following options are relevant.

Rule 1(a)   If the current speaker has identified, or selected, a particular next speaker, then that speaker should take a turn at that place.

(2.5) (From Sacks *et al*, 1974: 717)

> S: Oscar did you work for somebody before you worked for Zappa?
> O: Yeh, many many. (3.0) Canned Heat for a year.

In this case, S uses a person's name to identify the appropriate next speaker.

> **Rule 1(b)** If no such selection has been made, then any next speaker may (but need not) self-select at that point. If self-selection occurs, then first speaker has the right to the turn.

(2.6) (From Sacks *et al*, 1974: 707)

> Lil: Bertha's lost on our scale, about fourteen pounds.
> D: Oh⌜::no::.
> Jean: ⌊Twelve pounds I think wasn't it?

Here Lil's announcement is not directed to a specific recipient, and thus two people select themselves as next speakers at the transition relevance place at the end of 'pounds'.

> **Rule 1(c)** If no next speaker has been selected, then alternatively the current speaker may, but need not, continue talking with another turn constructional unit, unless another speaker has self-selected, in which case that speaker gains the right to the turn.

(2.7) (From Sacks *et al*, 1974: 704)

> Ava: He, he 'n Jo were like on the outs, yih know?
>   (0.7)
> Ava: ⌜ So uh,
> Bee: ⌊They always are

Here, after Ava's observation, no next speaker has self-selected up to nearly a second into the onset of a transition relevance place. Then Ava attempts to continue her turn ('so' indicating that what follows is somehow connected to a prior turn), at the same time that Bee self-selects. Ava then abandons her turn.

> **Rule 2** Whichever option has operated, then rules 1(a)–(c) come into play again for the next transition relevance place.

The procedures for turn allocation are described in the original Sacks *et al*'s paper as a series of *rules*. Before we go on, however, it is necessary to discuss what they meant by the word 'rule'. They are not claiming to have identified a set of determinate rules the application of which governs turn-taking. Rather, speaker transfer is taken to be an accomplishment, achieved as a consequence of mutually coordinated speaker sensitivity to those procedures or conventions for effecting such change. It is locally managed by the parties involved, that is, an interactional achievement coordinated 'on the spot' (Schegloff, 1992c).

There are some distinctive features about the system identified by Sacks *et al*. It can be said to be context independent because it does not rely on particulars of the circumstance to operate. People manage turn-taking in the street or at work as well as in their homes; it occurs between lovers and friends as well as between colleagues and strangers; and it works in periods of economic boom as well as during recessions. However, this system is also context sensitive, in that any actual instantiation of these options will be managed on a turn-by-turn basis. This is because these turn-taking options become relevant at the completion of each and every turn construction unit (unless the current speaker has indicated that she is engaged in an activity which requires the temporary suspension of turn-taking, for example, telling a story or a joke).

How does this system account for the features of mundane conversation we discussed earlier? For example, it was noted that it is routinely the case that one party speaks at a time; furthermore, that although there are gaps in the conversation during occasions of speaker transfer, these are very rare; and finally, that although there are instances of more than one party speaking at the same time, these spates of overlapping talk are very brief.

We observed that one way to achieve turn-transfer is for the current speaker to select the next speaker. Consequently, co-participants have at a least one motivating reason for not speaking while someone else is speaking, and that is to monitor the turn in progress to see if they will be selected by the current speaker as the next speaker. In those cases in which the turn in progress has not selected a next speaker, then turn-transfer may commence at the first available transition relevance place. Potential next speakers must therefore monitor the turn in progress to locate the end of the turn construction unit. Thus there are two respects in which close monitoring of the on-going turn is built into the system. Close monitoring is impeded if possible next speakers are engaged in simultaneous verbal activities. Thus the system provides an account for the observation that only one party tends to speak at any time.

There are several ways in which the system ensures that gaps between turns are minimised. We have already noted that the completion of turn construction units can be anticipated. Possible next speakers can thus anticipate with some accuracy the impending arrival of transition relevance places, and thus initiate their turns accordingly. But there are other features of the system's organisation which ensures minimal between turn gaps. For example, if the next speaker is not selected in the turn in production, then potential next speakers may self-select at the first transition place. If there is more than one possible next speaker, there is a premium in starting to talk as early as possible to ensure possession of the floor. So, the system provides a motivation for potential next speakers to begin talking as close as possible to the completion of the first turn construction unit. Similarly, it is possible that the current speaker may self-select and continue beyond the transition place. So, again, to ensure possession of the floor, any co-participant who wishes to take a turn needs to start talking as early as possible at the next available turn transition place.

If a current speaker selects next, the person so selected not only has the rights to start talking, but is obliged to do so, insofar as she has been allocated a turn in which to speak. Gaps after turns in which the next speaker has been selected will be heard by co-participants as the absence of a specific person's talk. In such instances, the absence of talk is a normatively accountable matter, in that negative inferences may be drawn about the speakers because they are not taking a turn allocated to them. Thus the system encourages allocated next speakers to start their turn at the earliest point.

This system also furnishes similar explanations for occasions in which more than one party is speaking, and also the briefness of such spates of overlapping talk. Because participants can project the onset of places where turn-transfer may be attempted, they are able to start up their talk just prior to the end of the current TCU. The following extract, from Pomerantz's study of responses to assessments, illustrates this.

(2.8)   (From Pomerantz, 1984: 59)

```
A:  Adeline's such a swell ⌐gal
P:                         └Oh God, wha̲dda gal
```

Overlaps can also arise when there is a 'collision' of a next speaker starting at a transition relevance place and the current speaker adding further turn components which do not significantly continue the turn. These non-continuing components can be tag questions (such as 'isn't it', 'didn't we', and so on), word repetitions, and politeness items. To illustrate, consider the next three extracts, which come from a corpus of calls to the British Airways flight information service.

(2.9)   (From Wooffitt *et al*, 1997: 107. 'A' is the British Airways flight information agent, and 'C' is the caller.)

```
14   A:  yes we've got the bee ay zero five six
15   C:  bee ay zero five six
16   A:  to arrive at oh seven hundred in the morning
17   C:  oh seven hundred and which uh
18       which te ⌐rminal⌐is it
19   A:           └·hh   └terminal four
```

The caller begins to ask a question concerning the terminal at which a particular flight will arrive. Before this turn is complete, the agent is able to predict that the next TRP will come at the end of the word 'terminal'. Evidence for this comes from the agent's in-breath after the initial sound of the word 'terminal', indicating she is gearing up to speak. She begins her next turn right at the anticipated end of the turn construction unit 'which terminal'. However, the caller's addition of a further component ('is it') at the TRP results in a short period of overlapping talk.

(2.10)   (From Wooffitt *et al*, 1997: 115)

```
127   A:   does he know you,
128   C:   yes he does ┌he does
129   A:              └right
```

Here, the overlap arises because the agent initiates her turn at the transition relevance place following the turn construction unit 'yes he does', at the same time that the caller repeats her last two words.

(2.11)   (From Wooffitt *et al*, 1997: 109)

```
10   A:   yes the four three one from amsterdam
11        came in at thirteen oh five madam
12        (1)
13   C:   thirteen oh five I ┌ovely thank you very
14   A:                     └that's right
15   C:   much indeed for your help
```

Here in line 13 the caller repeats the information the agent has provided. Pretty much at the anticipated end of the turn construction unit in which the repeat is done, the agent confirms the information, and thus overlaps with the caller who has now initiated another turn construction unit to thank the agent.

Jefferson has conducted extensive analyses of the organisation of overlapping talk (Jefferson, 1983, 1986). The clear finding from her studies is that instances of overlap are either the result of next speakers starting in anticipation of the forthcoming transition relevant place, or the consequence of speakers orienting to the relevance of different aspects of the rule set identified by Sacks *et al*. Routinely, then, instances of overlapping talk transpire to be an orderly consequence of that system, not a deviation from it.

The turn-by-turn development of interaction is not simply a series of utterances coming one after another from different participants. There are connections between turns which yield describable and consistent properties. To illustrate this we need to go back to Rule 1(a) of the model outlined by Sacks *et al*, and consider one powerful method by which a current speaker can select a next speaker.

In extract 2.5, S asks the question, 'Oscar did you work for somebody before you worked for Zappa?' and thereby issues the first part of a question–answer *paired action sequence*.

Intuitively, it seems that some kinds of conversational actions belong with each other. Greetings, such as 'hi'–'hi', seem to form a 'natural' pair. It also seems natural that questions will be followed by answers, and that offers will be followed by acceptances (or refusals), and so on. Right from the start of his studies of interaction Sacks was interested in these kinds of paired units. To provide a formal account of their generic properties, Sacks proposed the concept of the *adjacency pair* (more formally outlined in Schegloff and Sacks, 1973). Heritage (1984a) provides the following formulation. An adjacency pair is a sequence of two utterances which are adjacent, produced by different speakers, ordered as a first part and second part and typed, so that a first part requires a particular second, or range of second parts (Heritage, 1984a: 246). An invitation, then, would be the first part of an invitation–response pair, a question the first part of a question–answer pair, and a greeting the first part of a greeting–greeting pair.

There is a normative relationship between the turns that constitute paired sequences. A speaker's production of the first part of a pair generates the expectation that an allocated next speaker *should* produce the appropriate second part. The second part of a pair is said to be conditionally relevant after the production of a first part (Schegloff, 1972a). So, if a next speaker is selected via the first part of a pair, not only are they obliged to speak, but they will be expected to provide the appropriate second pair part, or an account for its absence.

Heritage (1984a: 247–53) discusses various kinds of evidence that participants in interaction are sensitive to these expectations. We will discuss just one: what happens when a first part of a pair has been produced, but the appropriate next part is not forthcoming. In extract 2.12, a child has asked her mother a question. After a gap of over a second, the mother has not answered, and the child speaks again.

(2.12)   (From Atkinson and Drew, 1979: 52; discussed in Heritage, 1984a: 248–9)

Child:	Have to cut the:se Mummy
	(1.3)
Child:	Won't we Mummy
	(1.5)
Child:	Won't we
Mother:	Yes

Had the child interpreted the mother's silence as indicating that she hadn't heard the question, it is likely that it would have been repeated, perhaps louder. Instead, the child provides increasingly truncated versions of the initial question.

This indicates that she is proceeding on the assumption that Mother has heard but has not answered. The normative expectation that the appropriate second part should be produced is still in force. The child's next two utterances thus constitute prompts to her mother to produce the now conditionally relevant appropriate second part. This illustrates a common phenomenon: first speakers will pursue the absent second part, thus displaying their tacit understanding that its absence is noticeable because it breaches a norm of paired action sequences.

This extract also illustrates a broader feature of the way interaction develops on a turn-by-turn basis. The child's subsequent turns exhibit her understanding of the current state-of-play at that precise moment in the interaction with her mother. That is, the design of her turn displays her interpretation of her mother's (non-)response. This is an intrinsic feature of interaction: the way we design our turns unavoidably displays the kind of inferences we are making. Heritage makes this point by reference to the following extract:

(2.13)   (From Heritage, 1984a: 254–5)

```
B:  Why don't you come and see me some ┌ times
A:                                      └ I would like to
```

As Heritage notes, B's turn 'Why don't you come and see me sometimes' could be interpreted in a number of ways: as an invitation, or as a genuine question, or as a complaint, and so on. But A's response displays her understanding of the activity performed by the prior turn. She produces an acceptance; this strongly suggests that she was interpreting B's prior turn as an invitation. In this sense, our on-going interpretations of interaction are publicly visible, as each turn successively exhibits its producers' interpretation of the prior turn (or, less commonly, a turn other than the immediately prior turn).

This is a valuable resource in establishing mutual intelligibility. Next positioning of utterances allows participants in interaction to monitor each other's understanding on a turn-by-turn basis. Through successive turns, participants can establish and revise their understanding of the interaction. It also provides the basis upon which misunderstandings can be identified and addressed. Moreover, next positioning is a significant methodological resource for the analyst: analytic claims about the organisation of participants' sense-making activities can be derived from inspection of, and warranted by reference to, the observable activities of the participants themselves. This in turn means that the analyst is liberated from having to make interpretative claims on behalf of the participants whose interaction is being studied (Sacks *et al*, 1974: 728–9).

Other approaches to the study of oral communication

One of the objectives of this book is to assess different ways of studying how people talk to each other in everyday and more formal settings. So, as we progress through the book we will consider a range of approaches to the study of language use in interaction. However, the study of language use is a wider and more diverse field than can be accommodated within this book. For example, in a review of methodologies for studying discourse, Schiffrin (1994) identifies:

- Speech Act Theory: the study of the activities performed by utterances and the investigation of the pre-conditions necessary for an utterance to be interpreted as a particular kind of act;
- interactional sociolinguistics: the analysis of the ways in which common grammatical knowledge may be mobilised by different social or ethnic groups, leading to misalignment in understanding, or the ways in which particular linguistic features are produced for particular settings and contexts;
- the ethnography of communication: a broadly anthropologically oriented approach which investigates communicative competencies specific to different cultures;
- pragmatics: the branch of linguistics which studies language use, as opposed to the structure of language;
- conversation analysis: the analysis of the sequential organisation of inter-action; and
- variation analysis: the formal investigation of the ways in which language use varies and changes between groups and across time.

This list reflects the range of methodological and substantive perspectives common to communication researchers in North America. But even this excludes approaches to language use conducted in experimental psychology. Furthermore, to this list we could add those approaches more associated with European communication research, such as that kind of discourse analysis which draws from linguistics (a brief discussion of which comes later in this chapter), the discourse analysis associated with Gilbert and Mulkay, Edwards, Potter and Wetherell, critical discourse analysis and Foucaldian discourse analysis (all of which receive extended treatments in this book).

There are, then, a range of approaches to the study of language use, communication and interaction. This book, though, has a specific focus on the relationship between CA and DA, and we will not have time to cover other approaches. But it is important for readers to be aware that there are methodologies and perspectives other than those being discussed in this book. To get a sense of the range and style of communication research being undertaken in addition to conversation analysis and discourse analysis, readers are advised to consult journals such as *Discourse and Society, Discourse Processes, Discourse Studies, Human Communication Research*, the *Journal of Language and Social Psychology*, the *Journal of Sociolinguistics, Language in Society, Language Variation and Change*, the *Journal of Pragmatics, Semiotica, Text*, the *Western Journal of Communication*, and the *Quarterly Journal of Speech*.

Summary

- Sacks *et al*'s study of turn-taking focused on the structure of turn design, and showed that speakers orient to particular locations in talk as places where turn-transfer may be initiated.
- Their study illustrated some of the normative conventions which underpin turn-transfer.
- Paired action sequences are fundamental units of interaction.
- CA examines how speakers' conduct displays a sensitivity to the normative expectations associated with sequential organisations, such as paired action sequences.
- There is a focus on people's own interpretation of on-going interaction as revealed in turn-by-turn unfolding of conversation.

Discourse analysis and interpretative repertoires in scientists' discourse

Gilbert and Mulkay's discourse analysis was based on the recognition of the variability in, and the context dependence of, participants' discourse. Their analytic goal was to discover the systematic features of scientists' discourse by which accounts of beliefs and actions were organised in 'contextually appropriate ways' (1984: 14). They were concerned with two kinds of contexts in which scientific discourse was produced: formal contexts, such as research papers published in academic journals; and informal contexts, such as interviews. They argued that for the purpose of analysis, no form of discourse could be considered to be superior to any other. The analyst was obliged, therefore, to consider all forms of discourse, thus having to address a wider range of data than was common in conventional sociological research.

Gilbert and Mulkay found that scientists' discourse in formal academic journals was systematically different from the discourse generated in informal interviews. It is important to keep in mind, though, that they were not claiming that the context should be viewed as somehow 'standing apart' from the discourse which occurs within it; nor that the context of discourse determines the features of accounts. Rather, they were indicating that these distinctive patterns of description construct and constitute the context, be that 'informal interaction' or 'formal research literature'.

Scientists constructed the formal and informal contexts through the use of two 'interpretative repertoires'. These are 'recurrently used systems of terms used for characterizing and evaluating actions, events and other phenomena' (Potter and Wetherell, 1987: 149). Repertoires may be characterised by a distinctive vocabulary, particular grammatical and stylistic features, and the occurrence of specific figures of speech, idiomatic expressions and metaphors. Formal contexts were constituted through the use of an *empiricist repertoire*, which derives from and endorses a 'common sense' or conventional view of scientific work: that the scientist is impartial as to the results of scientific work, and whose feelings, attitudes, personality, and so on, are irrelevant to the outcome of research. It also promotes the significance of experimental procedures as a reliable method by which to discover objective facts about the physical universe. It is also characterised by formal language which obscures the active role of individual scientists. For example, consider the following opening from a research paper on the chemical processes involved in the production of adenosine triphosphate (ATP).

(2.14)   (From Gilbert and Mulkay, 1984: 41)

> A long held assumption concerning oxidative phosphorylation has been that the energy available from oxidation-reduction reactions is used to drive the formation of the terminal covalent anhydride bond in ATP. Contrary to this view, recent results from several laboratories suggest that energy is used primarily to promote the binding of ADP and phosphate in a catalytically competent mode and … to facilitate the release of bound ATP.

Note that the 'long held assumption' is unattributed; it seems to be free standing, unconnected to the work or activities of particular scientists. This is a routine feature of formal scientific research papers: the use of phrases such as 'it was discovered that …', 'the results showed…' or 'the experiments confirmed …' portrays experimental findings as nuggets of knowledge which popped into existence without any assistance from the scientists and technicians conducting the experiment. Research papers do not state that 'Dr Evans believes that …' or 'Janet's results indicated …'. Note also that evidence which challenges this assumption is reported as coming from 'laboratories'; again, individual scientists are not named. The style of the quotation thus illustrates a powerful convention in scientific writing: the agency or personal commitments of the author are excluded. In this sense, the empiricist repertoire has the function of depicting the 'out-there-ness' of scientific phenomena (Woolgar, 1980: 256), in that it leads us to view scientific claims as representing objective features of the natural world, independent of the desires, motivation and personality of the people who individually or collectively conducted the research.

Informal contexts were characterised by the use of the *contingent repertoire*. In this, biographical or personalty features of the scientist are implicitly or explicitly invoked to account for scientific activities or claims; for example, the interpretation of experimental results, or why particular theories may be endorsed or rejected. Moreover, the laboratory and experimental procedures are characterised in terms of social factors: commitments or friendships between scientists, interpersonal rivalries, tacit knowledge about the ways in which experiments should be conducted, and so on. Consider the following extract, which comes from an informal interview conducted by Gilbert and Mulkay with a scientist involved in the dispute about oxidative phosphorylation.

(2.15) (From Gilbert and Mulkay, 1984: 65)

> But Waters didn't believe any of it. None of it. He'd been brought up with the chemical theory. He'd made several contributions to that. He'd interpreted all his work on [a particular reagent] in terms of it, in a complicated way. He was a great friend of Watson's. He knew Gowan. It was American anyway. The chemiosmotic theory, as far as he was concerned, was a little bit of a joke.

In this passage, the speaker accounts for the position of a senior scientist in the dispute by reference to a range of contingent or non-scientific factors: personality (a dogmatic refusal to consider alternative theories); biography (a history of personal commitment to a particular theory); career (a life of research informed by that theory); social commitments (friendships with leading scientists associated with the theory), and even geography (the alternative theory is promoted by a scientist in a different county).

In short, the empiricist repertoire sees the scientist as detached, working in accord with universally accepted experimental procedure, and humble before the facts, wherever they may lead. In the contingent repertoire, the scientist is portrayed as a social being, whose scientific work and beliefs are not easily divorced from wider nexus of desires, hopes and affiliations which characterise everyday human action.

Gilbert and Mulkay explored the ways in which these two repertoires provided scientists with discursive resources by which they could address a sensitive issue. Each scientist they interviewed took it that their own scientific beliefs were correct. They were warranted through the use of the empiricist repertoire: results from properly conducted experiments forced them to acknowledge the factual status of particular claims. But how, then, to account for the errors of other scientists who espoused different interpretations of experimental results and proposed alternative theories? If scientific method allows scientists to uncover objective facts about the universe, how come some scientists get it wrong? The contingent repertoire was invoked to deal with this: personal or social issues were distorting other scientists' research. Consider the following extract, which comes from interviews in which scientists were describing theories that differed from their own.

(2.16) (From Gilbert and Mulkay, 1984: 65)

> People like Gowan and Fennel especially and Milner, certainly had many publications … and they had a lot invested in that field and I think they were psychologically a little bit reluctant to follow the lead of … somebody else completely.

Factors which are not supposed to intrude upon scientific procedure (psychological traits, personal investment and individual friendships) are used to account for other scientists' error. (Similar kinds of accounting practices are illustrated in extract 2.15.)

There was, then, asymmetry in the ways in which scientists characterised and accounted for correct and incorrect beliefs. However, we should not treat these accounts at face value, as if they revealed that some scientists in fact were allowing their view to be distorted by social or psychological factors while others simply developed their theories on the basis of objective experimental results. Gilbert and Mulkay noted that almost everyone they had interviewed had their work explained away by reference to the contingent repertoire by someone else. As Potter and Wetherell note 'this seems a very good reason for not taking ... discourse as a model of what is the case' (Potter and Wetherell, 1987: 152).

While formal contexts such as published research papers were invariably constructed through the empiricist repertoire, both repertoires could be invoked during informal interviews. The availability of the empiricist and contingent repertoire presented some sharp interpretative problems for scientists during the interviews. Scientists account for others' beliefs in terms of distorting psychological or social influences. But given that science is meant to proceed according to the principles of objectivity and experimental method, does this constitute a more general threat to the value of scientific activity? That is,

> If scientists regularly draw upon and move between two quite different repertoires, how is it that potential contradictions between these repertoires do not require constant attention? (Gilbert and Mulkay, 1984: 90)

Gilbert and Mulkay identified a descriptive practice which allowed scientists to reconcile the contradictions inherent in these two repertoires. They called this the Truth Will Out Device, or TWOD. Examples of Truth Will Out-type formulations are 'in the fullness of time', 'with more experimental evidence', 'the facts will become clear', and so on. They are used to anticipate the (invariably unspecified) future date at which sufficient evidence will have been accumulated to settle any current debates. The device allows the scientist to draw upon the contingent repertoire to account for other scientists' erroneous beliefs, while at the same time implicitly supporting the broader principle that the scientific method does indeed provide a unique access to objective physical phenomena, and will ultimately reveal Nature's secrets. It also suggests that any on-going disagreements and conflicts are not an intrinsic part of scientific work but arise because the scientific method has not yet prevailed: 'Gradually, it is implied, the realities of the physical world will be recognised; and idiosyncratic, social, distorting influences will consequently be seen as such' (Gilbert and Mulkay, 1984: 94).

To illustrate, look at the following extract; this comes near the end of a scientist's description of the oxidative phosphorylation dispute in biochemistry.

(2.17)   (From Gilbert and Mulkay, 1984: 93; original italics)

> I think *ultimately* that science is so structured that none of those things are important and that what is important is scientific facts themselves, what comes out at the end.

The Truth Will Out Device has an elastic temporal dimension, in that confidence that any particular dispute *will* eventually be settled does not rely on having to specify *when* that closure will occur. This has the further interpretative advantage of allowing scientists to acknowledge that scientific controversies may be deep-rooted and long-lasting without also jeopardising the idea that the scientific method is infallible.

Discourse analysis, discourse analysis and discourse analysis

Gilbert and Mulkay adopted the term 'discourse analysis' to describe the kind of empirical work they were advocating. However, with hindsight, this was perhaps not a wise choice, as at the time there were two other forms of analysis which were known by this title. There was the work that drew from linguistic and socio-linguistics which tried to analyse the relationship between components of spoken discourse in much the same way that components of written language could be analysed. So, mirroring the analysis of grammatical rules which ordered the combination of clauses, verbs, nouns and so on, attempts were made to discover if episodes of verbal interaction displayed quasi-syntactical rules. In this way, analysts tried to identify the formal architecture of real-life speech situations and the formal rules which governed the production of speech acts. Introductions to and illustrations of this approach can be found in Brown and Yule (1983), Coulthard (1977) and Coulthard and Montgomery (1981). However, there have been a number of critical assessments of the assumptions which guide empirical analysis in this form of discourse analysis. Perhaps the most compelling critique has been offered by Levinson (1983: 286–94). He argues that the attempt to understand everyday talk in the same way that we can analyse the formal relationship between components of language is ill advised, as it does not take account of the socially organised, sequential organisation of verbal interaction. He goes on to conclude that CA's explicit focus on the way that utterances are designed to contribute to on-going sequences of actions offers greater insight to verbal communication in everyday and institutional settings.

The second kind of work known as discourse analysis was associated with the French social theorist and philosopher Michel Foucault (although he never consistently used the term to refer to his investigations). This form of discourse analysis tries to show how conventional ways of talking and writing within a culture serve political or ideological functions, in that they constrain or circumscribe how people think and act as social beings (for example, Foucault, 1970). Foucault's emphasis on the analysis of discourses, and its influence in critical social psychology, will be discussed in later chapters.

Gilbert and Mulkay argued that their version of discourse analysis occupied a middle ground between the formal linguistic method and the more socio-cultural studies influenced by Foucault. But adopting the term discourse analysis when it was already associated with established and markedly different empirical enterprises invited confusion. And the situation would become even more confusing with the subsequent emergence of critical discourse analysis (for example, Fairclough, 1995), and the fact that the term 'discourse analysis' came to be used in some quarters as a generic term to refer to all forms of language analysis, including sociolinguistics, conversation analysis, speech act theory, and so on (for example, Schiffrin, 1994; van Dijk, 1991). For the purposes of this book, we will use 'discourse analysis' to refer to the work associated with Gilbert and Mulkay, and Edwards, Potter and Wetherell. But it is important to recognise that very different styles of empirical work are also known by this term.

Summary

- Gilbert and Mulkay adopted and developed the concept of the linguistic repertoire as a tool by which to show how accounts are constructed in contextually appropriate ways.
- The empiricist repertoire endorses a 'common sense' view of scientific work: that the scientist is impartial as to the results of scientific research. Scientists' feelings, attitudes, personality, and so on, are irrelevant to the outcome of research.
- The contingent repertoire focuses on scientists' biography or personality to account for scientific action. Laboratory and experimental procedures are characterised in terms of social factors, such as commitments or friendships, interpersonal rivalries, and tacit knowledge about the ways in which experiments should be conducted.
- Discourse analysis entails radical implications for social sciences which continue to rely on a representational view of language.

The broader perspectives of CA and DA

Conversation analysis

Sacks *et al*'s study of turn-taking highlights a number of key features of conversation analytic research.

Methodology   Sacks *et al* developed their account of turn-taking practices from analysis of recordings taken from a variety of kinds of everyday interaction. Use of naturally occurring data has come to be a distinctive feature of CA's approach. The emphasis upon the study of real-life interaction stemmed from Sacks' broader objectives. What he was trying to do was develop a new method of sociology in which analytic observations were grounded in detailed analysis of actual instances of human behaviour. Thus he rejected artificially produced data, such as might be generated from an experimental setting (an approach associated with psychological studies of communication), or intuition, in which the analyst draws on his or her own experience and knowledge to examine how the social world is organised (associated by research informed by Austin's Speech Act Theory). Audio recordings of naturally occurring, 'real-life' interactions were relatively easy to obtain, and allowed the analyst to transcribe to whatever level of detail was needed, and permitted repeated listening and analysis.

On first viewing, the transcripts used by Sacks *et al* are not easy on the eye. However, to study turn-taking properly, it was necessary to have a representation of speech practices usually overlooked in transcripts which focus only on the spoken word. For example, the use of brackets cutting across lines of transcript to indicate periods of overlapping talk allows the analyst to show precisely when a potential next speaker initiates a turn. Using this transcription symbol allowed Sacks *et al* to establish that next turns are overwhelmingly built to occur at, or in close proximity to, the end of turn construction units.

As transcripts have come to provide detailed characterisations of the complexity of verbal interaction, so the rejection of intuition as an analytic guide has proved well founded. Introspection simply does not equip us to imagine, for example, how false starts to words, minor gaps between words and turns, and even the simple act of drawing breath can have real consequences for the way in which interaction unfolds. And as we saw earlier, the kind of work an utterance might be doing is crucially dependent on its location in a series of utterances. Even, say, a sophisticated appreciation of the formal syntactical and grammatical rules which govern the relationship between words would not equip the analyst to anticipate how those words might work in any particular setting.

Conversation analytic research proceeds by examination of collections of cases. Initially, analytic observations may be generated from the detailed examination of a particular case, for example, a sequence of turns which seems to display some interesting properties. Although the intensive analysis of single cases can yield important findings (for example, Schegloff, 1984; Whalen *et al*, 1988), the majority of conversation analytic research aims to provide an account of an interactional practice generated from a consideration of number of instances. So having found something that seems analytically interesting, it is necessary to return to the corpus from which the initial instance was taken (or additionally, to consult other corpora if they are available and relevant) to see if there are more sequences with similar properties. The next step is to develop a more formal and detailed account of the organisation of the target exchange. This involves examining the sequential context of the phenomenon: for example, if the focus of interest is a particular two turn exchange, what kinds of turns precede and follow that exchange? If patterns can be identified, then there is the basis for a systematic analytic description. Finally, the analyst can return to the data to determine if other instances of the phenomenon can be described in terms of this account. In this way a substantial collection of instances can be established, from the analysis of which a refined and formal account of the phenomena can be developed.

Research focus   Although Sacks *et al*'s paper deals with the precise topic of turn-taking, its more general approach illustrates concerns which continue to inform research in conversation analysis. First, there is the investigation of ordinary talk as the vehicle for interpersonal social actions: utterances are examined as activities people do to each other. Second, CA examines the highly patterned nature of these verbal activities in interaction. It seeks to identify and analyse the properties of recurrent sequences of interaction. Finally, it seeks to identify the normative expectations which underpin action sequences. In their analysis of turn-taking, Sacks *et al* discussed some of the properties of paired action sequences, such as question–answer sequences or invitation–response sequences. Paired action sequences illustrate these three points. They consist of clearly identifiable actions performed by the respective turns. They exhibit recurrent properties, for example, in the ordering of turns: answers tend to be produced after questions, not the other way round; invitations are met with acceptance or refusals, not greetings, and so on. Finally, they are informed by normative expectations, such that the producer of a first pair part might try to pursue an absent second part; while the allocated producer of the second part might try to account for its absence.

Discourse analysis

Gilbert and Mulkay's study of scientists' accounting practices illustrates a number of key features of discourse analytic research.

Methodology   There will be a detailed discussion of methodology of discourse analysis in a later chapter. In this section, then, I will just raise a few of the main broad features.

First, discourse analysts examine a variety of kinds of data. Gilbert and Mulkay studied spoken accounts generated during informal interviews, research papers published in formal academic journals, and letters between scientists. Later discourse analytic research would go on to examine an even wider range of verbal and textual materials: television current affairs programmes, the official record of speeches in the House of Commons and newspaper reports, for example. However, perhaps the most used sources of data in discourse analysis are accounts drawn from recordings of informal interviews between researchers and respondents.

As can be seen from the examples taken from Gilbert and Mulkay's book, the transcripts of verbal data are not as detailed as those found in conversation analysis. This still tends to be the case today, although more contemporary discourse analytic research papers do make more use of the range of symbols conventionally used in CA. Simpler transcripts mean that readers (especially those who may be unfamiliar with sociological studies of language) do not become distracted by strange and confusing transcription symbols. However, there is the worry that important details in the way the accounts are produced might be lost in the process of editing and 'tidying up' required to produce an uncluttered transcript.

Gilbert and Mulkay used the concept of the interpretative repertoire to characterise regular descriptive features in their data. As we shall see, the idea that there are varying kinds of repertoires from which we can choose to fashion our descriptions of actions and events is still powerful in some forms of discourse analysis. Repertoires are identified by the use of particular clusters of words and phrases. As such their presence can be diffuse through long stretches of talk. However, Gilbert and Mulkay also provided more fine-grained analysis when they discussed the Truth Will Out Device. This was identified by a much narrower set of phrases. Again this focus on descriptive devices has endured in subsequent discourse analytic work (although this may be due more to the increasing influence of conversation analysis, in which regular patterns in interaction may be described as 'devices'). However, the conceptual terms used in discourse analysis are considerably less formal than those found in conversation analytic research, where a technical vocabulary is routinely employed to describe the properties of talk-in-interaction.

Despite introducing discourse analysis to a wider sociological audience, Gilbert and Mulkay's book did not discuss in any depth the methodology involved in empirical research. It was not until Potter and Wetherell developed discourse analysis as a critical approach in social psychology that a formal account of the method was offered. They describe ten stages in discourse analytic research, but emphasise that these are a guide for research, not a definitive list of procedures which must be followed (Potter and Wetherell, 1987: 160–75). Of these ten stages, only two actually deal with analysis and the validation of analytic findings; the rest concern more practical steps in discourse research such as identifying research questions, sample selection, collecting data, transcription, coding, report writing and the application of discourse analytic findings.

But how is analysis actually done? This is a difficult question: even discourse analysts acknowledge that it is hard to capture in a formal guide what is essentially a series of interpretative engagements with data from which emerges a sense that the functional orientation of a section of discourse has been captured. Potter and Wetherell liken the process of analysis to the performance of a craft skill which relies on the development of largely tacit expertise.

Research focus   There are two broad goals of Gilbert and Mulkay's work which still inform discourse analysis. First, they wanted to 'document some of the methods by means of which scientists construct and reconstruct their actions and beliefs in diverse ways' (Gilbert and Mulkay, 1984: 188). The recognition of the intrinsic variability of accounts forced them to abandon their original aim of producing a singe, coherent sociological narrative and instead examine how these variable accounting practices fashion versions of the world. Second, they wanted to explore the functions achieved by different accounting practices: what have descriptions been constructed to do? Although this was not a major focus of Gilbert and Mulkay's study, it has become a key feature of many subsequent discourse analytic projects.

In conversation analysis the functional orientation of language is explored in the design of utterances and their placement within the turn-by-turn development of interaction. In discourse analysis the functional character of discourse may be located at a broader level. This does not mean that discourse analysts are uninterested in specific conversational activities or their sequential contexts; rather, their interest is not restricted to that level of action. This does allow a little more interpretative flexibility. However, analytic claims in conversation analysis can be grounded in the analysis of participants' own interpretations as they are displayed in subsequent turns; this resource is unavailable in the analysis of textual materials, and the kinds of lengthy monologic accounts which can occur in informal interviews (Heritage and Atkinson, 1984).

Further readings

Discourse analysis

While we have discussed some key features of Gilbert and Mulkay's analysis, their (1984) monograph merits close attention because it deals with a wider range of issues, including analysis of the use of humour in scientists' discourse, and the management of consensus in scientific debates. Many of the themes explored in the 1984 monograph (and other issues) are also explored in separate journal publications, for example: Mulkay and Gilbert (1982a, 1982b, 1983). The following two articles are early discussions of the broader methodological issues concerning the identification and analysis of interpretative repertoires: Potter and Mulkay (1985); and Wetherell and Potter (1988). More contemporary discussions can be found in Horton-Salway (2001), Potter (2004), Potter and Wetherell (1995) and Wood and Kroger (2000). Lawes (1999) and Widdicombe (1993) provide illustrative analyses.

Conversation analysis

There is a substantial number of studies in conversation analysis. Useful bibliographies can be found on Paul ten Have's excellent website: http://www2.fmg.uva.nl/emca/

The following is a very small selection of papers which illustrate the spirit and approach of CA: Jefferson (1990) on list construction; Pomerantz (1984) on agreements and disagreement with assessments; Schegloff, Jefferson and Sacks (1977) on repair and the preference for self-correction; Schegloff (1992b) on further issues in the organisation of repair; and Schegloff and Sacks (1973) on the organisation of terminal sequences in telephone calls.

Excellent CA studies can be found in the following edited collections: Atkinson and Heritage (1984); Button, Drew and Heritage (1986); Button and Lee (1987); and Psathas (1990). However, the first port of call for anyone interested in developing their knowledge of conversation analysis should be the lectures of Harvey Sacks (Sacks, 1992). Schegloff's (1992a) introduction to the first volume of Sacks' *Lectures on Conversation* is a sophisticated account of the emergence of Sacks' work and its context. Silverman (1998) offers an accessible introduction to Sacks' work and his legacy for sociology, particularly his work on membership categorisation. Wilson, Wiemann and Zimmerman (1984) situate the CA of turn-taking organisation in relation to other models of turn-transfer.

3
Method and Critique

In this chapter we explore conversation analysis and discourse analysis in more detail. However, each approach has generated a substantial literature of empirical and theoretical discussion. Consequently it is necessary to focus our discussion. Therefore, we will consider the methodology of conversation analysis in the context of studies of talk in work-related or institutional settings; but, first, we will examine how discourse analysis developed as a central part of a broader critique of experimental psychology, especially experimental social psychology. It is important to explain why these particular aspects have been selected for special attention.

It would be inappropriate to view discourse analysis merely as a critical movement within social psychology. Researchers in this area have written extensively on the methods of discourse analysis; and they have explored various substantive topics: for example, the organisation of racist discourse, and the ways in which identities are produced in talk and texts. However, it is appropriate to emphasise the critical stance of discourse analysis. It emerged in social psychology as part of a more widespread critique of the narrow experimental and cognitivist approach which characterised the discipline in western Europe during the mid- to late-1980s. And although not all critical social psychologists adopted discourse analysis – for example, some drew from more theoretical and psychoanalytic literatures – it became centrally associated with a critical assessment of the methods and assumptions of social psychology. Moreover, many of the core topics addressed in discourse analytic research, such as attitudes and attributions, grew out of a critique of the ways in which the constructive and functional features of language were overlooked in more conventional social psychological approaches.

Similarly, it would be incorrect to regard conversation analysis as primarily a novel methodological development: research in CA has a wide variety of substantive topics. Consider, for example, the range of topics covered by contributors to Atkinson and Heritage's (1984) collection of CA research papers: the management of agreement, disagreement, offers, invitations and requests; topic change; the relationship between talk and non-vocal activities, such as body movement; laughter; and the organisation of political rhetoric. However, what is remarkably consistent in CA research is a demonstrable adherence to a distinctive set of methodological steps. For example, CA's overriding concern with the interactional management of verbal activities between participants means that turn-taking is central to empirical research. Indeed, this focus on turn-taking is often reflected in the ways in which edited collections of CA research papers are organised. Thus we find that contributions to Drew and Heritage's (1992a) collection of studies of talk in work-related settings are distributed between sections entitled 'The Activities of Questioners', 'The Activities of Answerers' and 'The Interplay Between Questioning and Answering'. But there are other distinctive features of CA's method; in the previous chapter, we noted the importance of next turn analysis as a procedure to expose the participants' tacit understanding of the moment-by-moment development of interaction. And later in this chapter we will illustrate how studying cases in which participants deviate from an established sequential pattern can advance our understanding of that sequence. The distinctiveness of CA's approach thus warrants a more extended methodological discussion.

Discourse analysis as critique

DA and sociology

Discourse analysis was an influential development within the sociology of scientific knowledge, but it did not make a significant impact in sociology more generally. There are several reasons why this was the case. First, as we saw in the previous chapter, discourse analysis was proposed as a radical solution to what Gilbert and Mulkay argued were significant and possibly insurmountable methodological problems in sociological research which used people's accounts as data. They maintained that their form of discourse analysis had implications beyond the issues that motivated the sociology of scientific knowledge. As they say in the conclusion to their (1984) discussion of their studies,

> [O]ur basic argument ... that traditional forms of sociological analysis of action are derived in an unexplicated manner from participants' discourse and that discourse analysis is a necessary prelude to, and perhaps replacement for, the analysis of action and belief, is a completely general argument which applies equally well *to all areas of sociological inquiry*. (Gilbert and Mulkay, 1984: 190–1; italics added)

The implication was clear: sociological research which treated people's discourse as if it could in principle furnish literal descriptions of social actions and beliefs might be, at best, premature, or worse, in error. This was a challenging conclusion because most sociological research had traded – and continues to trade – on precisely that naive view of language. This means that a wider adoption of Gilbert and Mulkay's arguments for discourse analysis would entail an extensive re-evaluation of core methods and findings in sociology.

Second, there are differences between sociology in the UK, other European countries and the United States. This means that intellectual developments in one part of the world may not have the same influence elsewhere. For example, the radically qualitative focus on discourse may simply have failed to engage with the agenda of North American sociology, which traditionally tends towards more formal and quantitative approaches to sociological research.

Finally, although there was some discussion of the wider sociological relevance of discourse analysis (Gilbert and Abell, 1983) the key proponents did not offer a sustained development or exploration of its potential or implications. Mulkay began to consider the radical upshot of the constitutive nature of discourse, especially the analyst's discourse in the construction of academic texts. This led to a remarkable series of studies in which he and his colleagues adapted literary forms of writing to produce sociological texts. These new literary forms, such as plays, monologues, dialogues and fictional stories, were used to draw attention to the constructive nature of academic discourse, while at the same time addressing important substantive issues in the sociology of scientific knowledge (Ashmore, 1989; Ashmore *et al*, 1989, Mulkay, 1985, 1991; Woolgar, 1988). Gilbert went on to explore long-standing interests in human–computer interaction (Luff *et al*, 1990), statistical methods (Gilbert, 1993) and the use of computer simulation of social processes (Gilbert, 1994).

DA, psychology and social psychology

Although discourse analysis did not have a radical or sustained impact in sociology, it has had more influence in British and European social psychology, due primarily to the efforts of Derek Edwards, David Middleton, Jonathan Potter and Margaret Wetherell.

During the 1980s Edwards and Middleton published a series of papers in which they began to offer an approach to memory and recollections which was in marked contrast to the majority of psychological research in this area (Edwards and Middleton, 1986, 1987, 1988). They argued that, broadly, experimental studies of memory were of little value to our understanding of everyday remembering because they primarily investigated the effectiveness and accuracy of memory in highly controlled, artificial laboratory settings. Thus experiments were designed to assess what might intervene to degrade or enhance memory abilities. However, Edwards and Middleton argued that when people produce recollections in real-life situations, a variety of other issues come into play, all of which are overlooked by laboratory-based studies. First, they note that, for the most part, recollections are produced in talk, and as part of a series of discursive activities. So recollections may be offered during relaxed informal chat, in business meetings, as part of arguments and disputes, and so on. The discursive basis of recollections, and their role in social actions, is rarely explored in cognitive psychological research. Second, they noted that most traditional psychological research focused on the accuracy of recall (and what might affect it). But Edwards and Middleton argued that this was hardly an issue for people who offer recollections in everyday settings.

To explore these issues further, they conducted an analysis of the discourse produced during an informal group meeting at which participants were invited to discuss the (then) recently released popular film, Spielberg's *E.T.* (Edwards and Middleton, 1986). Their objective was not to assess the accuracy of the participants' recollections by comparing them to some objective record of what actually happened in the film, but to explore remembering as a situated and social activity. Their analysis revealed that the participants' accounts and recollections were oriented to various functional or situational issues: for example, the establishment of the criteria for what counted as an appropriate recollection, and the production and negotiation of consensus about the topic under discussion. In this way, Edwards and Middleton were able to show that everyday informal recollections are occasions in which participants engage in various kinds of discursive activities to ensure the appropriate-for-the-context accomplishment of memory. Accuracy of recall did not seem to be an issue; what informed the participants' memory discourse was what counted as a contextually appropriate recollection.

Broadly, then, Edwards and Middleton argued for an approach to memory and recollections which reflected a strongly ethnomethodological and social constructionist position. That is, they wanted to see how memories were produced as socially organised accomplishments through everyday discursive practices; and they wanted to see how those practices in turn informed the properties of the memories so offered. As we shall see, this approach to ostensibly cognitive or psychological phenomena became a key feature of discourse analytic research.

Potter, who had a background in psychology, had been one of Mulkay's postgraduate students. He had initially used the method to examine the discourse of psychologists as a community of scientists (Potter, 1984), but had become aware that discourse analytic arguments about the constitutive and variable qualities of language raised serious problems for the primarily experimental and cognitive orientation of social psychology. Wetherell was a social psychologist whose work was concerned to explore and incorporate the importance of wider ideological and political issues (Wetherell, 1983, 1986). These were often overlooked in psychological research because they were not amenable to the kinds of experimental procedures which dominated the discipline. In 1987 they published *Discourse and Social Psychology* in which they provided a sustained critical examination of the ways in which traditional methods in social psychology had failed to take account of the variable, functional and constructive nature of language.

It is important to note that during the 1980s in British social psychology there was a growing dissatisfaction with the experimental and cognitivist orientations of the discipline. Edwards and Middleton's ethnomethodologically oriented critique of memory research is a key example. But the critique reflected a number of other intellectual influences. For example, Parker's critique of social psychology drew from Foucauldian discourse analysis, and tried to explore the ways in which language embodies ideological positions (Parker, 1989, 1992). Billig's critique, on the other hand, stemmed from his interest in rhetorical psychology, which treats everyday thinking as a discursive activity in which people's accounts reflect their engagement with dilemmatic or contradictory positions (Billig, 1985, 1987). Harré and his colleagues were developing an account of the rules of conduct, self and the use of language which rejected the determinate primacy of cognition and focused instead on social rules (Marsh *et al*, 1978). He later went on to examine the ways in which notions of self and identity are implicated in the structure of grammatical expressions (Harré, 1995). Feminist psychologists were also beginning to explore language as the site in which psychological issues concerning sexuality and gender relations might be explored (Kitzinger, 1987). Potter and Wetherell's text was able to highlight common ground between many of these approaches, thus establishing a broad base for a sustained critique of cognitivism and experimental methods, while at the same time giving a greater prominence to alternative ways of doing social psychology.

In many respects, Potter and Wetherell's account of discourse analysis follows that offered in Gilbert and Mulkay's earlier book. They claim that discourse analysis stems from the following principles:

1   language is used for a variety of functions and its use has a variety of consequences;
2   language is both constructed and constructive;
3   the same phenomenon can be described in a number of different ways;
4   there will, therefore, be considerable variation in accounts;
5   there is, as yet, no foolproof way to deal with this variation and to sift accounts which are 'literal' or 'accurate' from those which are rhetorical or merely misguided thereby escaping the problems variation raises for researchers with a 'realist' model of language;
6   the constructive and flexible ways in which language is used should themselves become a central topic of study.
     (Potter and Wetherell, 1987: 35)

However, there are some key differences. For example, Potter and Wetherell discuss how the variability of people's discourse has figured in some work in social psychology, but point out that its radical implications have not been developed because it was accommodated within existing social psychological explanations. They also provide an account of the various methodological procedures which lead to the suppression of variability (Potter and Wetherell, 1987: 36–43). Moreover, as can be seen from Potter and Wetherell's list of the principles which inform their formulation of discourse analysis, they emphasise the importance of the functional and constructive nature of language. Gilbert and Mulkay's main concern, however, was to illustrate that scientists' accounts are constructions which 'depict scientific action and beliefs in various different ways' (Gilbert and Mulkay, 1984: 14). Although issues concerning the construction and function of accounts informed many parts of their analysis, these were not given the analytic prominence they subsequently received in Potter and Wetherell's account.

Potter and Wetherell also emphasise the ideological nature of everyday discourse. Ideologies are ways of thinking which support asymmetries in power and advantage. Potter and Wetherell argued that discourse analysis could examine how ideologies are embodied in and reproduced through everyday discourse practices. This argument was primarily developed in their subsequent analysis of the racist discourse of white New Zealanders, where they argued that discourse analysis could offer a more satisfactory account of the relationship between ideology, racism and social practice than provided by traditional Marxist conceptions of ideology (Wetherell and Potter, 1992).

A final and significant departure from Gilbert and Mulkay's discourse analysis, and one which reflected Edwards and Middleton's studies of discursive rememberings, was Potter and Wetherell's sustained critique of the cognitivist orientation of social psychology. This orientation is manifest in two man ways. First, it is assumed that cognitive processes and mental states drive social action. To understand social behaviour, therefore, it is necessary to study the psychological states and processes which give rise, say, to attitude formation (or change), or self-categorisation and group membership. Second, this orientation informs the methodological approach of traditional social psychology in that it is assumed that cognitive structures are best measured by experimental techniques, or can be inferred from people's discourse. To illustrate these issues, we will discuss how discourse analysis provided the basis of a critique of attribution research in social psychology and offered new lines of empirical inquiry.

Attributions, description and inference

Attribution theory is concerned with the ways in which ordinary people come to make causal explanations of social actions or events. Its focus is cognitive and perceptual, in that our attributions are treated as a form of social cognition which is informed by the way in which we perceive and interpret the world (Kelly, 1967). A common experimental technique has been to present subjects with vignettes: stories in which some set of events or relationships are described. The subject is then asked questions which are designed to elicit their understanding of, and inferences about, the causal relationship between events or actions in the vignette. Vignettes can then be altered. By comparing how subjects' inferences subsequently change (if at all), the researcher can begin to build a model about the variables that affect how we form causal relationships.

There are two senses in which the experimental procedure of attribution research rests on a naive theory of language. First, it is assumed that the composition of the stimulus materials – the vignettes – are neutral descriptions. They are taken to be 'straightforward stand-ins for the world' (Potter and Edwards, 1990: 407). Second, it is assumed that the subjects' reports of their inferences about the stimulus materials provide accurate or literal representations of inner mental processes. However, for discourse analysts, description is itself a form of social activity, and not just a decontextualised representation of cognitive events, or neutral versions of social reality. Thus the methodology of attribution studies is problematic because it ignores the functional, action orientation of language; it is not able to take account of the way that descriptions are constructed to do things.

Moreover, in real-life circumstances, even descriptions which seem to be neutral reports of events will be evaluatively loaded and thereby attending to attributional concerns. We can illustrate this by looking at Potter and Edwards' (1990) study of the controversy surrounding an off-the-record briefing by a senior figure in the Conservative government in 1988. Subsequent newspaper articles by the journalists who had been present claimed that the minister had said the government was planning to introduce means testing of pensioners. There was a fairly swift and unanimous condemnation of this policy in the press and from politicians from all parties. Shortly after, the minister stated that he had not said the government were planning to means test pensioners, claiming that the journalists had indulged in a 'farrago of invention'. At that point, journalists and political commentators began to focus on the dispute as to what actually had been said at the briefing. In numerous newspaper articles and speeches by politicians, the relative merits of the journalists' and the minister's case were debated. This presented Potter and Edwards with a collection of real-life accounts in which causal reasoning about who said what was explicitly displayed. Furthermore, it allowed them to address a key feature of attribution theory.

The social psychologist Roger Brown (1986) had proposed a 'causal calculus' to account for every attributional reasoning. According to this, causal responsibility is attributed in respect of information variables, one of which was consensus. So for example, a report that 'All people are afraid of this dog' is more likely to lead to conclusions that this dog is fierce than the statement 'Janet is afraid of this dog'. Potter and Edwards observed that all the journalists who had been at the briefing produced a similar account. This consensus was noted by many who were sceptical of the minister's protestations of innocence. Indeed, it was used as discursive resource in descriptions which were designed to cast doubt on the minister's story.

Extract 3.1 comprises two statements taken from a speech made in the House of Commons, and the third from an article in a broadsheet newspaper.

(3.1)   (From Potter and Edwards, 1990: 412)

How on earth did the Chancellor, as a former journalist, manage to mislead so many journalists at once about his intentions?

As all the Sunday newspapers carried virtually the same story, is the Chancellor saying that every journalist who came to the briefing – he has not denied that there was one – misunderstood what he said?

The reporters, it seemed, had unanimously got it wrong. Could so many messengers really be so much in error? It seems doubtful.

These descriptions appeal to the following lay or common sense logic: if a number of observers report the same thing, it is likely that the thing they are reporting is objective. However, this is not to endorse the naive view of language in which regularities in accounts are treated as providing accurate or objective representations of the world. As Gilbert and Mulkay pointed out, regularities in accounts might reflect recurrent features of the social contexts in which they are produced. And that is precisely what we see happening here. These accounts contributed to, and constituted, a dispute about who was telling the truth about what happened at the briefing. They were partial accounts which sought to establish the factual status of one version of what really happened. Common sense logic about consensus was not invoked because it simply indicated which accounts were, in fact, factual; it was being used as a resource to lend descriptions a rhetorical or persuasive force so that they would be heard or read *as* factual statements.

In attribution theory, consensus is just one of a variety of variables which are taken into consideration when we perform mental calculations about causal relationships. But in these real-life descriptions consensus is a live concern, managed in discourse to particular inferential ends: it can be 'worked up', or fashioned in various ways. In the statements in extract 3.1 consensus is deployed in various teasing and ironic ways. Moreover, it is established indirectly: as a consequence of 'so many' or 'every' journalist, and in the 'unanimity' of their reports. As such, it is marshalled with some delicacy as a resource to construct a version of the world which is hearably persuasive or factual.

Consensus, then, was a resource by which to warrant a version of what had happened. Potter and Edwards also noted, however, that consensus could be recast as collusion, thus working to support precisely the opposite account. The clearest example came from the minister at the centre of the dispute in an exchange in the House of Commons.

(3.2)   (Hansard, November 7, in Potter and Edwards, 1990: 416)

Opposition MP: They [the journalists] will have their shorthand notes.

Chancellor: Oh yes they will have their shorthand notes and they will know it, and they will know they went behind afterwards and they thought that there was not a good enough story and so they produced that.

Here the apparent similarities in the journalists' stories are depicted as a consequence of collaborative invention. Uniformity of accounts is thus depicted as an artefact of social activity, not reflection of objective reality.

Important points emerge from Potter and Edwards' study. First, consensus is not merely a category used by social psychologists to theorise about the way people interpret causal relationships: it is a resource which can fashioned, made inferentially available or undermined in various ways. Second, its occurrence was intimately tied to the kinds of discursive work being addressed: establishing the factual status of one version of events over competing versions. Whereas traditional attribution research had tended to see attributions as a decontextualised, cognitive phenomenon, Potter and Edwards showed that attributions should be understood in the first instance as social actions which are contingent on, and oriented to, a wider web of social and discursive activities, such as blamings, accusations and rebuttals. Experimental work which was based on subjects' interpretations of made-up vignettes simply overlooks the situated, complex and action-oriented nature of real-life attributive actions.

Ideologies in practice

We noted earlier that discourse analysis emerged at the same time as a variety of critical perspectives in social psychology, and that there were many points of overlap. One common concern was to explore how ideologies were embedded in discourse. In this, discourse analysts showed that their approach not only owed much to the empirical traditions of analysis, such as conversation analysis, but also drew from more theoretical approaches to discourse, such as semiotics (Barthes, 1972) and Foucault's philosophical and historical studies (Dreyfus and Rabinow, 1982). This area of discourse analytic research seeks to examine the broader ideological underpinnings of language use: it assumes that language embodies 'sediments' of social practices which serve to justify and perpetuate inequalities of power and opportunity in society. Consequently, Potter and Wetherell's discourse analysis was concerned not only with the organisation of accounts, but with the wider social and political consequences of that organisation.

A study by Wetherell *et al* (1987) provides an illustration. They examined interview data with university students in which they discussed their future career plans. Wetherell and her colleagues were interested in the linguistic resources by which the respondents addressed the issue of employment opportunities for women. The analysis thus focused on the 'practical ideologies' about women and their opportunities in the labour market which informed the respondents' accounting practices.

Wetherell *et al* found four primary themes in their data. These concerned the different ways in which the participants characterised women's opportunities in the workplace, especially in relation to child rearing, models of individualism, the relevance of social change and discussion of preference for present (and anticipated future) opportunities for women's employment compared to previous periods in history. To illustrate their approach we will concentrate on the first theme, which Wetherell *et al* characterised as unequal egalitarianism.

They found that the respondents' discourse about women, workplace, careers and children clustered around two issues. First, there was the issue of equal opportunities. In this people invoked a moral universe in which generally liberal values were endorsed: it was right for women to be able to work, equal opportunities should be extended, and so on. For example:

(3.3)   (From Wetherell *et al*, 1987: 62)

Female 2:   I would expect the father to do his equal share …
Male 3:   I think that equal opportunities should continue …

However, respondents also raised practical considerations, and presented an alternative formulation in which constraints upon women's equal opportunities were described as either reasonable or at least understandable.

(3.4)   (From Wetherell *et al*, 1987: 64)

Male 4:   (*With respect to employers' reluctance to employ young women who might start a family*) I suppose you can always see how an employer's mind will work, if he has a choice between two identically qualified and identically, identical personalities, and one is male and one is a female, you can sympathize with him for wondering if the female is not going to get married and have children and then there's always the risk that she may not come back after …
((*some lines omitted*))
Female 8:   But I think more and more nowadays companies are willing to take on women although I can (pause) it's understandable that sometimes they don't …

These kinds of formulations were drawn upon by the respondents at various times through the interviews. It was not the case that some people supported the principle of equal opportunities while others opposed it, or instead emphasised the practical considerations which might prevent women from enjoying equal opportunities with men. As in Gilbert and Mulkay's study of scientists' discourse, Wetherell and her colleagues found variability in the way their respondents described their attitudes, expectations and assumptions. Wetherell *et al* argued that these ways of reasoning about the world and constructing accounts were resources through which respondents could address particular issues as they emerged in the interview. In this they were able to point to how practical ideologies inform particular kinds of mundane discursive activities. This is where their discourse analytic approach provided an advantage over more traditional Marxist accounts in which the influence of ideologies was largely assumed.

However, there are drawbacks to discourse analytic studies of the ideologies which inform discursive practices. Because accounts are examined primarily to locate the workings of broad ideologies, there is a diminished sensitivity to the interactional environment in which utterances are produced. This in turn can lead the analyst to impute an ideological significance to utterances when their design may owe more to the particular turn-taking sequences which provide an immediate interactional context. There is, then, a tension between discourse analytic projects which are informed by wider political and social concerns and those which focus more on the inferential or interactional tasks served by language use. This tension will be explored more fully in later chapters.

Summary

- Discourse analysis emerged as a central part of a wider set of critiques of experimental psychology and social psychology.
- The focus on the variable, constructive and constitutive properties of language offered a powerful critique of the laboratory-based practices and cognitivist assumptions of mainstream social psychology.
- Discourse analysis was broadly concerned with the management of authority in disputes; the invocation of psychological states as social practices, and the relationship between everyday discourse, and the ideologies which maintained the *status quo*.

Exploring the method of conversation analysis: talk in work-related or institutional settings

In the last chapter, we discussed some properties of the ways in which turn exchange is organised in everyday interaction. This allowed us to identify and demonstrate some key goals of the conversation analytic approach: the analysis of the activities performed by turns at talk, and a concern to identify the ways in which successive utterances cohere into strongly patterned sequences of interaction. And this in turn illustrated how normative frameworks underpin the sequential organisation of interaction. In this part of the chapter, we will explore in more detail the approach and methodology of CA by looking at studies of interaction in formal institutional settings: televised news interviews. In particular, we will be focusing on the ways in which the organisation of turn-taking and turn design in these contexts differ markedly from that found in more conversational interaction. These kinds of data will also be used to illustrate the importance of paying close attention to those occasions in which participants seem to deviate from an established pattern or sequence.

We will look at a study conducted by Heritage and Greatbatch (1991) on the organisation of news interviews. This has been selected for a number of reasons. First, it is an excellent study of its kind. But more important, we are all familiar with the general character of interaction which happens in these political interviews. Interviews with leading political or public figures are a routine feature of news and current affairs programmes broadcast on television or on the radio. Indeed, during election campaigns, politicians and candidates are expected to submit themselves to regular televised interrogations from leading political journalists and news interviewers. The majority of us, therefore, have some degree of familiarity with the kinds of verbal activities which occur in news interviews.

Interaction in formal institutional settings

Drew and Heritage (1992b) draw a distinction between two types of institutional settings: formal and informal. In formal settings we find that participation is focused on particular tasks; that the order of participation is fairly rigid; and that the kind of turns expected of participants is limited, and to an extent pre-allocated. This captures many of the features of interaction in news interviews.

News interviews have two kinds of participant: the interviewer and the interviewee (hereafter the IR and IE, respectively). There is a clear ordering to the interaction between the IR and the IE: they alternate turns at talk. Thus we can observe the following kind of pattern: the IR talks, then the IE, then the IR and then the IE, and so on. Moreover, there is a clear difference in the kind of activity associated with each participant: so that we find IRs predominantly tend to ask questions, and IEs predominantly tend to answer them. This IR–IE interaction can be characterised thus: question–answer–question–answer, and so on. Immediately we can see that this is very different from ordinary conversation, where there is much greater flexibility in both the ordering and nature of participation.

What is interesting, however, is not merely that this is how interaction proceeds in news interviews, but that this is how participants tacitly *expect* it to proceed. It is a normative arrangement which bestows obligations and expectations on the participants in different ways. We can find evidence for this set of normative expectations if we consider some of the design features of questions and answers. To illustrate, we will consider some properties of news interview interaction from Heritage and Greatbatch's study.

Normative assumptions in news interview interaction

It is not uncommon to find that the IE's questions will have two components: a preface, such as a statement of fact (or what is offered as fact), and then a question. So for example:

(3.5)   (From Heritage and Greatbatch, 1991: 99)

```
IR:   ˙hhh The (.) price being asked for these
      letters is (.) three thousand pou::nds.
      Are you going to be able to raise it,
      (0.5)
IE:   At the moment it … ((continues))
```

Here there is a statement: 'The (.) price being asked for these letters is (.) three thousand pou::nds.', and then a question based on this statement 'Are you going to be able to raise it,'.

The statement component of the turn is a complete turn construction unit; at its completion, then, comes a transition relevance place: a location in which it would be appropriate for the IE to begin to speak. However, it is a routine feature of news interviews that IEs will not begin to speak at the end of prefatory statements, but will wait until a question component has been delivered.

People invited to take part in news interviews understand that they are being asked because they have expertise in or opinions on particular issues, or involvement in specific events or policies. It is often the case that the IEs will be precisely aware of the kinds of issues which will be raised during the interview. It is therefore very likely that IEs can anticipate (or will know in advance) the topics which will come up during the interview. And a prefatory statement will provide a clear signal as to the type of question which will be asked. But it is routinely the case that IEs will address the issue only when a question has been formulated.

This tells us that IEs orient to the expectation that their contributions should be hearable as answers; and for that, they need a question to be delivered. Furthermore, it tells us that there is an expectation that IRs should ask questions. Moreover, that IEs do not initiate turns at the completion of prefatory statements displays their understanding that a question is forthcoming.

What emerges, then, is a sense of the obligations and expectations attendant upon participation in a news interview. There is a normative framework which sustains the distinctive kinds of contributions which IRs and IEs make. This normative framework explains why IEs are unlikely to address the topics raised in prefatory statements directly after those statements (they anticipate a forthcoming question). It also explains why IRs can design turns with non-question components (they share the normative understanding that IEs' participation is contingent upon the production of a question).

This is a powerful normative framework, and it is relevant even when IEs are faced with prefatory statements which constitute significant challenges, accusations and damaging characterisations, all of which are eventually disputed. Consider the following extract.

(3.6) (From Heritage and Greatbatch, 1991: 100)

```
IR:   ˙hhh we What's the difference between your
      Marxism and Mister McGaehy's Communism.
IE:   er The difference is that it's the press that
      constantly call me a Ma:rxist when I do not,
      (.) and never have (.) er er given that
      description of myself.  ┌hh I -┐
IR:                           └But I ┘'ve heard you-
      I've heard you'd be very happy to: to:
```

er ˙hhhh er de<u>scribe</u> yourself as a Marxist.
<u>C</u>ould it be that with an election in the
<u>off</u>ing you're anxious to play down that you're a
Marx⌈ist.⌉
IE: ⌊ er ⌋ Not at all Mister Da:y.=And I'm (.)
<u>s</u>orry to say I must disagree with you,=you have
<u>nev</u>er <u>h</u>eard me describe my<u>self</u> ˙hhh er as a
Ma:rxist.=I have o:nly ... ((continues))

Heritage and Greatbatch observe that the IR has asked a question which assumes that the IE is a Marxist, and the IE has refuted this, claiming that it is the press who have labelled him as a Marxist. However, the IR then makes a prefatory statement which takes issue with the IE's response: 'But I-'ve <u>heard</u> you- I've heard you'd be very <u>happy</u> to: to: er ˙hhhh er de<u>scribe</u> yourself as a Marxist', and then asks a question: '<u>C</u>ould it be that with an election in the <u>off</u>ing you're anxious to play down that you're a Marxist.' This turn constitutes a potentially damaging challenge to the IE's credibility, for several reasons. First, the IE has claimed that he has never called himself a Marxist, which suggests that – at the very least – he has some reservations about Marxism; yet the IR's statement depicts the IE as sympathetic to the label and, by implication, the views associated with it. Second, it offers an account for the IE's resistance to being called a Marxist: he is denying his true beliefs just to enhance his credibility with the electorate. Finally it suggests that at that moment in the interview, the IE is being at best disingenuous, or worse, dishonest about his true political beliefs.

Perhaps the most damaging component of the IR's turn is the claim that he personally has heard that the IE would welcome being called a Marxist. Yet the IE does not attempt to address this at the transition relevance place at the end of the prefatory statement. Instead, he withholds participation until a point when it is normatively appropriate for him to speak: after a question. And even here, the first component of the IE's response deals (albeit briefly) with the question component of the previous turn, not the more damaging prefatory statement. Only when the question has been addressed does the IE go on to rebut the claim in the prefatory statement (Heritage and Greatbatch, 1991: 123). So even when there are clear matters of some importance and consequence, IEs will participate in normatively expected ways.

It is not only that participants in news interviews orient to the obligation to produce questions and answers; they orient to expectations about *the way* those activities should be done. We will take the case of IE answers.

In the previous chapter, we discussed how turns at talk are built out of turn construction units; at the end of each one is a place where turn-transfer may be initiated by a next speaker (if a next speaker has not been identified by the current speaker). This means that extended turns – ones built from several consecutive turn construction units – are not automatically available: they have to be designed so as to forestall possible other-initiated turns at transition relevance places. In ordinary conversational interaction, speakers use a variety of devices to maintain on-going speakership at points in their turns where they may be vulnerable to co-participants' turn initiations. Speakers may speed up their delivery as they approach a transition relevance, thus rushing through the place where turn initiation might be attempted (Schegloff, 1981). Alternatively, non-lexical items such as 'er' and 'mm' may be used to demonstrate further talk in the on-going turn. Or extended, multi-unit turns such as lengthy anecdotes, stories or accounts can be advertised by the use of story prefaces; these signal that normal procedures for turn-taking are momentarily suspended during the course of the projected turn (Sacks, 1992, Vol. II: Spring 1970, lecture 2). And co-participants can also facilitate an extended turn: by the use of minimal continuers, such as 'uh huh' and 'mm hm' they can display that there are passing opportunities in which turn transfer could be initiated (Jefferson, 1984a; Schegloff, 1981).

The normative expectation which underpins everyday interaction is that turn exchange can be attempted or initiated at the end of every turn construction unit. Therefore, multi-unit turns in everyday conversation, then, have to be warranted or sustained by the use of particular kinds of lexical or non-lexical activity. However, in news interview interaction, there is a very different normative expectation: IEs are *expected* to provide multi-unit answers.

Heritage and Greatbatch show how this expectation informs two features of news interview interaction. First, when IEs build multi-unit turns it is noticeable that there is an absence of those kinds of devices and practices which in everyday interaction are used to secure continuing speakership rights. Extract 3.7 comes from an interview with a man who was convicted of a crime which he claims he did not commit.

(3.7)   (From Heritage and Greatbatch, 1991: 101)

```
IR:  Have you any sort of criminal connections or
     anything,= ˙┌h      ┐
IE:             └No┘t at all.=                                [1]
     =I- I was working for the Gas Board at the time
     as a salesman,=                                          [2]
     =I had no: (0.2) emphatically no er: associates
     that (wo(h)old) had criminal records,=                   [3]
     =or I did not associate with people with criminal
     records.                                                 [4]
     ˙hhhh I- I- I was living a life o-o- of
     a family man in Stockton-on-Tees,                        [5]
     hhh where I was a representative for the Gas
     Board                                                    [6]
     ˙hhh and it was out of the blue to me                    [7]
IR:  ˙hh Were you surprise:d when You: w-went to
     court, an- and indeed went down,
```

In his answer to the IR's question, the IE produces a multi-unit turn with seven possible completion points (indicated in the square brackets.). It is noticeable that first, there are no attempts by the IR to initiate a turn at any of these possible completion points. Only after the IE provides a summary assessment to his experience ('and it was <u>out</u> of the blue to me') does the IR begin the next question. Second, the IE does not use any techniques to signal that he intends to continue speaking beyond possible completion points. He clearly expects to be able to extend his turn.

Finally, consider the following extract, in which an IE offers only a minimal answer.

(3.8)   (From Heritage and Greatbatch, 1991: 102)

IR: And d'you ex<u>pect</u> these reforms to be pa:ssed?
IE: Yes I do:.
        (1.2)
IE: The <u>ma</u>jor ones certainly

The IR does not move on to another question but withholds further talk. After a 1.2 second gap the IE speaks again to elaborate on his earlier answer. The IR was thus clearly orienting to the expectation that the IE should provide a more developed answer.

By examining the organisation of turn-taking and the ways in which questions and answers are built, we have established some of the normative expectations which underpin news interview interaction. The design of participants' turns displays their sensitivity to obligations and expectations regarding the kinds of contribution they can and should produce in this context. However, normative expectations do not determine behaviour: they are not law-like rules which govern conduct. Indeed, in extract 3.8 it is clear that the IE has deviated from the expectation to produce an extended answer. The analysis of these kinds of deviant cases is an important step in conversation analytic research.

Analysing deviant cases

A key stage in building a conversation analytic account of an interactional phenomenon is to examine cases in which there seems to have been some departure from an established pattern. We can analyse these deviant cases to investigate how participants' utterances display their understanding of the significance of that departure. So, if someone displays that they are 'noticing' the absence of a certain type of turn from a co-participant, then that demonstrates their own orientation to the normative expectation that it should have been produced.

To illustrate this, look at this fragment which we discussed in Chapter 2, in which a question is not followed by an answer.

(3.9)

Child:	Have to cut the:se Mummy
	(1.3)
Child:	Won't we Mummy
	(1.5)
Child:	Won't we
Mother:	Yes

It is clear that the child's second and third versions of the initial question display that she has 'noticed' the absence of the mother's answer. Moreover, her repeated attempts to solicit an answer display her orientation to the normative expectation that an answer should follow a question. Thus what seems on first inspection to provide evidence which undermines claims about the properties of paired action sequences (for example, that second parts should follow first parts), actually displays the participants' orientation to the normative relevance of those properties. So too in extract 3.8, we can see that the IR's withholding of a further question and the subsequent elaboration by the IE demonstrated that they were orienting the expectation (albeit belatedly in the case of the IE) that answers should be extended.

However, participants' orientation to normative expectations is not only exposed in those circumstances in which a specific kind of turn is noticeably absent: it is also revealed by the way in which participants engage in non-normative activities.

One of the overriding norms of news interview interaction is that it is the IRs who ask questions, and thereby guide the interview. It is not expected that the participants will initiate their own topical agenda. But there are circumstances in which IEs do offer comment or opinion which is not directly solicited by the IR. Some news interviews are conducted with more than one participant; and to generate a lively exchange, or to ensure that a wide range of perspectives will be represented, it is often the case that the IEs will hold different opinions. In such interviews it is not unusual to find disagreement between participants. This disagreement can result in attempts to by-pass the IR and address directly what the other IE has said. Yet when this happens, the IE asking the question will seek permission from the IR, thus displaying that they are aware that their question deviates from normative conventions.

Extracts 3.10 and 3.11 provide illustration. The two participants in this interview hold differing opinions about imprisonment as a deterrent to crime.

(3.10) (From Heritage and Greatbatch, 1991: 103)

IE 1:	... and therefore I'm not going to accept the
	criticism that I haven't tried to help victims=
	=I've (.) been trying to help them (0.2) off and
	on for twenty-five years.=

```
(?):     ='hhhh=
IE 2:    =Can I- can I say something abou⌐t this ⌐
IR:                                      └Yes in ┘deed.
         (0.5)
IE 2:    e:r (0.7) As (0.5) Frank (.) Longford knows so
         well 'hh er my views ... ((continues))
```

(3.11) (From Heritage and Greatbatch, 1991: 104)

```
IE 1:    ... there was no evidence whatever that stiffer
         penalties diminish crime.=
IE 2:    =Can I make a point about that.=hhh, Which is
         that if only this country ... ((continues))
```

In these cases IE2 responds to the point made in IE1's answer to a prior question. However, instead of simply embarking on a response, IE2 seeks permission from the IR. In extract 3.10, this is treated as a literal request in that the IR gives permission; in extract 3.11, IE2 makes a token request, in that he begins to address IE1's point before being authorised by the IR. We can see, then, that the normative expectations which underpin news interview interaction are of a markedly different kind to those which inform more conversational interaction. These normative expectations are most clearly visible in the way that participants restrict themselves to – and exhibit an expectation of – a limited range of primarily question–answer activities.

Context and interaction

In this section I want to make some points about the relationship between sequences and possible characterisations of participants. A common sense assumption would be that prior to analysis, it is necessary, or at least useful, to have some understanding of the participants: their history, their relationship to each other, their personality, the topic of their talk or the context in which they are speaking. It seems intuitively sensible to assume that all these things must cohere together and influence the way people speak, and therefore, that it is appropriate to take account of these factors when analysing talk. In CA, however, there is a principled reluctance to draw on ethnographic characterisations of the setting and its participants in the analysis. The first reason for this is that there is a very real problem in formulating what the context might be (Schegloff, 1991, 1997). This is because, as we have seen in earlier chapters, the description of any event, situation, place, or person can be done in a variety of ways (Heritage, 1978; Schegloff, 1972b). The point is that any description or reference is produced from a potentially inexhaustible list of possible utterances, each of which is 'logically' correct or 'true' by any test of correspondence. How is the analyst to decide which particular version of the context is most appropriate?

This is not to say the context of interaction is analytically irrelevant. Context is a relevant issue for the participants. During interaction speakers orient to, and display to each other in the design of their turns, what they understand to be the salient features of their context. And in the same way that we can discover speakers' own interpretations by examining the design of their turns, so we can discover what *they* take to be the relevant features of the context of their interaction. We can investigate if the participants' turns are designed to display, for example, that they are orienting to each other's work or gender identities; or we can explore how the relevance of the relationship between the participants is invoked, if at all, and so on.

However, features of the interaction may themselves be the relevant context for any subsequent contributions. For example, what might be relevant to the way an utterance is produced is the activity performed by the prior turn: a question, an excuse, a repair, an instruction, and so on. Consider extract 3.9 again.

```
Child:    Have to cut the:se Mummy
          (1.3)
Child:    Won't we Mummy
          (1.5)
Child:    Won't we
Mother:   Yes
```

This child's first turn is the first part of an adjacency pair. However, after 1.3 seconds, the child produces two further turns, both of which display the understanding that the conditionally relevant second turn has not been produced. Her turns suggest that the salient context, on this occasion, is an accountably absent turn.

Because participants' turns will exhibit their analysis of relevant features of the context, the analyst is provided with a significant methodological advantage. We do not have to speculate what *might* be relevant, we can see directly what *is* relevant to the participants. And as the 'relevant context' may be as immediate and transitory as the prior turn, CA treats context as a fluid and contingent achievement:

> a notion like 'context' will have to remain substantively contentless, and uncommitted to any prespecified referent and be instead 'programmatically relevant' [that is] relevant in principle, but with a sense always to-be-discovered rather than given-to-be-applied. (Schegloff, 1987b: 112)

The second reason that conversation analysts do not rely in their research on a characterisation of the context is because interaction is viewed as a domain of activity in its own right, and not a reflection of individual personalities or social or cultural constraints. Following Goffman, who was the first to focus on the organisation of mundane, everyday activities, interactional practices are regarded as exhibiting an order which is not reducible to the personality, intentions or mood of the speakers, nor the social or cultural context in which they are speaking. As Heritage puts it, 'the institution of interaction largely antedates the characteristics of those who staff it' (Heritage, 2001: 52).

Research in CA, then, focuses on detailed description and analysis of structured interactional practices unencumbered by any formal account of the identity of the participants, speculation about their intentions or goals, or a characterisation of the context of the interaction. Moreover, it does not incorporate explanatory terms or hypotheses associated with more conventional social scientific theories and explanations of human action. Analysis is not directed to confirming or disconfirming, for example, the impact of class, status or gender variables in interaction. For these reasons, analysis is said to be data driven, not led by theory.

Summary

- CA studies of institutional interaction examine how turn-taking patterns depart from those observed in informal conversational exchanges.
- CA research shows how participants display their orientation to the appropriateness of these distinctive turn-taking patterns.
- It thereby identifies participants' sensitivity to the normative conventions which underpin these turn-taking arrangements.
- Departures from established sequential patterns, and the participants' responses to, or 'noticings of' these departures are a useful methodological resource because they display their understanding of the significance of those departures.
- CA seeks to show how participants' orientation to the relevance of the context (physical setting, topic, respective identities, etc.) demonstrably informs their talk.

Developments, divergences, continuities and convergences

In this section I want to trace how the later studies discussed in this chapter relate to the earlier work in each field.

Discourse analysis: divergence, convergence and implications

What, then, is the relationship between the form of discourse analysis described in Gilbert and Mulkay's study of scientists' discourse, and the empirical approach and theoretical arguments developed in social psychology? We start by noting some differences.

Influences   With the exception of a discussion of Halliday's work on language and social context, and a brief mention of Foucauldian and sociolinguistic discourse analysis, Gilbert and Mulkay rarely acknowledge the influence, or even existence, of related approaches to the study of language. For example, except for a passing reference to Sacks *et al*'s study of turn-taking procedures in everyday conversation, there is no discussion of conversation analysis. This is a curious omission: Gilbert and Mulkay were trying to establish the need to study discourse as a topic, and to demonstrate the complexity of language use, to a largely sceptical sociological community which had hitherto regarded language as an unproblematic research resource. Acknowledgement of CA's findings about the action-orientation of utterances, and the level of detail at which turns can be designed, would have been useful in establishing the relevance of their arguments. It would have at the very least supported their claim that language use can be studied sociologically as a topic in its own right. Discourse analysts, however, are much more explicit about the range of intellectual influences. For example, Potter and Wetherell cite the importance of speech act theory, ethnomethodology and semiotics. The findings from conversation analytic studies are regularly used to illustrate general claims about language, or to strengthen the force of criticisms of traditional social psychological approaches. Their chapter on accounts uses Atkinson and Drew's (1979) research on courtroom interaction; and their critique of social psychological attempts to study how people categorise themselves into social groups is informed directly by material from Sacks' early lectures. Edwards' work on categorisations in everyday speech and the use of scripts in social life is informed, respectively, by Sacks' work on membership categorisation devices and ethnomethodological arguments about the constitutive nature of rule following in social life (Edwards, 1991, 1995a).

Focus Although Gilbert and Mulkay's discourse analysis was forged from a consideration of methodological issues which have a wider relevance in sociology, their research concerned issues in the sociology of scientific knowledge. (This was also true of colleagues who were sympathetic to discourse analysis.) This reduced the likelihood that their broader arguments would be influential in the discipline as a whole. Edwards, Potter and Wetherell, however, explored the implications of the variable and constructive properties of language in a variety of sub-topics within social psychology: for example, the study of attitudes, categorisation, social representation theory and theories of the self. This ensured that the analytic method they offered as an alternative to traditional approaches in social psychology enjoyed a wider currency. It also allowed them to identify several important new lines of empirical inquiry, thus stimulating further research.

Repertoires One major difference between the initial work in DA in sociology of scientific knowledge and the subsequent emergence in social psychology research concerns the use of the concept of repertoires. There is no clear-cut distinction, but it seems reasonable to propose that the investigation of repertoires was a much more prominent feature of the earlier discourse analytic work. There was discussion of repertoires in Potter and Wetherell's key DA text; but even here many of the analytic themes which they addressed did not rely on the notion of repertoires. Their chapter on accounts, for example, draws much more heavily from conversation analytic work on courtroom interaction. And Edwards and Potter's subsequent analysis of attributions in discourse concerning a political dispute focused more on the ways in which versions of events and descriptions of people had been formulated so as to manage imputations of blame and responsibility. In the subsequent development of discourse analysis, the use of repertoires has been variable. For example, in studies of the way we use psychological terms, or invoke cognitive or mental phenomena – a branch of discourse analysis which has become known as discursive psychology – there is little use of the concept of repertoires (for example, Edwards, 1991, 1994). But in some more ideologically oriented discourse analysis, analysts still seek to identify the repertoires through which versions of the world are constructed (for example, Edley, 2001).

Implications: from representations to action   What unites these two strands of discourse analysis are their radical methodological implications.

Discourse analysis proposes the language we use, and the way we use it, is not determined by, nor anchored in, some set of objective properties of the events to which we refer. Any state of affairs, any event, any person or group of people, yield potentially inexhaustible descriptive possibilities (Waismann, 1965; Wittgenstein, 1953). Moreover, we do things with our words: they are not inert representations of social action, nor neutral disclosures which either exhibit the operation of underlying cognitive processes, or from which such processes may be inferred. They are actions, designed for the 'here-and-now' of their production.

Social scientists are aware of the difficulties in using people's accounts as data for research, but perhaps for the wrong reason. It has been assumed that such data are either anecdotal, and therefore of little analytic value, or that they are subject to distortion, revision, omission and so on, and thereby unreliable. A variety of methodological techniques have been developed in sociology and social psychology to overcome the perceived shortcomings of discursive data. However, these methodological responses still embody the assumption that language is a medium of representation, when in fact it is a medium of social action. Unless we recognise this key property of the language through which social and psychological life is conducted, and make it a central feature of our analytic enterprise, sociology and social psychology will rest on fragile foundations.

Conversation analysis: continuities and implications

Earlier we examined some findings from studies of interaction in particular kinds of work-related or institutional settings. How has this discussion advanced our understanding of the core methodological principles of CA and the significance of its findings?

Continuities It might be objected that a method known as *conversation* analysis is inappropriate for the study of more constrained forms of interaction such as those we would expect to find in formal work or institutional settings. Despite its name, however, conversation analysis is not exclusively concerned with forms of everyday interaction which might be loosely termed 'conversational'. Indeed, it is common in more contemporary literature to see references to CA as the study of *talk-in-interaction* (Schegloff, 1987b); this term embraces ordinary mundane conversation and forms of talk which exhibit more formal properties. Moreover, CA developed as a distinct approach to interaction in part from Sacks' analysis of calls from members of the public to a suicide prevention centre, and recordings of discussions in therapy group meetings. In these contexts, many of the participants at various points were performing specific work-related tasks which reflected the broader goals of the institution or organisation for which they worked: for example, in the calls to the suicide prevention centre, the centre's staff were employed to provide help and guidance. In this sense, then, even some of Sacks' earliest lectures were concerned with how people use everyday language to accomplish particular work-related tasks. The study of interaction in formal and informal work settings thus develops concerns which were explored in early studies in conversation analysis.

A key feature of studies of interaction in institutional settings is a concern to show how the business of the institution is addressed through distinctive patterns of turn-taking. Clearly, these are not the only features of institutional talk which set it apart from more conversational interaction: there may be distinct specialist vocabularies; interaction will reflect the relevance of work-related identities ('manager', 'interviewer', 'barrister', and so on); and participants will be concerned with particular work-related tasks. But to an important degree it is necessary to prioritise examination of the turn-taking organisation because it underpins and facilitates these other activities and relevancies (Drew and Heritage, 1992a).

Implications Institutions and their activities are profoundly implicated in shaping our lives. However, social scientists have tended to examine their effects at a macro or statistical level, studying, for example, what is the social class background of those who tend to succeed in education, or who are convicted for crime, or who occupy senior managerial posts in industry or the civil service? However, the most immediate and everyday impacts of institutions are manifest and felt in patterns of verbal interaction. We are educated in schools, and the daily intellectual, moral and personal growth of children and young adults is encouraged and nurtured through classroom interaction with our teachers. In workplaces we develop an understanding of the rules of procedure, both formal and informal, through verbal instruction from and interaction with supervisors and colleagues. Our health is monitored and maintained in interaction with our doctors, but also, if necessary, in consultations with other medical professionals in hospitals and clinics. And if we do fall foul of the law, or are required to give evidence or serve as jurors, or qualify as barristers or judges, our courtroom participation will be conducted through talk. In an important sense, people will walk free or lose their liberty on the basis of verbal activities such as providing testimony and cross-examination.

Conversation analysis can thus offer a great deal to our understanding of institutions and their relevance in our lives. It offers a novel perspective on institutions, in two ways. It examines the ways in which participants attend to work-related tasks or the core functions of the institution. In this sense CA has been able to develop our understanding of the ways in which, for example, teachers and pupils, doctors and patients, and barristers and witnesses conduct the business of schools, hospitals and courts through their talk. By focusing on the features of turn-taking in particular work contexts, and the normative frameworks which underpin those turn-taking organisations, we have developed a sophisticated and empirically grounded appreciation of what makes conduct in these settings so distinctive. And this in turn has a more radical implication. It suggests that instead of viewing institutions as somehow constraining or simply determining conduct which occurs in institutional settings, we can explore how particular kinds of interactional practices 'enable' or 'realise' the institution (Schegloff, 1991; Zimmerman and Boden, 1991). Thus CA offers an alternative to the view – enshrined in many social science approaches – that our conduct automatically reflects the context in which it occurs.

Further readings

Discourse analysis and critical developments in social psychology

Hepburn's (2003) introductory text provides an excellent and comprehensive overview of the kinds of critical positions in contemporary social psychology. The following texts draw upon Foucault's writings and address broadly political issues in psychological practice and research: Burman, Aitken, Aldred, Allwood, Billington, Goldberg, Gordo-Lopez, Heenan, Marks and Warner (1996); Burman and Parker (1993a); and Parker (1989). The two following edited collections offer diverse ways of thinking about the discipline of psychology, and the practices of psychological research: Smith, Harré and Van Langenhove (1995a, 1995b). The following text offers a distinctive and stimulating position on the ideological nature of everyday life, and its implications for social psychological research across a variety of substantive areas: Billig, Condor, Edwards, Gane, Middleton and Radley (1988).

One feature of DA work which we do not have space to discuss is the DAM: the Discourse Action Model. This was formulated by Edwards and Potter to sensitise researchers to three deficiencies with traditional social psychological approaches: a failure to explore the relationship between ordinary communication and psychological analysis; the use of methodologies which ignore the sequential organisation of natural discourse; and a failure to recognise how descriptions and versions of events are constructed to perform social actions. It is described in the following two texts: Edwards and Potter (1992, 1995). Horton-Salway (2001) illustrates the use of the DAM approach in a study of accounts of ME (myalgic encephalomyelitis).

Conversation analysis and interaction in institutional settings

The best collection of papers on CA studies of institutional talk is Drew and Heritage (1992a); and their introductory paper in this collection (Drew and Heritage, 1992b) provides an excellent overview of the main dimensions of the work in this area, and also situates the CA approach to institutional discourse in relation to other social science perspectives. Although Atkinson and Drew's (1979) study is exclusively concerned with courtroom interaction, it is an excellent example of the use of CA to study more formally constrained kinds of interaction. It also contains a very useful comparative discussion of conversation analytic and ethnographic perspectives.

Chapter-length introductions can be found in Drew and Sorjonen (1997) and Heritage (1997). McHoul and Rapley's (2001) edited collection provides introductions to and illustrations of various approaches to the analysis of institutional interaction, including conversation analysis, discursive psychology and critical discourse analysis. The following collection has some key papers on the relationship between CA and social structure more generally, many of which explore issues which overlap with the study of institutional interaction: Boden and Zimmerman (1991). Finally, Schegloff's (1987b) discussion offers a clear account of the CA position on the relationship between talk and the (macro) contexts in which it occurs. For further discussion of the relationship between talk and its contexts from an ethnomethodological/CA perspective, see the papers in Duranti and Goodwin (1992) and Watson and Seiler (1992).

4
Similarities and Differences

Many social scientists regard conversation analysis and discourse analysis as roughly similar kinds of approaches: they both offer qualitative analyses of the functional and sense-making properties of language. And viewed from the standpoint of traditional social science, which by and large has not been concerned to understand the role or nature of language use, there do appear to be overlaps. In the first part of this chapter we will examine some of these similarities. However, it will become apparent that conversation analysis and discourse analysis share assumptions and approaches only at a broad level. When we consider in more detail the substantive focus of research, and the methodological assumptions which inform empirical analysis, significant differences begin to emerge.

Similarities

Our discussion will be organised around four themes: talk as topic for analysis; attention to properties of data; the influence of ethnomethodology; and accusations of triviality.

Talk as topic

It is simple to get a sense of sociology's priorities: look at the contents page of any introductory textbook and see what kinds of areas are covered by the chapter headings. While it is likely there will be chapters on classic theoretical approaches and some methodological discussion, the core of the book will be concerned with topics such as education, the family, gender and social inequality, work, crime, deviance and the criminal justice system, religion, health and illness, and so on. The sociology of language is simply not one of the core topics of the discipline. And although some psychologists have studied mundane interaction, the approach has been largely experimental (for example, Beattie, 1983). Moreover, psychologists tend to focus on the cognitive and developmental aspects of language. In this sense, both conversation analysis and discourse analysis are distinctive because they focus explicitly on language as social action.

Of course, as Gilbert and Mulkay pointed out, a significant proportion of sociological research relies heavily on people's discourse. One of the main methods of data collection in sociology is the informal or semi-formal interview, through which researchers solicit various kinds of discourse – accounts, reports, descriptions, anecdotes – which then become the data for analysis. Invariably, however, these discursive data will be analysed as a resource to allow the researcher to make claims about some non-discursive topic. They will be interpreted in terms of the researcher's theoretical or substantive concerns, be that health care provision for older people, perceptions of crime, or the nature of religious observance in contemporary society. The analytic focus concerns what the discourse is about; the properties and significance of the discourse itself are largely unexplored.

In this sense, CA and DA are truly radical developments, because they examine discourse as a topic in its own right, and not as a reflection of wider structural conditions. So, for example, Sacks *et al* did not examine the turn-taking system for ordinary interaction to allow them to draw conclusions about wider social inequalities. And neither did Gilbert and Mulkay analyse scientists' accounts to make broader claims about the relative differences in research culture between laboratories in the UK and the US. Their prime concern was with language in use: the systematic ways it was being used, and what it was being used to do.

Attention to properties of data

In keeping with their explicit focus on language, conversation and discourse analysis are attentive to the properties of how language is actually used. Research questions derive from observations on features plainly exhibited by the data. For example, Sacks and his colleagues' careful transcription of talk-in-interaction revealed that there were few gaps between turns; moreover they noted that although periods of overlapping speech were common, these were relatively short-lived. These simple observations informed their empirical research. They argued that any adequate analysis of the methods for turn-taking had to be able to account for these properties of talk-in-interaction. Similarly, Gilbert and Mulkay realised that in their interview data, scientists were producing variable accounts. Instead of trying to expunge this variability from their data in order to produce a single, coherent sociological narrative, they began to examine the organisation of these varied accounting practices to identify the functions they performed. In both cases empirical research questions were thus generated from an open-minded assessment of the data. In this sense, neither Sacks and his colleagues nor Gilbert and Mulkay approached their data with pre-established research questions in mind. Indeed, it has become a distinctive (and controversial) feature of conversation analysis (and, to a lesser degree, discourse analysis) that premature theorising is actively resisted.

The influence of ethnomethodology

Both conversation analysis and discourse analysis reflect and develop the concerns of ethnomethodology. Pioneered by Harold Garfinkel (1967) the fundamental tenet of ethnomethodology is that the sense of social action is accomplished through the participants' use of tacit, practical reasoning skills and competencies. These skills are referred to as 'tacit' and 'practical' because they are not the kinds of 'rules' or norms of behaviour which we could consciously articulate, or on which we would routinely reflect. Instead, they inhabit the very weave of social life, and thereby become invisible and unnoticeable. As so much of social life is mediated through spoken and written communication, the study of language was placed at the very heart of ethnomethodology's sociological enterprise. Sacks was a colleague of Garfinkel, and their work shares many concerns: for example, analysing the normative basis of social action, and the way that sense-making procedures are embedded in mundane activities. However, Sacks' work was focused exclusively on the communicative competencies that informed ordinary, everyday conversation. Moreover, as his distinctive style of analysis developed it became much more positivistic in its outlook. CA subsequently emerged as the study of objective structures in the way that interaction is patterned. This is at odds with ethnomethodology's more interpretative stance, and its focus on the ways in which members achieve the sense of any particular event or moment. In recent years, some ethnomethodologists have been critical of this positivistic turn in CA, arguing that it betrays the more ethnomethodological spirit which was important in some of Sacks' earlier lectures (Lynch and Bogen, 1994).

Although Gilbert and Mulkay (1984) were interested in the interpretative practices which informed scientists' accounts of a scientific dispute, their analyses were not ethnomethodological in orientation. However, ethnomethodology's focus on the situated and constitutive use of tacit sense-making activities was reflected in Edwards and Middleton's studies of the joint production of discursive remembering. And Garfinkel's work was explicitly influential in Potter and Wetherell's (1987) subsequent development of discourse analysis, in two senses. First, ethnomethodological research was cited to establish that the study of people's own sense-making should be a central part of social psychology. But it was also important as part of their wider critique of experimental methods in social psychology. Thus although discourse analysis was informed by a range of intellectual traditions, ethnomethodology was central to their attempt to highlight the implications for social psychology of the constructive and constitutive properties of ordinary language.

Accusations of triviality

In the early stages of their development, both CA and DA were criticised for making trivial claims. So, critics of Gilbert and Mulkay's discourse analysis argued that variation in participants' accounts was already well-known and not an intractable problem (Abell, 1983). Alternatively, it was claimed that empirical results amounted to little more than a superficial gloss of different forms of description, and that discourse analysis offered little more than the observation that 'some scientists write their scientific papers in impersonal terms but in interviews talk about science personally'. Moreover, it was argued that the focus on spoken and verbal discourse was an unnecessary and unhelpful diversion from the proper topics of inquiry in the sociology of scientific knowledge (Halfpenny, 1988: 177; but see Potter and McKinley, 1989, for a rebuttal of Halfpenny's critique). The upshot, though, was clear: DA is a largely trivial affair, dealing primarily with unimportant methodological matters, and offering no new and significant insight to the way that science and scientists work.

Conversation analysis has attracted a more sustained critical inspection, and sometimes generated extreme responses. For example, in his (1975) polemic, Gellner argues that there is a cult of personality surrounding ethnomethodology, and by implication conversation analysis. He suggests that the lecturing style of its practitioners owes more to pop stars than respected sociologists. His claim that an ethnomethodology conference seemed to attract a higher number of attractive 'chicks' than would be found at other academic conferences implies that interest in the nature of the work is secondary to the more superficial attraction of the way it is presented, and the cultish aspects of the movement (Gellner, 1975: 435).

Gellner's critique focuses on relatively unimportant matters, and his arguments have not had much bearing on the development of ethnomethodology or conversation analysis. But the tone of his review is of more significance: in many places he simply abandons conventional academic standards of argument and presentation, and instead resorts to sarcasm, flippancy and gross caricature. Clearly, Gellner felt the arguments presented by ethnomethodologists and conversation analysts did not merit the kind of serious consideration afforded other developments in sociology.

Gellner's paper was an extreme response to the kind of work advanced by conversation analysis, but not untypical. But perhaps it was to be expected: CA is a form of sociology which departs radically from that practised by most sociologists. Whereas conventional sociology is informed by wider theoretical issues, CA is rigorously empirical and in fact rejects premature theorising. And whereas sociology is traditionally concerned with intuitively pressing issues such as power, class, gender and asymmetries in status and opportunity, CA attends to what might seem to be on first inspection utterly trivial features of human conduct: turn-taking in mundane conversation, or the fact that questions and answers seem to form 'natural' pairs, and so on. Again, the basis for the criticisms is that CA fails to address core sociological issues, attending instead to matters of little wider relevance.

So, are CA and DA unimportant because they fail to address what we can intuitively recognise to be important issues? There are several responses. First, it can be argued that CA and DA do address 'core issues' in the social sciences, but in ways distinctive to their own epistemological and methodological orientations. So, for example, we will see later in this book how power can be studied using conversation analysis. This treatment of power may not chime with those found in more traditional sociological perspectives – it is concerned, broadly, with the management of interactional advantage through turn-taking – but it is a treatment of power nonetheless. Second, we may question the assumption that the social sciences have adequately identified the core issues for empirical research and theorising. For example: sociology is an empirical discipline concerned with the social organisation of individual and collective human action. However,

> Talk is at the heart of human existence. It is pervasive and central to human history, in every setting of human affairs, at all levels of society, in virtually every social context. (Zimmerman and Boden, 1991: 3)

Our communicative competencies facilitate the intricate and complex inter-relationships which sociologists (and social psychologists) seek to understand, whether they occur in classrooms, in family homes, at work, in hospitals, or in the courtroom. This means that if we do not properly understand the way that language is used in the performance of social activities, in talk and in texts, then we have, at best, an incomplete account of a key dimension of human behaviour as it affects precisely those areas of inquiry which have traditionally been conceived as the core topics of social science disciplines. And thus we have to question the adequacy of any theoretical account, or the reliability of an empirical research project, which fails to address the centrality of language use in social life. In this sense, the concerns of conversation analysis and discourse analysis should be at the heart of any social scientific enterprise. Indeed, it is possible to make an even bolder claim: that CA and DA offer analyses which are the necessary starting points for any adequate social science.

But more important – and more telling – it is possible to identify numerous empirical studies in discourse and conversation analysis which have clear practical implications for people's lives. We will consider just two.

Understanding public disturbances: Potter and Reicher and the Bristol riots   What empirical gains come from analysing the descriptive and referential patterns in everyday language? To illustrate we will consider Potter and Reicher's (1987) study of the public debate which followed a major disturbance (or riot) in the city of Bristol in the UK. Potter and Reicher's data consisted of, among other things, newspaper reports, the texts of television programmes about the events, and transcripts of interviews with people involved. In all these forms of data, participants were concerned to identify which groups were to blame and what could be done to prevent further outbreaks of violence.

Potter and Reicher were interested broadly in the way that categorisations of the protagonists in the riot, and relevant others, were accomplished in texts and talk. In particular they focused on the way that a linguistic repertoire of 'community' presented its users with a variety of inferential and descriptive resources.

Remember that a repertoire is a 'broadly discernible clusters of terms, descriptions, commonplaces ... and figures of speech often clustered around metaphors of vivid images and often using distinct grammatical constructions and styles' (Potter *et al*, 1990: 212). The community repertoire was characterised by words and phrases which invoke cohesive social relationships: for example, 'closeness', 'integration' and 'friendliness'. It was also marked by the use of certain metaphors concerning space and proximity ('a close knit community'), organism ('the growth of the community') and agency ('the community acts').

While 'the community' was always regarded positively, the use of the community repertoire was varied. On some occasions it was used to depict community members reacting bravely to unwarranted police harassment; on other occasions, it was used to include the police as part of the community. However, this descriptive variability was consequential, because there was a lot at stake: these two uses of the community repertoire entailed very different implications for the wider public understanding of what had happened and, more important, what should be done about it. For example, portraying the police as part of the community paved the way for greater integration and involvement in the form of community policing. But depictions of the disturbance as a consequence of antagonism between the community and the police as an external body invoked a very different set of interpretations. It focused attention on the differences between the community and the police: in this case, the mainly black local residents and the predominantly white police officers. Thus the problem revolved around race relations, as much as, for example, the relative poverty and poor facilities of the area where the riots occurred. This use of the repertoire presupposes a very different set of personal and institutional responses to the disturbances.

By focusing on the use of a particular repertoire, Potter and Reicher were able to avoid trying to marshal these variable and contradictory accounts into a single story of 'what really happened' or 'what the community's response should be', and so on. Instead, they were able to give analytic priority to the rich tapestry of interpretations and their inferential implications which followed as people tried to make sense of the Bristol riots.

Getting help: Whalen, Zimmerman and Whalen and misunderstanding in a call to emergency services

In 1984, in Dallas, Texas, a call was made to the city emergency services. A man reported that his stepmother was dying – she was having trouble breathing – and that he needed help. But the person taking the call (called the dispatcher, although a qualified nurse) did not immediately alert the various medical services available. This was because the caller and the dispatcher became embroiled in an argument. And because the medical services were not alerted immediately, the caller's stepmother died.

This was a tragic and unusual case, and city officials and journalists alike wondered how could it be that, in a case where the caller has stated that his stepmother was experiencing breathing difficulties – clearly a life threatening state – emergency medical services were not alerted at once? Recriminations followed, and eventually the nurse who took the call was fired.

All calls to emergency services are recorded as a matter of routine. Whalen *et al* (1988) examined the recording and transcript of this call. Unlike officials responsible for investigating this case, they were not concerned to allocate blame. Instead, they wanted to use conversation analysis 'to understand how the fateful denouement of this event was achieved as an orderly outcome' (Whalen *et al*, 1988: 340). That is, they did not want to study the argument in vernacular terms – as a result of rudeness, interpersonal friction or insensitivity – but as an interactionally coherent consequence of the way that the participants interpreted the activities performed by the other's utterances.

Whalen *et al* note that a cursory inspection and summary of the caller's initial utterances would indicate the seriousness of the problem. But they point out that utterances are used in specific sequential contexts, and that their sense, or the activity they are performing, is linked to that sequential context (Schegloff, 1984). Through a detailed analysis of the call, they show how the respective participants clearly had a different understanding of the kinds of sequential contexts in which their talk was occurring. There was, then, misalignment between caller and dispatcher in their analysis of the actions performed by the other's turns. There is no space here to provide an illustrated instance, but a summary will suffice. During one phase of the call, the caller was reporting symptoms of his stepmother's condition. Clearly for the caller, he was engaged in the activity of providing 'news' – informing the dispatcher about matters relevant to securing help. But the dispatcher's utterances indicate that she is working with a different interpretation of the current sequential context: 'the caller's informings failed as news of priority symptoms because they were for the most part embedded/placed in sequential positions where they did the work of, or were tied to, *disputing and opposing*' (Whalen *et al*, 1988: 358; italics added). And from such misalignments throughout the course of the call, a full-blown dispute developed, as a consequence of which the caller's stepmother did not receive the help she needed.

This conversation analytic study has many practical implications. For example, it revealed that the dispute was not the fault of one person, but was an interactionally generated outcome. This suggests that the City of Dallas may have been premature to fire the nurse dispatcher who took the call. Moreover, it exposed the internal sequential machinery through which such calls can become problematic, which at least offers the possibility for some formal training for dispatchers to ensure such misalignments are in future recognised and dealt with before serious consequences develop. And, finally, it is useful to bear in mind that Whalen *et al*'s insight about the distinctive features of this case drew from studies of the sequential organisation of more routine and unexceptional calls to the emergency services (Whalen and Zimmerman, 1987).

Summary

- When compared to traditional social science approaches, CA and DA are distinctive in their focus on discourse/language use as a topic in its own right.
- Both CA and DA have been dismissed either because they focus on trivial or unimportant matters, or because they are said to add little to existing knowledge.
- CA and DA are not exclusively concerned with the routine or mundane, but can be harnessed to address and explore intuitively important matters.

Differences

The discussion of the differences between conversation analysis and discourse analysis will be organised around various substantive and methodological issues.

Substantive issues

In this section we examine the different kinds of substantive topics or issues which are studied in conversation analysis and discourse analysis.

Analysing actions vs analysing action orientations in accounting practices   In this section I will try to identify in general terms broad differences in the focus of empirical research. I will argue that, as a heuristic, it is useful to identify the core analytic concern of CA as the study of *social action* through language, and to identify the core analytic concern of DA as the investigation of the way that accounts and formulations display an *action orientation*. But before I go on to articulate this distinction, it is important to acknowledge that there are some blurry areas where this distinction does not hold. Conversation analytic studies of interaction, on the whole, tend to exhibit specific methodological characteristics, and there is a consistent style to formal published studies. There is, however, greater diversity in discourse analytic research, in terms of both the treatment of data and the range of analytic issues being explored, and some later discourse analytic studies have much in common with conversation analytic research. For example, the data in Edwards' (1995a) analysis of interaction in a relationship counselling session are transcribed according to CA conventions, and his analytic claims are grounded in close description of the activities constituted through the participants' turns; and Potter and Hepburn (2003) examine the sequential basis of the use of psychological terms in calls to a telephone child protection helpline. Moreover, some areas of research associated with CA, such as Sacks' earlier writing on the organisation and use of membership categories, exhibit a less formal and more interpretative stance characteristic of DA studies. So it is important to bear in mind that there will be exceptions to the argument which follows in this and subsequent sections. With that caveat in mind, let us turn to the broad differences in the style and focus of empirical analysis.

Put simply, in conversation analysis, the topic of research is the social organisation of activities conducted through talk. CA research seeks to discover sequential patterns of interaction, and to explicate the web of normative expectations and assumptions which inform and underpin the production of those sequences.

Analysis of any particular utterance proceeds by examining its placement in the turn-by-turn development of interaction. This is because the goal of analysis is to examine sequences of interaction, not isolated utterances; but also, because empirical analysis has revealed that turns at talk are designed in various ways to show their relationship to the activity performed by prior turns. Turns at talk are built to display how they 'fit' with prior turns. And of course each turn establishes a range of possible next actions, and the subsequent turn will be constructed to display its fit to that sequential environment. This is how interaction proceeds: each successive turn building on the prior turn and setting up an environment for particular kinds of next activities.

CA, then, is focused on interaction; discourse analysis, however, is primarily concerned with a broader set of language practices: accounts in talk or texts. The word 'accounts' has two senses: it can be used to refer to specific discursive acts which excuse or justify some course of action; or it can be used in a non-technical sense to refer to passage of text or talk which expresses opinions, formulates versions of events and so on. Discourse analysis has been primarily concerned with accounts in this non-technical sense. Thus Gilbert and Mulkay (1984) studied scientists' accounts of experiments, theories and people involved in a scientific dispute; and Potter and Reicher (1987) studied reports of riots from newspapers and from interviews with people involved. The goal of analysis is to study the ways in which accounts are constructed flexibly and used functionally.

This is a key difference between CA and DA. Conversation analytic research examines how participants manage interaction as it proceeds: how they make sense of the moment-by-moment unfolding of interaction; it describes the highly patterned sequential structures through which particular activities are accomplished; and it discovers the methods used to effect turn-transfer, or to identify and address troubles, such as misunderstandings, errors and corrections, and so on. CA has revealed that verbal activities are coordinated at an extremely fine level of detail: it is therefore argued that it is incumbent upon analysts who are interested in studying interaction, or who use inter-actional materials as data, to analyse their data at the same level of detail and organisation as was demonstrably relevant to the participants in the record-ing. In this sense, CA offers formal analyses at a greater level of detail, and relies upon a distinctive vocabulary of technical terms to capture this detailed organisation.

In discourse analytic research, however, the action orientation of language is located at a broader level, and, traditionally, empirical analysis of the organ-isation of talk (and texts) has focused on the wider interpersonal or social functions served by a passage of talk. Thus Gilbert and Mulkay examined extended descriptions and reports to reveal how they had been constructed to portray a set of experimental results in a negative manner, or to depict the contingent social or psychological factors that informed scientists' work. And although interactional materials are often used as data in discourse analytic studies, the management of interaction *per se* is rarely the focus of research. (However, as we shall see in later chapters, in some forms of analysis which developed from discourse analysis, such as discursive psychology, there is greater analytic attention to the interactional organisation of verbal data.)

The broader analytic focus of DA is reflected in its main conceptual tool, the linguistic repertoire. Linguistic repertoires are related or themed terms, such as metaphors or figures of speech, used in particular kinds of ways. The linguistic repertoire, then, offers considerably less descriptive precision than, say, 'first pair parts' and 'second pair parts' of 'paired action sequences', 'turn construction units' or 'transfer relevance places'. Consequently, because dis-course analysis has not developed the same kind of specialised, formal vocab-ulary, research papers are often more accessible than conversation analytic papers, especially to those new to the study of language.

We can illustrate these differences by comparing two passages from published research in which analytic claims about data are presented. For con-venience, we will refer to studies discussed in the previous chapter. The first comes from Potter and Edwards' (1990) discourse analytic study of the dispute about 'what was really said' at a meeting between the then Chancellor of the Exchequer and ten political journalists.

Potter and Edwards consider these data.

(4.1)   (From Potter and Edwards, 1990: 412)

[1]   How on earth did the Chancellor, as a former journalist, manage to mislead so many journalists at once about his intentions?

[2]   As all the Sunday newspapers carried virtually the same story, is the Chancellor saying that every journalist who came to the briefing – he has not denied that there was one – misunderstood what he said?

[3]   The reporters, it seemed, had unanimously got it wrong. Could so many messengers really be so much in error? It seems doubtful.

Their analysis is:

> In the sequence of events, Extracts 1 to 3 follow Lawson's [the Chancellor] claim that the reporters were wrong. That is, he has questioned the factual status of the reports. Using the idea of witnesses corroborating versions, we take the rhetorical force of these accounts to be something like this: it is reasonable to imagine that some of the journalists might be misled in a briefing of this kind but not that they all should. If a number of observers report the same thing, that encourages us to treat the status of that thing as factual. The consensuality of the reports' accounts is offered as the basis for scepticism about the Chancellor's ... the passages do not merely state that the consensus is present, but provide the basis for a rhetorical appeal to the reader to construct it herself. For example, the extracts work on the quality or adequacy of the consensus and its unanimity ... The large size of the consensus is worked up using the description 'so many' journalists, which pick out the number of journalists as exceptionable or notable. (Potter and Edwards, 1990: 412)

Now consider the following passage from Heritage and Greatbatch's conversation analytic study of news interview interaction. Here they are discussing how the interviewee observes the normative expectation that the interviewer should be seen to be neutral, and not offering his or her own opinions.

(4.2) (From Heritage and Greatbatch, 1991: 117)

    IR: 'hhh we What's the difference between your
          Marxism and Mister McGaehy's Communism.
    IE: er The difference is that it's the <u>press</u> that
          constantly call me a <u>Ma</u>:rxist when I do <u>not</u>,
          (.) and never <u>have</u> (.) er er given that
          description of myself. -

Heritage and Greatbatch offer the following analysis:

> The question rests on two claims about the individuals involved: first, that Mr McGahey is a communist, and second, that Mr Scargill [the interviewee] is a Marxist. Within the format of the IR's turn, neither of these claims is overtly asserted as either a fact or as an opinion. Rather the claims are embedded within the question as factual presuppositions about the individuals involved ... In his response to the question, the IE (Scargill) rejects one of the presuppositions – that he is a Marxist. But it is noticeable that this rejection (which is framed as an 'answer' to the question – note the answer preface 'the difference is') is managed as the rejection of an error of fact (ascribed to 'the press') and not as the rejection of an opinion expressed by the IR. In this, and innumerable other cases, IEs treat IR questions – no matter how hostile or in other ways prejudicial to their viewpoints – as activities which are not accountable as the 'expressions of opinion'. (Heritage and Greatbatch, 1991: 117)

There are clear differences: Potter and Edwards examine sections from newspaper reports, and seek to distil a general orientation in these texts to the use of consensus information; Heritage and Greatbatch explicate from one question–answer sequence to show how both participants orient to and reproduce the neutrality conventionally associated with news interviews. Potter and Edwards argue that their data are organised to have a 'rhetorical force'; Heritage and Greatbatch discuss activities at the level of turn design. Potter and Edwards' analysis is not couched in a technical vocabulary; Heritage and Greatbatch's analysis is more technical in that it refers to 'turn format'; and in the discussion of the way Scargill's turn is constructed invokes the properties of paired action sequences. Finally, Potter and Edwards examine the way the details of the extracts are organised to portray the broad factual status of the journalists' claims; Heritage and Greatbatch's analysis reveals how the participants have designed their turns to accomplish a specific interactional task, namely, achieving neutrality within a news interview.

One feature of CA analysis illustrated by the passage from Heritage and Greatbatch is the focus on explicating the participants' own understanding in next turn analysis. Thus we see the claim that Scargill is orienting to the expectation that news interviewers should be neutral is warranted by close description of the design of his turn: he treats the IR's question as offering factual statements, as opposed to opinions. This simple methodological step has important implications which will be discussed when we consider the differing methodological emphases of CA and DA.

Engagement with disciplinary topics and methods   It is reasonable to describe conversation analysis and discourse analysis as having different disciplinary 'homes'. So, although DA emerged in the sociology of scientific knowledge, it has primarily flourished in social psychology. And although CA has clear overlaps with linguistics, it is branch of sociology.

CA and DA have very different relationships with their home discipline. Discourse analysts have addressed some of the core research areas in social psychology, both critically and substantively. In his collaboration with Middleton, and in his own work, Edwards has focused on the way in which the ethnomethodological and conversation analytic perspective on language and interaction can be used as the basis for a radical critique of the assumptions and experimental methods of cognitive psychology (Edwards, 1991, 1994, 1995a; Edwards and Middleton, 1986, 1988). Potter and Wetherell's (1987) introduction to discourse analysis explored how a concern with the constitutive properties of language use had important implications for (amongst others) the study of attitudes, self-identity, and social representation theory. Take the study of attitudes, for example: in cognitive psychology, these were regarded as fairly static mental constructs which either were examined experimentally, or were taken to be simply revealed or expressed through people's talk. Discourse analysis argued that the functional, variable and constructive properties of language meant that it was methodologically unwise to regard people's discourse as a neutral conduit to a realm of objective cognitive phenomena.

But discourse analysis did not only offer a set of methodological critiques. Analysts offered new ways of conducting empirical research, and identified new research topics. Again, take the concept of attitudes: instead of assuming that attitudes exist as mental constructs, discourse analysts argued that it was more important to study how people formulate attitudes or opinions in everyday contexts to see how they have been designed to perform particular functions. But discourse analysis also focused on research topics which were hitherto ignored by social psychologists. As we shall see in the next section of this book, one key area of research which emerged from discourse analysis was the study of the ways in which accounts of controversial events were built to be robust and resistant to sceptical or alternative accounts. Because it could offer alternative ways of empirically approaching core topics, and opened up new areas for research, discourse analysis was able very quickly to establish itself as a significant new methodological specialism within the discipline.

There is another related reason why discourse analysis was able to consolidate its position within academic psychology. It offered a significant and explicit challenge to traditional experimental methods and cognitivist assumptions of social psychology. But not everyone was convinced of its argument, and, naturally, many experimental social psychologists offered a vigorous defence of their practices and theories, and also subjected discourse analysis to a critical assessment (as many working in the sociology of scientific knowledge had challenged Gilbert and Mulkay's arguments about the intractable problem of variability in scientists' accounts). And, indeed, other critical psychologists offered their critiques of discourse analysis. Thus discourse analysis stimulated intense debates, many of which were conducted in academic journals which served the discipline more generally (see, for example, Abrams and Hogg, 1990; Parker, 1990; Potter *et al*, 1990; see also the contributions to Conway, 1992, for other examples of responses to DA from mainstream psychologists). This meant that a wide audience was exposed to the approach and claims of discourse analysis, as well as arguments about its merits and drawbacks.

Conversation analysis, however, has not had the same kind of impact on sociology. It has been influential in a range of related disciplines, such as linguistics and, as we shall see, social psychology, but it has remained marginal in sociology. Perhaps the key reason is that sociology does not address the core topics of the discipline: talk-in-interaction is studied as a topic in its own right, and is not viewed automatically as an adjunct to, nor indicator of, the operation of broader structural variables such as class and power.

There are some important caveats to this claim. First, an argument which will be developed later in this book is that CA can begin to address these kinds of mainstream sociological topics, albeit in a novel way. Second, there is a strong tradition in sociology of research into the organisation of everyday activities, and these seem to have much in common with CA's focus on the organisation of everyday verbal conduct. We have already discussed ethno-methodological studies of sense-making practices. Goffman's studies of the practices we use to present an image of ourselves to others is another example. And ethnographies of mundane urban environments and settings were a feature of the influential Chicago school of sociology. Although these kinds of sociological approaches seem to have much in common with CA, there are some clear departures, some of which will be raised later. But perhaps the key reason why CA has not been as influential in sociology as, say, Goffman, is that its analyses are highly technical, and they do not easily lend themselves to assimilation into the broader knowledge base of the discipline. Indeed, they seem to offer an understanding of social life couched in a vocabulary which is alien to most sociological theorising and research. Moreover, in CA, the analytic focus is on people's own sense-making practices as they are revealed in the turn-by-turn unfolding of interaction. The discovery and description of these sense-making practices is thus elevated over more conventional socio-logical concerns, such as the wider context in which interaction occurs, the relationship between participants, and the superficial meaning or 'obvious' significance of what they say.

Methodological issues

We now turn to some more specific methodological differences between con-versation analysis and discourse analysis. Our discussion is organised around three themes: influences, data, the formality of empirical analysis and warranting analytic claims.

Influences   Put simply, Sacks started conversation analysis. Sacks was well read in a diverse set of literatures, to which he frequently refers in his lectures; but we should not assume that CA emerged as a product of his wide reading. Despite his erudition, it is clear that the work Sacks developed was truly original: it sprang from his unique mind, and cannot be easily traced back to particular traditions or approaches. Sacks began working with his colleagues Emmanuel Schegloff and Gail Jefferson, both of whom are distinguished ana-lysts in their own right; and their work, independently or in collaboration with Sacks, has been extraordinarily influential in developing the distinctive style of research now associated with CA. But it is fair to say that Sacks' work was the cornerstone upon which subsequent research was built.

Discourse analysis, however, has a more eclectic pedigree, as it drew from observations and insights from a variety of related disciplines and approaches: ethnomethodology, sociolinguistics, structuralism, speech act theory and literary criticism. For example, Potter and Wetherell's (1987) introduction to discourse analysis and its implications for social psychology is rich in its references to ethnomethodology and semiotics.

In their introduction to discourse analysis, Gilbert and Mulkay made no reference to CA research. But in their discussion of DA in the context of social psychology, Potter and Wetherell used CA as a valuable resource. It provided a set of findings which could inform critiques of experimental approaches. Thus their critique of social representation theory drew from Sacks' work on the fluid and dynamic ways in which we categorise ourselves and others in every-day interaction (Sacks, 1979, 1984b). And their discussion of the study of accounts in social psychology made use of Atkinson and Drew's analysis of the kinds of activities which can be accomplished in question–answer sequences in courtroom cross-examination. More generally CA had established that everyday interaction exhibited a hitherto unimagined degree of order-liness, and offered a method for the analysis of that orderliness. This method-ological achievement allowed Potter and Wetherell to make the broader argument that naturally occurring discourse – of all kinds – was an appropriate site in which to explore social psychological issues. Finally, the transcription symbols used in CA have become more or less standard in discourse analysis; again, this was due to Potter and Wetherell's account, in which they included an amended set of the symbols developed by Gail Jefferson.

Conversation analysis has been an important influence in discourse analysis. Analysts still draw from CA studies of everyday interaction, and Sacks' lectures provide an invaluable resource in shaping analytic projects. Moreover, as we shall see later, even some critical discourse analysts who have reservations about CA's apparent reluctance to engage in wider debates about political or social issues still offer analyses which are couched in CA terms, or which reflect CA's methodo-logical concern with sequences and the action orientation of turns at talk.

But here we find a striking asymmetry: whereas discourse analytic research routinely draws from and refers to CA research, conversation analytic research rarely refers to findings from or approaches of discourse analysis.

Data   There are two points with regard to data that separate CA and DA. First, conversation analysis examines audio or, less frequently, video recordings of naturally occurring talk-in-interaction, and transcripts are used as an aid in that analysis. Sacks' work on the use of categories in everyday interaction has been used to examine textual materials, such as newspaper article headlines (Atkinson,1978; Jayussi, 1991) and interview data (Baker, 1997; Widdicombe and Wooffitt, 1995); but on the whole, CA research focuses on recordings of verbal interaction. Discourse analytic projects, however, consider a much wider range of empirical materials: in the previous chapter we discussed studies in which the analysts had examined newspaper articles, statements made by politicians in the House of Commons, and accounts generated from informal interviews. And in the later chapter on critical approaches to dis-course analysis we will encounter an argument that analysts should analyse *texts*: any events, objects or processes which are imbued with meaning and subject to interpretation. This broadens considerably the range of materials discourse analysts can examine as data in their research.

Second, discourse analytic research gives greater prominence to disputes or controversial events, whereas CA focuses on the mundane and routine. Gilbert and Mulkay's discourse analysis, for example, sprang from studies of accounts from scientists involved in a debate about the relative merits of two competing perspectives on biochemical processes. Potter and Edwards' critique of social psychological studies of attributions drew from their analysis of accounts surrounding a political controversy: whether or not a senior member of the government had said things attributed to him by political journalists. And in more recent years, there have been several discourse analytic papers which examine materials from a televised interview with Diana, Princess of Wales, in which she talked controversially about her marital and health problems. These kinds of events offer fascinating materials for discourse analysis. Moreover, they generate a large amount of secondary discourse: commentaries on newspaper, discussions in news broadcasts, and so on.

Conversation analysis, on the other hand, tends to focus on the management of routine activities: turn-taking, repair, sequence organisation, and so on. Even when the data come from non-everyday settings, such as courtrooms or news interviews, the focus is on the way in which the participants manage those activities which routinely feature in these settings, such as questioning and answering.

It is important to stress that this is not a hard and fast distinction. As we saw in the previous chapter, Wetherell *et al*'s discourse analytic study of practical ideologies in accounts from interview respondents was not driven by any notable event; and there have been CA studies of notable events, such as the notoriously fractious interview in 1988 between (then) Vice President George Bush and the CBS news presenter Dan Rather (Clayman and Whalen, 1988/9; Schegloff, 1988/9). But predominantly discourse analytic papers are more likely to examine discourse surrounding controversial events; and that CA research overwhelmingly focuses on routine features of the management of interaction.

Warranting analytic claims   One of the key problems in any research project is to warrant whatever empirical statements are made. In psychology, research has been conducted in laboratory and experimental settings, thus allowing some degree of control over the manipulation of relevant variables. This means the researcher can have greater confidence in any subsequent interpretations of their experimental results. And in sociology and psychology, the use of sophisticated statistical procedures is standard practice. However, if the research aim is to study naturally occurring interaction, without imposing artificial experimental controls, how are we to justify our claims? This is a real problem in many kinds of qualitative research: how do we know that the researcher's interpretations are valid, accurate depictions of objective phenomena, and do not simply reflect their particular interpretative approach?

In CA, however, it is not the job of the analyst to interpret the significance or nature of conversational activities, but to reveal how participants' own interpretations of the on-going exchange inform their conduct. Because of this, CA has a distinctive resolution to the problems involved in warranting analytic claims. In Chapter 1, we discussed how next positioning of utterances allows participants in interaction to monitor each other's understanding on a turn-by-turn basis. But because their particular interpretations are exhibited publicly in the construction of subsequent turns for each other, so too are they publicly available for analysts.

> [W]hile understandings of other turns' talk are displayed to co-participants, they are available as well to professional analysts who are thereby afforded a proof criterion (and search procedure) for the analysis of what a turns' talk is occupied with. Since it is the parties' understandings of prior turns' talk that is relevant to their construction of next turns, it is *their* understandings that are wanted for analysis. The display of those understandings in the talk of subsequent turns afforded both a resource for the analysis of prior turns and a proof procedure for professional analysis of prior turns – resources that are intrinsic to the data themselves. (Sacks *et al*, 1974: 702; original italics)

Next turn analysis, then, means that the analyst is not expected to guess or infer how the participants are making sense of interaction as it unfolds: their understanding is publicly displayed in the kinds of activities they produce and the way in which they produce them. Analyses can be grounded in the observable activities of the participants themselves.

As we saw in Chapter 3, an important step in building a conversation analytic account of an interactional phenomenon is to examine cases in which there seems to have been some departure from the established pattern, and investigating how participants' utterances display their understanding of the significance of that departure. To illustrate this, look at these fragments. The first comes from the corpus of calls to the British Airways flight information service, and the second comes from a courtroom cross-examination.

(4.3) (From Wooffitt *et al*, 1997: 80)

```
1   A:  British Airways ^flight information
2       can I help you
3       (1.3)
4   A:  hel↑lo↑
```

(4.4) (From Atkinson and Drew, 1979: 52)

```
C:  Is there something bothering you?
    (1.0)
C:  Yes or no?
```

The concept of the adjacency pair suggests that an acceptance or a refusal should follow an offer; and after a question, there should be an answer. In each case, though, the recipient does not produce the appropriate second pair part. On first inspection, these extracts seem to provide evidence which undermines claims about the properties of paired actions. However, the speakers' responses to these absences demonstrate that for them the normative expectations which underpin paired sequences are still relevant. In extract 4.3 the agent's 'hel↑lo' is designed to check that there's a caller on the line, thus not only demonstrating her understanding that the caller should produce a request for flight information, but displaying her reasoning as to why it is not forthcoming (there may be a problem with the line); and in 4.4, the counsel's 'Yes or no?' stands as a prompt for the answer. In both cases, but in different ways, the speakers' turns indicate that the absence of the appropriate second pair part is a noticeable and accountable deviation from the norms of interactional practice.

Discourse analysts do not have the same kinds of resources by which to ground their empirical observations. There is no next turn position, for example, when studying the use of consensus information in newspaper articles. Similarly, it is difficult to envisage how a concern with deviant cases might be of use to discourse analytic studies: they are not focused on the kinds of normative expectations which deviant cases so neatly expose. Other ways of grounding analytic claims, however, have been developed. As in conversation analysis, there is an emphasis on the presentation of data in the body of research reports to substantiate the analyst's empirical statements, and to allow the reader to check analytic claims against the data from which they were generated. And with respect to verbal data, such as those generated by informal interviews, Wetherell and Potter (1988) have argued that participants will seek to address inconsistencies which arise from the clash of mutually competing or incompatible linguistic repertoires. This reparative work provides evidence, intrinsic to the participants' conduct, of the operation of those repertoires, and to some degree mirrors the resources provided by next turn analysis available to the conversation analyst. Despite these steps, though, it is clear that the burden of warranting analytic claims is greater for the discourse analyst than for the conversation analyst.

Finally, it is clear that CA has some distinctive methodological steps: analytic claims are (usually) generated from analysis of a collection of instances of a particular interactional phenomenon; the sequential organisation of activities is explicated and warranted by analysis of the turn-by-turn unfolding of utterances in which participants exhibit their understanding of the on-going interaction; and the participants' orientation to the web of normative expectations which underpin interaction can be identified through analysis of sequences which seem to depart from an established pattern. Consequently, conversation analysis can be said to offer a repeatable and consistent method for the analysis of interaction. Discourse analysis does not offer the same degree of formal methodological procedure.

Summary

- CA and DA differ substantively in respect to the focus of empirical analysis, varying engagement with traditional disciplinary topics, and the range of empirical questions which are addressed.
- CA and DA differ methodologically with respect to the range of intellectual influences, the kinds of data which are studied, the nature of analytic findings and the resources available to warrant empirical claims.

This brings us to the end of the first stage of this book. It should be clear by now that in relation to the general approach of the social sciences, CA and DA are aligned in their focus on discourse and language use as a topic in its own right. But once we examine closely how that focus is mobilised in empirical research, we see there are significant differences, in terms of both what is studied and how it is studied.

Conversation analytic studies are highly focused on the sense-making practices which inform the turn-by-turn management of interactional activities. This is true whether the data come from everyday conversation, news interviews, radio talk shows, doctor–patient consultations and so on. Discourse analytic studies, however, display a greater diversity of approaches and goals. To illustrate this diversity, let us return to the discourse analytic studies we discussed in the previous chapter.

Potter and Edwards (1992) studied accounts from journalists and politicians during a political controversy. Their empirical analysis revealed that even descriptions which seem to be neutral reports of events will be evaluatively loaded, and thereby attending to attributions of truth and falsehood. Their analysis thus addressed two sets of issues: how was the ostensibly cognitive matter of causal reasoning managed in everyday discourse? And second, how were particular viewpoints or claims warranted by the use of consensus information? By contrast, Wetherell *et al* (1987) had a different goal: they wanted to explore how practical ideologies informed interview respondents' accounts about gender and employment rights. In this their objective was implicitly political: to show how ways of thinking about the world informed discourse, and thereby justified and maintained the asymmetrical work opportunities between men and women.

These two studies illustrate three strands of discourse analysis research:

- the analysis of discursive resources through which the truth or factual status of a claim or version of events can be established;
- the analysis of reports of mental states, and discourse in which mental states become relevant, as a form of social action which is oriented to interactional and inferential concerns;
- the analysis of discourse to reveal how it is underpinned by ideologies which in turn reflect wider societal inequalities.

Gilbert and Mulkay's (1984) analysis of scientists' discourse did not exhibit this variety of empirical concerns; their analysis focused primarily on the way in which scientists' discourse was organised to establish or undermine the factual status of competing positions in a dispute. However, all three strands of research were represented in Potter and Wetherell's (1987) discussion of the implications of discourse analysis for social psychology. Indeed, at that time, it would be fair to say that the term 'discourse analysis' subsumed these three distinct sets of empirical concerns. It was not unusual, for example, to find the same researchers publishing critical, ideologically oriented papers and analyses of the use of psychological vocabulary in talk and texts (Edwards and Potter, 1992; Wetherell and Potter, 1992).

During the 1990s, however, discourse analytic work began to take on a more specialised character as researchers tended to focus on either the study of factual accounts, or discursive psychology or more critical forms of discourse analysis. And there were clear tensions between the broad goals of these strands of discourse analysis. For example, whereas discursive psychologists wanted to show how cognitive terms were used in interaction – thus moving closer to a conversation analytic position – critical discourse analysts wanted to identify the wider structural and political implications of discursive prac- tices. In the next three chapters we will consider these dimensions of discourse analytic work in more detail, and in turn explore the often complex relation- ships with conversation analysis.

Further readings

Critical accounts of CA and DA

What follows is a list of critical accounts of CA and DA. Where relevant, responses by practitioners have also been listed.

Many of the issues which inform contemporary critiques of CA will be discussed later in this book. But some older critical discussions of CA can be found in: Bostrom and Donohew (1992); and Searle (1986). Schegloff (1992c) offers a response to Searle's critique of CA and its approach to conversation. Taylor and Cameron (1987) also offer an interesting critical appraisal of CA. A critical but sympathetic account of CA in the context of other broadly sociolinguistic approaches to the study of discourse can be found in Schiffrin (1994).

Critical assessments of discourse analysis and responses from practitioners can be found in a published debate. Abrams and Hogg (1990) evaluate DA's contribution from the perspective of cognitivist and experimental social psychology. They argue that although it can offer insight to the analysis of language use, ultimately it needs to be directed towards the exploration of more traditionally conceived social psychological topics. Parker (1990) offers a more critical and Foucauldian assessment, emphasising the importance of the analysis of discourses. Potter, Wetherell, Gill and Edwards (1990) offer a defence of DA against these experimental and Foucauldian critiques. More recently, Coulter (1999) has questioned the underlying conceptual framework of discourse analysis, but Potter and Edwards (2003) offer a robust defence, claiming that Coulter confuses various approaches in his argument.

Recently Hammersley (2003a, 2003b) has criticised both CA and DA: he criticises CA because he believes it is too ethnomethodological; and DA is attacked because it is too constructionist. For these reasons Hammersley believes that neither CA nor DA offer a new paradigm for social science. Potter (2003a, 2003b, 2003c) defends discourse analysis, arguing that Hammersley misunderstands its constructionist elements.

5
Persuasion and Authority: CA and the Rhetorical Turn in Discourse Studies

A major development in discourse analysis has been the study of the organisation of persuasive, authoritative or factual language (terms I shall use interchangeably throughout this chapter). Why is this? There are several reasons.

First, discourse analysis grew from the sociological study of scientific knowledge. This approach adopted a radical position in that it did not accept the orthodox scientific consensus that some knowledge claims were simply true, and others were simply false. Instead, it sought to expose and investigate the social processes which informed the way in which the scientific community came to regard some knowledge claims as objective representations of the physical world and others as errors, or false claims. This was reflected in Gilbert and Mulkay's (1984) analysis of scientists' discourse. Their discussion of the empiricist and contingent repertoires illustrated some of the discursive practices through which the factual status of a knowledge claim could be constructed or undermined. The empiricist repertoire is used to establish that (some) scientific knowledge claims are simple representations of objective reality, while the contingent repertoire is drawn upon to show that (other) knowledge claims are a consequence of scientists' social circumstances or personality. These repertoires are thus used to speak or write about scientific disputes while at the same time providing a particular sense or significance for those events or actions being reported. They are resources by which scientists can establish the factual status of some knowledge claims, and portray other claims as being false.

Gilbert and Mulkay's (1984) study supported a more general finding from sociological studies of science: facts do not speak for themselves in resolving a scientific dispute because what 'the facts are' are subject to argument and interpretation. This in turn reflects the (broadly social constructionist) position that social factors inextricably underpin the processes through which knowledge claims come to be accepted as accurate accounts of the properties of an objective universe.

Potter and Edwards (1990) also adopted a constructionist perspective (but see Potter, 1996b) in their study of how journalists reported a dispute about what had really been said at a meeting between a government minister and political journalists. They observed that articles about this dispute invoked consensus information to support the claims of the journalists: as they all reported the same story, their version must be factual. However, the minister drew upon the uniformity of the journalists' accounts to suggest collusion in the production of a sensationalised and thereby false account. Thus the unanimity of the journalists' versions was employed either as a resource to support the factual status of their claims or to undermine them.

These studies suggest that we can examine accounts which ostensibly offer a factual version of events to see how they are 'worked up' so that they are heard (or read) as a factual, authoritative or objective report. That is, if we accept that accounts and descriptions do things, we may therefore investigate the ways in which their own status as factual accounts is accomplished.

This can be explored in more mundane settings, as well as in controversies about cutting-edge science or high-profile political disputes. Our everyday life is marked by minor dispute and disagreement: mundane interaction is rife with arguments, accusations, rebuttals, blamings, criticisms, complaints and justifications. And there are occasions in our lives when we make more contentious claims, for example, accusing someone of inappropriate behaviour, or reporting unusual experiences. It is possible that these kinds of discursive actions will receive unsympathetic, sceptical or, indeed, hostile responses. Here again we can ask: what are the resources through which controversial reports are constructed so as to appear reasonable and robust, and to anticipate sceptical responses?

There is another reason why we may be interested in factual statements. Conversation analytic studies of utterance design, and discourse analytic studies of accounts, are both informed by an understanding that we can describe any particular state of affairs in a variety of ways. That is, our descriptions of the world are not determined by the objective properties of the things we are describing. To illustrate, consider the many different ways we might refer to a person: in terms of their gender, occupation, marital status, religion, and so on. All of these would be logically correct, and therefore offer a factual reference. But of course, in everyday settings, references to people are accomplished with a minimal number of descriptive terms (Sacks and Schegloff, 1979). So the issue arises, even with factually correct statements, why have they been constructed in this way, at this time?

Because of these kinds of concerns, the study of factual discourse – or, more accurately, discourse which is designed to be factual or authoritative – has become a key feature of discourse analytic research. It is prominent in later accounts of discourse analytic research. For example, in their (1995) account of the Discourse Action Model (formulated to outline the broad rationale of discourse analysis, and to indicate lines of empirical inquiry), Edwards and Potter emphasised that reports and descriptions are constructed and displayed as factual through various discursive devices; and that reports and descriptions are rhetorically organised to undermine actual or possible alternatives (Edwards and Potter, 1995: 88–9).

Note the reference to the rhetorical organisation of discourse. This term reflects the influence of a renewed interest in the study of rhetoric generally, and, more specifically, the emergence of an approach called rhetorical psychology. Rhetorical psychology is primarily associated with the work of Michael Billig. It shares many concerns with discursive psychology (of which more in the next chapter) and discourse analysis more generally. Both discourse analysis and the rhetorical approach seek to identify and redress what are perceived to be fundamental fault lines in the way traditional social psychology has viewed language and its role in social life. There are also historical and institutional links: Billig's key text in rhetorical psychology, *Arguing and Thinking: A Rhetorical Approach to Social Psychology*, was published in 1987, the same year that saw the publication of Potter and Wetherell's *Discourse and Social Psychology*. Moreover, Billig, Edwards and Potter all work in the Department of Social Sciences at Loughborough University, UK, and were responsible for establishing the Discourse and Rhetoric Group (DARG) in that department. This is an extremely active research group, and its members have been responsible for key research in discourse studies, and have trained numerous doctoral students in discourse analysis and related critical approaches in social psychology.

There are, then, close institutional links between leading figures in discourse analysis and rhetorical psychology. It is no surprise, then, that there are close intellectual links as well. As we have seen, Edwards and Potter (1995) incorporate a concern with the rhetorical organisation of discourse in their account of the broad discourse analytic project. Other introductory accounts of DA also refer to the importance of rhetoric, thereby recognising Billig's contribution to the discourse-based critique of social psychology (for example, Edwards and Potter, 1992; Gill, 1996; Potter, 1996b; Potter and Wetherell, 1995). And in his (1997) account, Billig emphasises the common ground between rhetorical psychology, discursive psychology and discourse analysis.

Although Billig's writings about rhetoric have clearly been influential in studies of factual discourse, his own research is more diverse and eclectic, and it would be fair to say that he has not been centrally concerned to document resources in the production of authoritative or factual language to the same degree as other discourse researchers. The core of this chapter, then, draws from Potter's (1996a) excellent overview and assessment of research into factual discourse. As we shall see, the body of work Potter reviews is broadly sympathetic to CA's methods and findings. We will end the chapter by exploring some of the substantive and methodological advantages offered by CA.

Rhetorical psychology

So, what is rhetoric? The *Collins Shorter English Dictionary* provides four definitions of rhetoric:

1. the study of the technique of using language effectively. **2.** the art of using speech to persuade, influence, or please; oratory. **3.** excessive ornamentation and contrivance in spoken or written discourse; bombast. **4.** speech or discourse that pretends to be significant but lacks true meaning: *mere rhetoric.* (1993 edition: 997; original italics)

The latter two definitions probably more accurately reflect what people today understand by rhetoric: that it is a superficially clever but ultimately shallow type of speaking, or the use of words concerned more with effect and style than with content and meaning. Indeed, the phrase 'a rhetorical question' – a question which requires no answer – seems to encapsulate the common belief that rhetoric is somehow an empty and insubstantial form of speech. This negative view of rhetoric, however, is a comparatively recent development. For nearly two thousand years, people viewed rhetoric and the study of rhetoric positively, an attitude reflected more accurately by the first two definitions presented above. Indeed, rhetoric was taught in the Roman era and in ancient Greek society, and classical rhetoric used to be taught in Britain until the latter part of the nineteenth century.

However, in the past thirty years, there has been renewed interest in the study of rhetoric and its implications for social and natural sciences (Nelson *et al*, 1987; Perelman and Olbrechts-Tyteca, 1969; Simons, 1989). This has coincided with a dissatisfaction with positivism and its claims to permit an objective account of physical and social reality. In this, it has much in common with social constructionist approaches. However, it focuses explicitly on the way in which discourse is a persuasive activity.

> Most centrally, perhaps, rhetoric is about persuasion. Thus, for example, we might wish to examine the discourse of economists, philosophers, or historians *as* persuasion; in other words, as discourse that is in some sense akin to what such prototypical persuaders as editorialists, advertisers, and politicians do … Fleshing out the ties between rhetoric and persuasion a bit more, we can say that rhetoric is the form that discourse takes when it goes public … that is, when it has been geared to an audience, readied for an occasion, adapted to its ends … Rhetoric is thus a pragmatic art; its functions those of symbolic inducement. (Simons, 1989: 2–3; original italics)

Billig argues that the study of rhetoric has much to offer contemporary social psychology. His rhetorical approach begins with the observation that common sense – maxims, idioms, clichéd appeals to values and so on – is essentially contradictory. For every maxim or saying, there is another which proposes the opposite view. Thus we might extol the virtue of collaborative effort by asserting 'many hands make light work', but then equally disparage joint activity by saying 'too many cooks spoil the broth'. But even in more mundane, less clichéd forms of talk, there is the possibility of an argumentative counter-position. Indeed, he asserts that to express an opinion or an attitude is necessarily to acknowledge and implicitly counter alternative possible viewpoints. (Billig claims that this is another explanation for the variability in accounts observed by discourse analysts: there is always an alternative position.) Discourse, then, is inevitably argumentative; and common sense is essentially dilemmatic. This has implications for empirical research because 'it could be suggested that we cannot understand the meaning of a piece of reasoned discourse, unless we know what counter positions are being implicitly or explicitly rejected' (Billig, 1991: 44). This means that rhetorical psychology focuses less on the action orientation of language use, as in conversation analysis and discourse analysis, and more on the argumentative or persuasive character of discourse.

But more than that, the argumentative nature of discourse has serious implications for social psychology. This is because, like discourse analysts, Billig rejects a simple cognitivist explanation of social action. He does not assume that people have inner thoughts or opinions which are then merely expressed in talk. Rather he sees talk, and its essentially argumentative character, as being *thinking in action*.

> Cognitive psychologists have assumed that thinking is a mysterious process, lying behind outward behaviour. However, the response and counter response of conversation is too quick for it to be the outward manifestation of the 'real' processes of thought. The remarks are the thoughts: one need not search for something extra, as if there is always something lying behind the words, which we should call the 'thought'. (Billig, 2001b: 215)

This does not mean that Billig rejects that we think. Rather, he accords primacy to social activities: he says that 'deliberative thought is internalised argumentation' (1991: 72).

Billig's focus on the oppositional orientation of discourse and the internalisation of argumentative activity is the basis for a critique of two dominant approaches in cognitive psychology. First, there is the attempt to identify the most effective thinking practices, as studied in experiments in problem solving. Second, there is a focus on actual reasoning procedures, as revealed in the way we process information. He does not argue with the methods or findings from these kinds of experimental studies, but he suggests that the picture of thinking which emerges is incomplete because it fails to take account of the essentially argumentative nature of thinking and talking.

Another respect in which rhetorical psychology and discourse analysis are similar is in their focus on ideology. Billig subscribes to the idea that ideologies – ways of thinking which support asymmetries in power and advantage – are sedimented in discourse. Thus the ways we have for talking about the world (which, in Billig's approach, constitute the ways we think about the world) are invariably laden with attitudes and assumptions which implicitly perpetuate particular forms of social organisation. Moreover, 'ideologies are intrinsically rhetorical, for they provide the resources and topics for argumentation, and thereby for thinking about the world' (Billig, 1990: 18).

Billig has examined a range of topics: for example, fascist propaganda (1988), tabloid newspaper coverage of Royal events (1990), family discourse about the Royal Family (1992) and jokes contained in the web pages of racist groups (2001a). Throughout all of these studies he has sought to show how ideological forces inhabit both the mundane and less mundane forms of discourse.

Discourse analysis and the study of factual language

In this section we are going to discuss discourse analytic research into the organisation of factual language. The key text in this area is Potter's *Representing Reality* (1996a), in which he reviews a wide range of empirical and theoretical literature dealing with the relationship between discourse and the social and physical world. His main argument, baldly stated, is that the ways in which we represent the world are invariably constructions. Moreover, the practices through which we represent the world also constitute its properties: discourse is a constructive and constitutive medium, and brings the world into being. In this sense, Potter locates the concern with factual language within a broadly social constructionist perspective.

There is a caveat to this statement. Social constructionism is a complex topic, and many strands of social scientific work can be described as adopting a constructionist stance. There are also many varieties of constructionism (see the discussions in Burningham and Cooper, 1998; Burr, 1995; Woolgar, 1988). The classic text, however, is Berger and Luckmann's *The Social Construction of Reality* (1966), in which they argue that customs, habits, practices and knowledge are the products of social arrangements; this includes knowledge claims which are taken to be factual, such as scientific knowledge. Potter's text is not a straightforward endorsement of social constructionism. Instead, he explores various kinds of constructionist thought, and shows how the discourse analytic approach, informed by conversation analysis, raises and addresses a number of conceptual and empirical problems. By doing this he is able to trace the trajectory of complex arguments about the relationship between words and the worlds they construct, thereby forging a distinctive contribution to constructionist theory and research. (See also some of the contributions to Potter's debate with Hammersley: Hammersley, 2003a, 2003b, 2003c; Potter, 2003a, 2003b.)

Potter's text is an introduction to, and provides a review of, many studies of fact construction and the organisation of authoritative accounts. Many of these studies have been informed by the argument at the heart of rhetorical psychology: that accounts, descriptions and reports are constructed with respect to actual or potential alternative versions of events. In various ways these studies offer an empirically grounded account of the communicative resources we have for producing factual discourse. In part, this is due to the influence of Sacks' writings, and the focus on the action orientation of language which is at the heart of conversation analytic research. We will consider three clusters of practices through which the authority of accounts can be established or undermined: how reports can be used to invoke or deny the relevance of personal interest in a particular point of view or claim; the management of tacit conventions about category membership, and ways in which the objective status of a state of affairs can be established.

Stake management

'Stake' here refers to personal interest in a claim or report. It is crucial to the production of authoritative or factual accounts for this reason: the authority of claims can easily be undermined by the retort 'well you would say that, wouldn't you'. This expresses the lay or common sense view that a person may be advancing a point of view, or making a statement about the world, because it is in their interest to do so, and not because the view is reasonable, or the claim accurately depicts a real situation. Thus it is necessary to show that our claims are not motivated by what we would simply like to be the case. Potter calls this stake management, and identifies several discursive practices through which accounts can be 'inoculated' from imputations of stake or personal interest.

To illustrate, we will look at some data from a study by Dorothy Smith (1978). This is a famous analysis of a written report of 'K', a young woman, and her apparent decline into mental illness, as reported by one of her peers/friends, Angela. Smith was interested in the way that the text was organised to facilitate the inference that K's mental health problems were real and objective and not, say, the result of malicious fabrication or naive misidentification of unusual – but not pathological – personality quirks. Smith was not working in a discourse analytic tradition; and her paper has a more ethnomethodological flavour to it. Her general goals, however, mirror many of the objectives of DA studies, in that she seeks to identify the way that the account constructs an object: in this case, K's status as mentally ill person. But it is important to bear in mind that although the following empirical claims resonate with Smith's broad goals, these are not derived from her analysis. Readers are advised to consult Smith's paper as it is a distinctive and sophisticated contribution to the ethnomethodological literature.

We can see stake inoculation working in the first part of the account which is written from the perspective of K's friend, Angela.

(5.1)   (From Smith, 1978: 28)

> Angela: I was actually the last of her close friends who was openly willing to admit that she was becoming mentally ill.

In extract 5.1 Angela characterises herself as one of K's 'close friends', thus indexing qualities such as loyalty, mutual respect, concern, and common interests and activities. This works to resist the possible interpretation that Angela's account was, for example, a malicious act motivated by her dislike of K. It establishes that Angela has no vested interest in describing K in this way; therefore, it is more likely to be heard as a report of an objective state of affairs.

Imputations of stake can be resisted by displays of indifference to issues or events which are sensitive matters for the participants. For example, Edwards (1995a) discusses a case from a counselling session in which a couple are in dispute about the cause of the problems in their relationship. The man believes his partner is overly flirtatious with other men; the woman claims that she does not act inappropriately, and that his criticisms are the result of extreme jealousy. At one point the man describes an incident to illustrate his partner's inappropriate behaviour. In doing so he reports that 'Connie had a short skirt on, I don't know' (Edwards, 1995a: 333). Edwards argues that the man is in a delicate position. The mere fact that he had monitored and mentioned the shortness of his partner's skirt could be cited as evidence of overbearing jealously, thus lending credence to his partner's version of the problem. However, the inferential implications are managed by the inclusion of the throwaway remark 'I don't know'. This marks his lack of concern for the matter: he thus portrays the comment about her clothes as simple 'noticing', rather than 'motivated scrutiny' (Edwards, 1995a: 334).

These inferential concerns are evident in the following section from Smith's account.

(5.2)   (From Smith, 1978: 29–30)

> ... At that time Angela's mother thought, well she misunderstood me. But later she noticed that K was unable to put on a tea pot cover correctly, she would not reverse the position to make it fit in, but would simply keep slamming it down on the pot.

K's inability to perform simple domestic tasks is presented as further evidence of her mental deterioration. But note how the mother came to be aware of K's difficulty: it was merely 'noticed'. This portrays the mother's indifference to K's activity. An account which implied a systematic observation of K might sustain an alternative interpretation: that the mother was aware of concerns about K's mental health and was thus explicitly monitoring her behaviour. Such motivated looking might suggest that the observer saw what she wanted or expected to see. 'Noticing', however, depicts the observer as 'just happening' to come upon a pre-existing state of affairs. This formulation thus reinforces the underlying claim that K's problems were objectively real, and not a matter of interpretation.

Sacks, membership categorisation devices and category entitlement

How do we refer to ourselves and other people? Consider other kinds of categories we have available to us: we could refer to a person in terms of their occupation, or their religious affiliation, or their nationality, or their gender, and so on. These kinds of categories are culturally available resources which allow us to describe, identify or make reference to other people or to ourselves. And the interesting thing is that they are not exclusive. For example, it is not hard to imagine a single individual who could be accurately described via a number of categories. For example, all the following correctly describe a friend who – conveniently – happened to call me right at the time I was writing this section: male, father, liberal, atheist, brother, son, account director, resident of York, graduate in sociology, friend, diver, Manchester United season ticket holder, Welsh – the list could go on. This means that when we come to describe other people or ourselves, there is an issue of selection: why did we characterise our social identity, or the social identity of someone else, in that particular way at that particular time?

The way in which categories are selected and their interactional implications was a feature of Sacks' early work in CA. He showed that categories are not neutral labels with which to describe ourselves and other people: they are what Sacks calls 'inference rich': we all have a stock of culturally available, tacit knowledge about categories and their members. When we come to see a person as a member of a particular category, the normative expectations associated with that category become available as an inferential resource by which we can interpret and anticipate the actions of this particular person. Categorisations of people thus entail significant implications for the way in which their conduct and claims will be interpreted (Sacks, 1979; 1984b; see also the references to membership categorisation in the 1992 publication of Sacks' lectures).

In his review, Potter focused on category entitlements: what sorts of tacit conventions about expertise, knowledge, attitudes and so on become inferentially available when people are ascribed to particular categories, and how might these entitlements be exploited to produce factual or authoritative accounts? We can illustrate this by examining some further data from Smith's study. In this extract, Angela is describing one of the events which led her to conclude that K had serious mental health problems.

(5.3) (From Smith, 1978: 29)

> ... a mutual friend, Trudi who was majoring in English, had looked over one of her [K's] essays, and told me afterward: She writes like a 12 year old –
> I think there is something wrong with her.

Note that Trudi is characterised as 'majoring in English'. When Trudi is reported as making a damaging assessment of K's writing style, the reader is thus assured of her relative expertise to form such a judgement. It is unlikely that this episode would be so convincing if Trudi's authority had not been established via this particular categorical identification. Moreover, it is not simply that K's writing is weak, or less sophisticated than one might expect of a university student: K is said to write like a *12 year old*. When applied to an adult at university, this categorisation invites the interpretation that she was extremely or pathologically immature.

Externalising devices

How can we use language to establish that something is 'out there', and that it has an independent objective existence? In his study of the ways in which scientific texts present knowledge claims as factual, Woolgar (1980) made some observations about metaphors which depict the scientist on a journey of discovery. For example, the following instance comes from the opening part of a Nobel Prize acceptance speech.

(5.4)   (From Woolgar, 1980: 253)

The trail which ultimately led to the first pulsar ...

Woolgar argues that the objectivity of the pulsar is established through the description of a trail which leads ultimately to its discovery. This section offers a metaphor for the process of scientific discovery: a trail. This metaphor and others which characterise the scientific process in a similar way, such as 'the road to truth' and 'the path of discovery', suggest movement towards a goal or target. Woolgar argues that this feature of the speech warrants the reader/hearer's understanding of the objective existence of the pulsar. He states:

> We would suppose that an entity of our own creation might be fairly readily at hand at the time when it was first noticed as existing. But 'the first pulsar' is to be understood as having a pre-existence, a quality of *out-there-ness* which required that it be *approached*. (Woolgar, 1980: 256; original italics)

What kinds of descriptive practices are available to establish the objectivity or 'out-there-ness' (Woolgar, 1980: 256) of the phenomenon being reported? We will illustrate just one: reported speech.

Reported speech has a variety of functions, and can work in various ways to affirm a position or claim, or attest to the facticity of an experience (Holt, 1996; Li, 1986; Mayes, 1990; Phillips, 1986). The following extract comes from a study of tape-recorded accounts of paranormal experiences (Wooffitt, 1992). The speaker uses reported speech to establish that the apparition of a malevolent entity was not a figment of her imagination, but was an objective event in the world.

(5.5)   (From Wooffitt, 1992: 163–4; speech marks added to identify
          reported speech)

tha:t night: (1.5) I don't know wh<u>a</u>t time it was: (1.3) my: husband (.) and I both woke up: (0.7) with the mo:st (.) dr<u>ead</u>ful (0.5) feeling of (1.7) hhh

°well° being (nyrie) smothered (0.3) but the <u>powerful</u> smell ˙h and a
<u>blackness</u> (0.3) that w's that was (0.2) blacker than black I can' describe it like
(.) <u>anything</u> else (.)˙hh it was the most penetrating (0.3) type of blackness ˙hh
and there was this (1.7) what I assumed to be th- the shape of a man (.) in a
cloak (2) it was the most (0.3) formidable (1.2) sight (1) my husband said
"my G<u>o</u>d what is it" (.) an' I just said "now keep quiet and say the Lord's
prayer"

Here the speaker invokes the urgency of the encounter by dealing with three
features of the experience: the smell, the 'blackness' and the description of the
figure itself. Immediately after this elaborate and evocative descriptive work,
she introduces her husband's utterance 'my G<u>o</u>d what is it'. This establishes
that he could see the figure, and also corroborates the description provided by
the speaker. That is, the severity of the husband's verbal reaction confirms that
the thing in the room, and the associated sensations, were as powerful and
alarming as the speaker had reported. This confirms the speaker's reliability as
an accurate reporter of the event. Of course the speaker could merely have
reported 'and my husband saw it too'. But the use of reported speech adds an
immediacy absent from such a neutral report, and this in turn works to establish the event as a truly unusual and dramatic experience.

  There are, then, several different ways language can be shaped to warrant the
factuality or authority of our claims about the world: the management of category entitlements, externalising devices and the ascription and negotiation of
the relevance of stake or personal investment. These are not necessarily discrete
discursive practices, but offer flexible and interrelated resources.

Summary

- Both discourse analysis and rhetorical psychology are concerned to
  explore the ways in which language can be shaped to warrant the factuality or authority of our claims about the world.
- The management of category entitlements, externalising devices, and the
  ascription and negotiation of the relevance of stake or personal investment are some of the kinds of discursive resources through which the
  factuality of opinions or claims can be managed in everyday talk and in
  accounts of controversial or contested events.

From the rhetoric of authority to practices of being: some implications of a CA approach to factual discourse

Rhetorical psychology and the discourse analytic study of factual language
have much in common, mainly a concern to highlight the dynamic nature of
everyday discourse as it is used persuasively. But discourse analysis offers a

more substantial and compelling account. This is due, at least in part, to the willingness of discourse analysts generally to embrace the findings from conversation analytic research and, to a lesser extent, its methodological stance. Thus whereas rhetorical psychology can offer a broad characterisation of the argumentative nature of everyday language, discourse analysis has tried to provide analytic claims grounded in the close description of the detail of specific discursive practices. Moreover, discourse analysts have attempted to identify particular devices, or clusters of practices, through which the authority of a claim can be established. Thus Potter has catalogued and analysed a range of devices through which we can manage 'stake inoculation': ensuring that a position or claim is not dismissed as a mere expression of personal interest (Potter, 1996a: 125–32). This focus on devices reflects the way in which CA tried to identify recurrent and robust patterns in the organisation of inter-action. Perhaps more important, DA offers a more sophisticated understanding of the way language is used persuasively in everyday discourse. In rhetorical psychology, it is claimed that discourse is argumentative, and that argumenta-tive activity is, at some fundamental level, the expression of overarching ideo-logical tensions. This position suggests that we are ensnared in webs of ideologies which constrain and shape our actions. Even if we accept this argument – and we might be cautious about endorsing a view which is both highly speculative and overly deterministic – it offers only a narrow view of the kinds of concerns which inform how we use language. The discourse analytic position, however, takes more seriously the findings from CA that interaction is complex and varied. This is reflected in the broad range of interpersonal, inferential and interactional contingencies which have been explored in discourse analytic research on authoritative language. Finally, rhetorical psychology has a limited – and limiting – focus on argumentation and ideology; empirical research thus revolves around a circumscribed set of issues. But DA studies are unen-cumbered by narrow theoretical frameworks, and are thus better placed to explore the implications of empirical findings, wherever they may lead. It is the application of CA-informed discourse studies of factual language to which we now turn.

Normalising: doing 'being ordinary'

In one of his lectures, Sacks made some observations on the ways in which people make reports of extraordinary experiences, such as being witness to hijackings or shootings. He had observed that, even when reporting such unusual events, people do so in routine and predictable ways, as if to under-line their own normality (published as Sacks, 1984b). Building on Sacks' obser-vations, Jefferson (1984b) examined a particular descriptive pattern which occurs in accounts of unusual events. Witnesses to these extraordinary events often employ a format identified as 'At first I thought … but then I realized'. A well-known example is the way that witnesses to the shooting of J.F. Kennedy reported a loud bang, which they first thought to be a car backfiring, but which they then realised was gunfire. The following example comes from Sacks' (1984b) initial identification of the phenomenon, and comes from the report of a witness to an aeroplane hijacking.

> I was walking up towards the front of the airplane and I saw by the cabin, the stewardess standing facing the cabin, and a fellow standing with a gun in her back. *And my first thought was he's showing her the gun, and then I realized that couldn't be, and then it turned out he was hi-jacking the plane.*
> (Sacks, 1984b: 419; emphasis added)

'First thought' formulations are invariably incorrect, and so Jefferson was puzzled: why would people present incorrect assumptions about the events they have seen? Her analysis revealed that people use the 'first thought' part of the device to present, as their normal first assumption, an innocuous reading of the state of affairs on which they are reporting. Through their 'first thought' formulations they display that they did not immediately assume that anything untoward was happening. They saw the world as any normal person might see it. Through this device, the perspective of the person telling the story is constructed so as to demonstrate their normality; in Sacks' (1984b) term, they are doing 'being ordinary': orienting to the world in a non-exceptional way.

In the following sections we will explore the way in which Sacks' observations on doing 'being ordinary' have implications for research projects in a range of academic disciplines: parapsychology, cognitive psychology and psychiatry.

Implications for parapsychology: the study of accounts of spontaneous experiences Parapsychology is the scientific investigation of the possibility that communication can occur between people without the use of the normal five senses. Although in part stimulated by anecdotal reports of precognition, ghosts and apparitions, telepathy and contact with spirits, it has modelled itself on the natural sciences. Thus the vast majority of parapsychological studies have been conducted in laboratories, involving thousands of experimental trials with undistinguished or ordinary subjects, the results of which are analysed using rigorous statistical techniques. The objective of these experiments was, first, to find evidence for psi, the mental facility which is taken to underpin various forms of ostensible parapsychological phenomena, such as mind-to-mind communication or the ability of the mind to influence the external physical environment. The second objective was to examine the physical and psychological factors that influenced the operation of psi (Broughton, 1991; Edge *et al*, 1986; Irwin, 1999; Radin, 1997).

Reports of spontaneous psychic experiences which happened to people in their everyday lives motivated the earliest serious investigation of paranormal phenomena (Gurney *et al*, 1886). But as parapsychology developed as a laboratory-based discipline, the study of reports of spontaneous experiences became marginalised. They were felt to have a limited use, perhaps as a way of guiding experimental design (J.B. Rhine, 1948), or as a way of indicating broad features of the way psi worked (L. Rhine, 1981). The reluctance of parapsychologists to study reports of spontaneous experiences reflects a suspicion about their evidential value. Even if it is assumed that experients are not deliberately fabricating stories, there is still a sense that the value of accounts is diminished by the possibility of unconscious distortion, the vagaries of memory, the experient's emotional involvement in the experience, and so on (for example, see West, 1948: 265; and Pekala and Cardena, 2000). Ultimately, then, parapsychologists are wary of accounts of paranormal experiences, viewing them as broadly unreliable records of 'what really happened'.

A CA-informed perspective offers a very different kind of position altogether. Drawing from a range of arguments in philosophy and the social sciences, it is assumed that language does not operate like a mirror of reality: '[e]xperience does not and cannot *determine* its expression in language' (Yamane, 2000: 177; original italics). This in turn invites us to ask: if accounts are not determined by the experience, what communicative and pragmatic concerns *do* inform the ways accounts are organised?

A CA-informed analysis reveals some recurrent features in the structure and design of accounts of spontaneous paranormal experiences. There is a descriptive device which can be used by speakers to demonstrate their 'ordinariness' (Wooffitt, 1992). When describing the onset of a particular paranormal episode, speakers regularly report what they were doing at the time. These reports have similar properties, in that they take the form 'I was just doing X ... when Y'. In the following extract, for example, the speaker is reporting an apparition of her recently deceased husband, which occurred during his (military) funeral service.

(5.6)   (From Wooffitt, 1992: 123–4)

```
 1   S:   an' I went in there (.) er:m w- with my mother in law
 2        and uhm: (.4) friends that were with me
 3        (1.3)
 4   X    ˙hhh (.) and I was just looking at the coffin
 5   Y    and there was David standing there (.3)
 6        he was in Blues
 7        (1)
 8        ˙hh he wasn't wearing his hat
 9        his hat was on the coffin
10        and he was there
```

Here the 'I was just doing X' component is 'I was just looking at the coffin'; and the ' ... when Y' component is the report of the apparition 'and there was David standing there'. The 'X' component is constructed from a report of an utterly mundane activity: 'just looking'. This is not unusual: 'X' component formulations are routinely used to depict distinctly mundane activities or locations; here are some other cases.

(5.7)   (From Wooffitt, 1992: 117ff)

'an' ah musta bin do:zin' there or somethin' ...'

'as I was going through the doorway ...'

'I was sitting in bed one night ...'

'un' driving fairly slowly ...'

'I were lookin' out that way ...'

'and we're just sitting watching the tele ...'

'and I was sat on a chair ...'

'I were just thinkin' ...'

'we were all sat round (.) ehm in a room ...'

'we were laid (.7) in the front bedroom ...'

These data indicate that speakers routinely use the 'I was just doing X ...' component as a way of portraying the mundane and routine features of their environment just prior to going on to report their first awareness of the particular paranormal event.

This addresses a variety of inferential concerns. First, by focusing on mundane, unexceptional activities, the speakers are able to demonstrate their normality at the time of a paranormal event. Indeed, there is evidence that the speakers build their X formulations so that they emphasise or construct their circumstances as a routine environment. In this study, some experiences occurred while speakers either were engaged in distinctly out of the ordinary activities, or were in clearly unusual circumstances: for example, engaged on a lengthy meditation about the nature of God; or in a life threatening illness, or in a state of grief following a bereavement. Yet in each case, the X formulations glossed the more evocative aspects of the speakers' environment to furnish a mundane and routine characterisation of what they were doing just prior to the onset of the experience (see also Heritage and Watson, 1979). Second, it established a contrastive organisation for the first introduction of the paranormal phenomenon into the narrative. Contrast structures have been shown to be powerful persuasive devices in a range of discursive contexts (Atkinson, 1984a, 1984b; Heritage and Greatbatch, 1986; Pinch and Clark, 1986; Smith, 1978). In the accounts of paranormal experiences, the report of the speakers' mundane circumstances acts as a contrastive context which serves to underline the strangeness of the particular incident.

The way in which accounts of this type are designed displays a lay or tacit logic which informs how we assess testimony from people reporting unusual or controversial events: we are less likely to give credence to accounts from people whose general assumptions about and perceptions of the world are demonstrably unusual. The 'X ... when Y' format is a device through which we can display that we are sensitive to, and orient our conduct towards, socially organised conventions about what counts as normal in the world. It establishes our social competence, in that it exhibits our understanding of, and commitment to, what counts as an appropriate response to truly unusual experiences. And establishing one's own normality and social competence is a central feature of warranting the factual basis of our claims.

This kind of approach to the study of reports of subjective paranormal experiences has numerous advantages. First, a CA-informed analysis is neutral as to the ultimate truth or falsity of the accounts; indeed, it seeks to explore how participants themselves address and establish the factual status of the experience. This means that it offers a way of examining accounts which liberates parapsychologists from having to endorse or reject accounts of specific experiences.

Because of its controversial nature, parapsychological work, and parapsychologists themselves, have been the subject of intense critical scrutiny by sceptics and debunkers (for example, Alcock, 1981, 1987, Hanlon, 1974; Kurtz, 1985; Zusne and Jones, 1989). The main thrust of the sceptics' arguments was that parapsychology was a pseudo-science: it had failed to produce cumulative and replicable evidence of the existence of psi. Moreover, it was claimed that parapsychology had not developed sophisticated theories, either of the functioning of psi or how it might relate to established physical and psychological principles. In their defence, parapsychologists claimed that their procedures were scientific, that experimental results consistently produced statistically significant evidence of anomalous communication, and that theoretical advances were slow because of the limited number of full-time parapsychologists employed in universities, and the relative lack of research funding compared to established psychological research (see, for example, the arguments put forward by Honorton, 1993, and Radin, 1997). Despite these counter arguments, parapsychology's position in the scientific and academic community is, at best, insecure (Mauskopf and McVaugh, 1980). Consequently many parapsychologists have considered ways in which their discipline's academic standing might be strengthened. One argument is to establish links with and draw from established disciplines, such as the social sciences (White, 1985, 1990; Zingrone, 2002), thereby facilitating innovative research links, and refreshing the theoretical and methodological resources of parapsychology. The use of conversation analysis to study accounts of paranormal experiences provides one example of the way in which parapsychology and the social sciences could establish closer links (Wooffitt, 1988, 1993). This would help secure parapsychology's status as a legitimate scientific discipline, while at the same time generating new interdisciplinary lines of inquiry (Wooffitt, forthcoming).

Finally, detailed analysis of the communicative practices through which accounts are assembled allows us to explore the range of inferential matters which are relevant when people present themselves as having experiences which are controversial and contested. It thereby affords a deeper understanding of the cultural and interpersonal consequences of paranormal experiences, their relationship to the experients' sense of self, and insight to lay standards of authority and reliability. All of this rich insight about the relationship between culture, the individual and anomalous experiences is lost if we merely treat accounts as more or less adequate mirrors of an external reality.

Implications for cognitive psychology: new approaches to the study of autobiographical memory   Consider the following report: the speaker is describing one of a series of violent encounters with a poltergeist, and introduces the onset of this episode with an 'I was just doing X ... when Y' formulation.

(5.8)   (From Wooffitt, 1992: 117)

```
1   S:   anyway I got to the kitchen door an as ah ·hh
2        I had the teapot in my hand like this and I walked
3        through the kitchen door (.5) ·hhh
4   X    as I was going through the doorway
5        (.7)
6   Y    I was just (.) jammed against the doorpost (.) like
7        this with the teapot sti(h)ll stu(h)ck
8        out in front of me
         ((Continues))
```

The speaker is not reporting something that was happening right at the time the account was being taped: it is a report of his *memory* of the event.

These kinds of memories are called autobiographical memories: recollections of events of personal significance. There has been a considerable amount of research in cognitive psychology on autobiographical memories. Much of this has been directed at understanding the basic cognitive processes which underpin memory formation, storage and retrieval (Brown and Kulik, 1977; Conway, 1995), and the degree to which memory processes are prone to distortion or error (McCloskey *et al*, 1988; Neisser and Harsch, 1992; Neisser *et al*, 1996). But there are other reasons why psychologists are interested in autobiographical memories. For example, it is thought that they offer insight as to the formation of the self: everyday memories are 'some of the things of which selves are made' (Barclay and DeCooke, 1988; see also Neisser and Fivush, 1994).

A recent development in this area has been an attempt to understand the functions of these memories as they occur in real-life settings. For example, Pillemer (1992) argues that there has been too much emphasis upon examining the accuracy of autobiographical memories, and that the research agenda should be expanded to include memory functions hitherto not considered in cognitive psychology, for example, their communicative functions. He suggests we need to consider some of the broader social contexts of memory sharing. He notes that the simple act of telling of one's own memories, and hearing those of others, performs functions beyond the mere transmission of information. Pillemer cites Tenney's (1989) study of the ways in which new parents inform friends of the birth of a child, which suggests that what gets reported owes more to social and interactional norms rather than any memory of the events being reported. Pillemer argues that it is necessary to study the underlying norms which inform the ways we report memories, claiming that the '*grammar* of memorial expression ... has yet to be fully described' (Pillemer, 1992: 242; original italics).

Pillemer is just one of a number of cognitive psychologists who are pressing for a more sustained analysis of the ways in which memory formulations are produced in discourse, and the kinds of functions they are designed to achieve. Given their overriding focus on the action orientation of language and interaction, conversation analysts and discourse analysts would appear to be well placed to contribute to, and indeed carry forwards, this work. For example, Edwards and Potter (1992) have already made important contributions to debates in cognitive psychology, and conversation analysts have studied the interactional basis of rememberings and forgettings (Drew, 1989; Goodwin, 1987). But even just a cursory summary of the study of the 'X ... when Y' formulations indicates that CA has much more to offer cognitive psychology. It offers a method for the analysis of the ways in which autobiographical recollections of this type are produced in everyday discourse, and in more distinctive contexts, such as research interviews. It shows that inferential matters clearly inform the ways in which recollections are designed, for example, to attend to possible sceptical responses. This in turn begins to flesh out the interest in the functions of memory sharings. Finally it reveals the ways in which speakers orient to expectations regarding 'normal' or 'competent' conduct, thereby exposing the kinds of socially organised normative frameworks which underpin memory production. In this sense, CA-informed discourse research can make a significant contribution to cognitive psychology's understanding of the grammar of memorial expression in everyday contexts.

Implications for psychiatry: the normative basis of recognising delusional talk Palmer (1997, 2000) has examined the discourse of people who have been diagnosed as having severe psychiatric problems. He shows how such people routinely deviate from the conventions of interactional practice, for example, in the way they produce narratives or anecdotes, and shows how these deviations are not addressed by the speakers as accountable or noticeable matters. He uses this analysis to suggest an interactional basis for the ways in which both professional psychiatrists and lay members of society come to see particular individuals as displaying signs of psychopathology.

This interactional approach to the discourse of psychopathology is an innovative contribution to our understanding of the ways in which people come to be seen as having serious psychological problems. Palmer argues that in psychiatry 'much of the important work in recognising delusions is performed through tacit skills' (Palmer, 2000: 667). By using CA, Palmer is able to lay bare some of the distinctive features of what we might term delusional talk. To illustrate his argument we can consider his analysis of the following account, which comes from a person who is diagnosed as having schizophrenia.

(5.9) (From Palmer, 2000: 669. 'C' is the interviewer, 'R' is the person with delusions.)

```
 1  C:  So you believe there's an afterlife then?
 2      (.)
 3  R:  Ye:s I do no:w. No:w I've see a god as
 4      well you jknow. Well he doesn't call himself
 5      God he calls himself Tho:r
 6      (0.8)
 7  C:  Ye:ah
 8  R:  I saw him on a f:- (.) I've se:en him a couple of
 9      ti:mes on a field up in Leicestershire I saw him
10      once.
11  C:  Ri:ght ((Questioning tone))
12  R:  Right out in the countryside where I was wo:rking.
13      (.)
14  C:  Yeah.
15  R:  I had a job as a ga:mekeeper there for Mr. Burnett
16      the animal food manufacturer.
17  C:  Uh huh.
18      (0.5)
19  R:  And e:r he visited me while I was up the::re.
20      (.)
21  R:  For some re:ason.
22  C:  Wuh-What kind of thing does
23      What did Floor-Thor look like?
24      (0.8)
25  R:  Well he's uh quite looks qui:te impressive
26      he's gotta ˙hhh catsuit on.
27  C:  Ri:ght.
28  R:  With an orange fla:sh down the front
29      like a: flash of li:ghtning would look
30      like sometimes

        ((Lines omitted about what Thor created))

47  C:  Is he kind of hu:ge.
48      (0.4)
```

```
49   C:   a big bloke or?
50   R:   No: he's not hu:ge he's a biggis:h looking
51        bloke though.
52   C:   Right
53        (0.7)
54   R:   a bih- ter:: (.) not bigger than (0.5) no:rmal
55        big men but (.) big you know
56   C:   Ri:ght. Couldn't he:- (1.) pahh! I don't want
57        to sound s(h)keptical but- couldn't he have just
58        been a jo:gger or something like that?
```

One feature of Palmer's analysis is that he shows how the structure of R's account deviates markedly from the kinds of accounts of unusual experiences reported by non-delusional people. For example, accounts of paranormal experiences are designed to address evidential issues: to warrant the claim that something objectively real happened, and which was not merely hallucination, wish fulfilment, or the misidentification of mundane phenomena. And one way in which this is managed is to build the report of what happened to undercut the relevance of possible sceptical explanations. The 'X ... when Y' device allows speakers to demonstrate their 'normality' and 'social compe-tence', thus defusing the likelihood that the veracity of the story can be under-mined by reference to deviation from cultural norms and expectations.

Palmer focuses on the stretch of talk in lines 47 to 58. It is apparent the inter-viewer, C, is seeking some kind of evidence for R's claim to have met Thor, the God of Thunder. C's question about Thor's size invites a consideration of his supernatural qualities: thus 'Is he kind of hu:ge.' invites a response which focuses on the ways in which Thor was not like normal men. However, R does not offer any evidential work. Instead he provides a merely factual answer. Moreover, he does not provide a factual answer and then corroborate the claimed paranormal status of the figure: he does not say, for example, 'No he wasn't huge but he did appear out of nowhere and alter the weather' (Palmer, 2000: 673). R offers the claim that Thor was normal in size *and no more*.

This is in marked contrast to accounts of paranormal experiences from non-delusional people. It is clear that their accounts are organised to display their evidence for the paranormal status of the event, and explicitly to address possible sceptical alternative accounts. This defensive work is conspicuously absent from the account from the delusional person, the organisation of which suggests a lack of concern that the story may be doubted. It is as if the norms of everyday conduct have not informed this account. In Palmer's terms 'he appears disengaged from interactional concerns which constitute the normal social world' (2000: 673).

Palmer goes on to argue that clinicians and psychiatrists have to assess their patients' mental states from the things their patients tell them. And this story is precisely the kind of claimed experience which might lead to the conclusion that this person is delusional. But there is a problem: the *content* of this story is not that different from the experiences reported by non-delusional people, and which are studied by parapsychologists. What is different, though, is the way the story is reported. In non-delusional people it is apparent that accounts are constructed to display the speaker's normality, and this entails showing an awareness and rebuttal of alternative, sceptical versions of 'what really happened'. But the delusional person whose account is discussed in Palmer's paper shows no interest in this kind of delicate interactional work. His story seems to be informed by a different set of expectations and norms from those which demonstrably inform accounts from non-delusional people. Palmer goes on to suggest that psychiatry would benefit from these kinds of conversation analytic observations, because they lay bare the complex and subtle interactional practices on the basis of which we might come to see some people as sane and others as delusional.

Summary

- Rhetorical psychology restricts its focus to argumentation and ideology; and empirical research thus concerns a limited set of issues.
- Discourse analytic studies of factual or authoritative language offer close description of the organisation and use of communicative resources, and in this they resemble conversation analytic studies of interactional devices and their inferential consequences.
- Sacks' substantive and methodological observations constitute an invaluable resource for a range of discourse analytic projects.

It is clear that conversation analysis can make a significant contribution to studies of how language can be used to produce authoritative formulations of events and opinions, both in the context of everyday discourse and in the production of controversial or contested accounts. But it may have a greater influence and reach. In the last section I discussed three instances in which Sacks' work on doing being ordinary connected with the concerns of other disciplines, and suggested new avenues of research. But all of these disciplines are concerned with (broadly) cognitive phenomena: parapsychological experiences, autobiographical memory and the recognition and diagnosis of psychopathologies. Can conversation analysis contribute to the study of ostensibly psychological phenomena? To answer this, we have to consider discursive psychology, and that will be the topic of the next chapter.

6
Discursive Psychology

Discursive psychology is nothing less than a thorough reworking of the subject matter of psychology. Reflecting the concerns of Wittgensteinian philosophy (Wittgenstein, 1953) and ethnomethodological sociology (Coulter, 1979, 1989), it seeks to analyse reports of mental states, and discourse in which mental states become relevant, as social actions oriented to interactional and inferential concerns. It can be characterised by the claim that

> Attributions of agency, intelligence, mental states … are *in the first place* participants' categories and concerns (manifested in descriptions, accusations, claims, error accounts, membership disputes etc.), just as much as reality, imitation and authenticity are. (Edwards, 1997: 319)

Moreover, it is a critique of the assumptions which inform traditional psychological research (that cognitive processes and mental states drive social action) and a critique of the methods which have been developed as a consequence of those assumptions (that cognitive structures are best measured by experimental techniques, or can be inferred from discourse).

There are two key texts in discursive psychology: a useful discussion of some early studies can be found in Edwards and Potter (1992), but Edwards (1997) provides the most comprehensive account, offering a critical analysis of the architecture of assumptions which inform theory and research across a range of topics in cognitive psychology, and pointing to new ways of conducting psychological research. In addition to these texts, te Molder and Potter's (2004) edited collection on discourse and cognition has significant contributions from conversation and discourse analysts which reflect a range of perspectives on the relationship between language and the mind.

In this chapter we shall be mainly concerned to explore the empirical orientation of discursive psychology. To do this, we need to consider instances of language use in which cognitive states or mental processes seem to have an importance for the participants.

Cognitions in action

The next three extracts show speakers using a variety of words and phrases which either report or invoke the relevance of cognitive processes or mental states. The first comes from routine conversational interaction.

(6.1)   (From JS:II: 219–20)

```
Ben:     Lissena pigeons
Ellen:   ⌈⌈Coo-coo:::coo:::
Bill:    ⌊⌊Quail, I think
```

Ben notices the sound made by pigeons. But at the same time that Ellen begins to mimic the sound of the birds, Bill corrects Ben by pointing out that they are quail, not pigeons. This correction is accompanied by a report of Ben's state of mind concerning the birds: he *thinks* they are quail.

The second illustration is taken from McGuiniss' (1983) account of the investigation of a notorious murder in 1970. Captain Jeffrey MacDonald, a respected army doctor, claimed that drug-crazed hippies broke into his apartment, knocked him unconscious and brutally murdered his family. The police, however, suspected that MacDonald was the murderer. McGuiniss was able to interview the main people involved in the investigation, including MacDonald himself. The following passage comes from a taped interview with MacDonald in which he is describing how, during a mealtime in the Officers' Mess, he first heard that the police had named him as the prime suspect in their investigation.

(6.2)   (From McGuiniss, 1983: 168)

> I was standing in line getting food, and I had just gotten through the cash register area and was beginning to sit down, when they had a news bulletin that Captain Jeffrey MacDonald, the Green Beret officer from Fort Bragg who six weeks earlier had claimed that his wife and children were brutally beaten and stabbed by four hippies, was himself named chief suspect.
>   And I remember the truly – I don't mean to use clichés, but I don't know how else to explain it – the room was spinning again.

MacDonald is able to recall in some detail this traumatic moment. He has clear and detailed recall of his movements at the time, and recollection of the news broadcast itself. Clearly then, here is evidence for the operation of memory, and a good one at that: the detail of MacDonald's description implies the successful operation of processes by which information or perceptions at the time are stored as memories and than later retrieved.

Finally, the last instance comes from an interview with two young women about personal style, appearance and membership of youth subcultures.

(6.3) (From Widdicombe and Wooffitt, 1995: 96–7)

```
 1  I:    can you tell me something about your style and the way
 2        you look,
 3        (0.7)
 4  I:    how would you descri:be yourselves
 5        (0.7)
 6  R1:   hh
 7        (0.7)
 8  R1:   I dunno >I hate those sorts of quest⌈ions uhm
 9  R2:                                        ⌊yeah horrible
10        isn't it
```

Consider the first respondent's (R1) reply to the interviewer's question: what kinds of inner psychological conditions are being reported here? First, she refers to her knowledge: 'I dunno' indicates that the speaker either does not know how to describe herself, or is at least uncertain as to how to go about that task. Second, her claim, 'I hate those sorts of questions', displays a firm stance towards a particular object. We can see, then, that in the space of a few words, the speaker has drawn upon and described her state of knowledge and has expressed an attitude.

We might be tempted to assume that cognitive terms are used because they correspond to or represent inner mental states: we say 'I dunno' because our brains do not contain the relevant information; we provide detailed reports of past experiences because the information is stored in our memory, and so on. This is a common assumption in traditional psychology. It may not be so crudely expressed: psychologists may work on the assumption that *in principle* language can reveal the workings of the mind while taking account of the various ways in which those processes might be obscured or distorted. But it is not hard to find instances in which, broadly, the way language is used is taken to reveal the causal influence of mental states, or the basic properties of cognitive entities. For example, in social representation research, it is assumed that talk can be examined to investigate the expression and use of underlying cognitive representations (for example, Jodelet, 1991). And in research on various kinds of autobiographical memory, the contents of reports of past experience are taken as more or less accurate indicators of what information is actually stored in the head; the goal for the psychologist is to explain how it got there, and how it was subsequently accessed (for example, Brown and Kulik, 1977). Thus traditional cognitivist psychology regards language as a window on, or expression of, the workings of cognitive procedures.

Discourse analysis, however, challenges this version of the relationship between discourse and cognition. It examines talk and texts to show how descriptions and reports have been constructed to perform interactional or interpersonal functions. It studies what people *do* in language. The discourse analytic focus on the way that language is used to do things has implications for the study of cognition. First, it means that we cannot rely on people's accounts to reveal the inner properties of the mind as the organisation of discursive acts might be informed by the social actions for which they have been designed. But more radically, it suggests a new research programme which takes as its subject the ways in which references to and descriptions of mental states, and a cognitivist vocabulary, are used to perform social actions. For example, in discourse analysis, the attribution of causal relationships is analysed as a discursive activity, designed and performed with respect to the interpersonal context for which it is produced. A speaker may be attributing a relationship between two events not because of the operation of some cognitive processes by which causal relationships are identified, but to attend to inferential concerns such as managing the imputation of blame, warranting the factual basis of a claim, and so on.

There was a concern to explore the implications of the action orientation of language for traditional psychological concerns early on in discourse analytic research. The term 'discursive psychology' was adopted to focus on this aspect of discourse studies.

> Discourse analysis is particularly concerned with examining discourse for how cognitive issues are dealt with. … It is a further development of these issues here which leads us to move beyond talking of discourse analysis and to describe the enterprise as 'discursive psychology'. (Edwards and Potter, 1992: 29)

Discursive psychology, then, is focused on the ways in which cognitive notions can be treated analytically as situated practices which address interactional and inferential concerns in everyday circumstances.

> Discursive psychologists ask: What does a 'memory' *do* in some interaction? How is a version of the past constructed to sustain some *action*? Or: what is an 'attitude' used to *do*? How is an evaluation built to assign blame to a minority group, say, or how is an evaluation used to persuade a reluctant adolescent to eat tuna pasta? (Potter, 2000: 35; original italics)

So what do they do? How do they work? We will begin to sketch some of the main analytic issues by considering the three kinds of cognitive states illustrated in extracts 6.1 to 6.3: reports of 'thinking', memory; and in particular, memory formulations which indicate good recall, and 'I dunno'-type reports of a lack of knowledge.

Thinking

What happens when we characterise a claim or position as something we 'think' is the case? Consider the following example.

(6.4)   (From Atkinson and Drew, 1979: 58)

```
1   B:   Uh if you'd care to come over and
2        visit a little while this morning
3        I'll give you a cup of coffee
4   A:   hehh   Well that's awfully sweet of you,
5        I don't think I can make it this morning
6        hh uhm I'm running an ad in the paper and and uh I
7        have  to stay near the phone.
```

B invites A round for coffee. In declining this offer, A says 'I don't think I can make it this morning'. This is the refusal component of a dispreferred response to an invitation or offer (Heritage, 1984a: 266). As such it handles delicate issues concerning the face of the person making the inviting. A blunt refusal might well appear brusque and insensitive. To say 'I don't think (X)', however, modulates the strength of the refusal, in that it portrays the uncertain or conditional basis of the action.

Now consider the exchange in extract 6.1.

```
Ben:     Lissena pigeons
Ellen:   ⌈Coo-coo:::coo:::
Bill:    ⌊Quail, I think
```

Again, sensitive matters are at hand, as Bill is *correcting* Ben. Overt repair of this kind is a delicate interactional activity because it may be taken as a slight, a 'put down' or deliberate rudeness. Repair work, then, has potential implications for the coordination of the interpersonal relations of the relevant parties (Jefferson, 1987). 'I think' formulations address this potential sensitivity because they modify the force of the correction (Schegloff *et al*, 1977).

'I think' formulations of knowledge claims are rooted in social activities. They allow speakers to manage sensitive interpersonal matters in delicate and subtle ways. Of course, this is not to say that this is the only kind of work they do: a withering scepticism can be achieved by following a report of someone's stated plans or intentions with 'I don't think so'. The point is that the design of utterances is informed by the discursive actions and contexts for which they are produced. It is a mistake to assume that reference to a speaker's 'thoughts', 'thinking' and so on simply expresses the operations of inner mental states.

Memory/remembering

For discursive psychology, the focus is on remembering (and forgetting), and these are treated as social actions embodied in everyday social practices. Verbalised recollections are treated as 'pragmatically variable versions that are constructed with regard to particular communicative circumstances' (Middleton and Edwards, 1990: 11). For example, Edwards and Potter's study of John Dean's testimony to the senate committee investigating the 'Watergate' scandal explores the contextualised and pragmatic work embedded in memory formulations (Edwards and Potter, 1992: 30–53).

Their analysis was prompted by an earlier study by Ulric Neisser, a cognitive psychologist who had been trying to broaden the scope of psychological research on memory to take account of ecologically valid data, such as memories of real events (for example, Neisser, 1982; Neisser and Harsch, 1992; Neisser and Winograd, 1988). The publication of the transcripts of the senate hearings allowed Neisser to investigate the extent to which Dean's recall, noted at the time for its extensiveness and apparent detail, was accurate. He claimed to have identified three kinds of memory functioning in Dean's testimony: verbatim, gist and repisodic memory. Neisser argued that repisodic memory works to preserve the key themes of an event or discussion while allowing for errors. In short, it allowed Dean to be telling the truth while ostensibly getting things wrong (Neisser, 1981).

While welcoming Neisser's attempt to move the study of memory beyond the laboratory, Edwards and Potter argued that his analysis was problematic because it confused accounting practices with memory processes. Aspects of the testimony which Neisser had seen as evidence of good recall, bad recall or a certain type of recall (verbatim, gist, repisodic) were ways of managing Dean's accountability in a courtroom setting; they were methods for dealing with actual or implied attributions of guilt, and so on. So, for example, producing the gist of a prior event or conversation allows the speaker to perform delicate descriptive operations: they can preserve, delete or transform aspects of the prior talk to attend to current interactional purposes (Heritage and Watson, 1979). Moreover, verbatim recall of prior conversation is a rhetorical strategy through which the speaker is able to manage the evidential value of their claims (Goffman, 1981; Holt, 1996; Wooffitt, 1992). Thus what Neisser interpreted as expressions of the workings of memory were discursive practices oriented to inferential tasks generated in the context of official hearings to identify responsibility and blame for illegal activities (see also Molotch and Boden, 1985).

Dean was noted for his good memory: he drew attention to it at various points in the hearings, and on occasions was able to give detailed accounts of past events. Edwards and Potter (1992) select some illustrative examples from Neisser's (1981) paper, which serve to show that Dean presented himself as

> ... someone with a virtually direct perceptual access to the original events: 'you know the way there are two chairs at the side of the President's desk ... on the left hand chair Mr. Haldeman was sitting' ([Neisser] 1981: 11); 'I can very vividly recall the way he sort of rolled his chair back from the desk and leaned over to Mr. Haldeman and said "A million dollars is no problem"'. (1981: 18, cited in Edwards and Potter, 1992: 42)

However, Edwards and Potter argue that we must not take Dean's pronouncements on his own memory abilities as literal or neutral statements as they are produced for rhetorical ends, to attend to matters of culpability and blame. (See also Lynch and Bogen, 1998, for an analysis of the strategic orientation of Oliver North's accounts of his memory capabilities in his testimony to the Iran–Contra hearings.)

Moreover, the vivid narrative detail provided by Dean may be produced as a device to warrant the claim to have exceptional recall, thus strengthening any specific version of events. In their study of the various debates following a con-troversial off-the-record briefing by the then Chancellor of the Exchequer, Potter and Edwards noted that the grounds for a particular version of what really happened could be established through detailed memory narratives. The follow-ing extract comes from one of the journalist's accounts of the disputed meeting.

> Mr Lawson (the Chancellor) sat in an armchair in one corner, next to a window looking over the garden of No. 11 Downing Street. The Press Secretary, Mr John Gieve, hovered by the door. The rest of us, notebooks in our laps, perched on chairs and sofas in a circle around the Chancellor. It was 10.15 on the morning of Friday 4 November … . (Potter and Edwards, 1990: 419)

The journalist's account contains what Potter and Edwards call 'collateral information' (1990: 419); his recall thus seems fresh and vivid. The provision of collateral detail thus advances and substantiates a claim to have veridical recall, which in turn grounds the authority of that particular version of what really happened. (See also Bell and Loftus, 1989, on the power of ostensibly 'trivial' information in courtroom testimony.) Neisser treated this kind of collateral detail in Dean's testimony as an expression of particular memory processes. However, if we take account of the context in which it was produced – an official, governmental hearing to determine knowledge of and involvement in the President's wrongdoings – we can see that it establishes the *grounds for* the credibility of Dean's version of events.

The upshot is that rememberings are social actions enmeshed in and built with respect to inferential concerns. In the senate hearing at which Dean gave his testimony, and in the dispute about what was really said at an off-the-record ministerial briefing with political journalists, matters of truth and responsibility were of paramount concern: the reputations of public figures – and possibly their careers – were at stake. Detailed narratives not only worked to provide vivid depictions of contested events, but established the authority of those versions. (See also Locke and Edwards' 2003 study of Bill Clinton's testimony to the Grand Jury investigating his relationship with White House intern Monica Lewinsky.)

We can now return to the extract (6.2) from the interview with Captain MacDonald in which he reports the moment when he heard that he was suspected of murdering his wife and two children.

> I was standing in line getting food, and I had just gotten through the cash register area and was beginning to sit down, when they had a news bulletin

that Captain Jeffrey MacDonald, the Green Beret officer from Fort Bragg who six weeks earlier had claimed that his wife and children were brutally beaten and stabbed by four hippies, was himself named chief suspect.

Matters of truth and responsibility are clearly relevant to individuals implicated in murder inquiries. It is no surprise, then, that we find MacDonald's recollection of first hearing that the police suspected him of murdering his family is vivid and sharp, as though the moment was indelibly burned into his mind. How does this detailed account address the broader inferential implications of being a murder suspect?

In the last chapter we discussed some of the descriptive resources through which accounts of personal paranormal experiences could be designed to mitigate possible sceptical responses. One device was characterised as 'I was just doing X … when Y', a format through which the speaker's first awareness of the phenomenon was introduced into the narrative. Of course, this device is not restricted to accounts of paranormal experiences, but regularly occurs when people are reporting extraordinary or traumatic events. MacDonald's account of hearing that he was the police suspect is organised around the 'X … then Y' format:

X   I was standing in line getting food, and I had just gotten through the cash register area and was beginning to sit down,
Y   when they had a news bulletin that Captain Jeffrey MacDonald …

A 'just X … when Y' formulation is a normalising device: X components are used to portray the speaker's mundane activities at the time of events which have personal significance. MacDonald is drawing on everyday communicative practices to establish his normality via reports of the routine aspects of his environment. And establishing one's orientation to culturally organised normative requirements – behaving 'normally' – may be a matter of real concern for people accused of serious crimes, regardless of their guilt or innocence.

Discursive psychology treats recollections as reportings oriented to interpersonal and inferential matter. To expose the pragmatic and rhetorical aspects of memory formulations, we have examined instances taken from participants in disputes as to 'what really happened'. Was the President implicated in illegal activities? What was said at a meeting between a government minister and political journalists? Did MacDonald murder his family? In each case we have seen how recollections of events are fashioned to address issues of blame and responsibility. Also, following Edwards' and Potter's arguments, we have examined the way that detailed recollection may be a way of warranting the authority of a particular version of what happened. These disputes are not everyday events, but they illustrate a general point which is relevant to more mundane forms of interaction: 'common sense' or vernacular characterisations of ostensibly cognitive memory processes may be invoked and constructed with respect to specific inferential tasks. There is, then, a clear point of contact between the concerns of discursive psychology and the study of factual language.

'I dunno'

Initially, claims such as 'I dunno' seem unpromising targets for detailed attention because they seem to be a verbalised 'shrug of the shoulders', a simple claim that we lack knowledge of some matter. Moreover, we might be tempted to regard these formulations as 'uncertainty markers', thus underlining the cognitive psychological perspective that language use is ultimately a representation of inner cognitive states or psychological processes.

The discourse view, however, treats 'I dunno' formulations as activities produced to address particular kinds of interpersonal work. In his study of interaction in relationship counselling sessions, Edwards (1995a) showed how 'I don't know' was used by a man reporting his partner's clothing to display a lack of concern for the topic, when disclosing such close monitoring could itself be cited as warranting accusations of overbearing jealousy. 'I don't know' or 'I dunno' formulations, then, can be used by speakers to display their uninterest in, or distance from, claims, opinions or descriptions which are in some way sensitive, or which may be taken as the basis for sceptical or negative inferences about them.

Potter (1997) has illustrated some of the work being done by 'I dunno' formulations in his analysis of a now famous interview between a television journalist, Martin Bashir, and Diana, Princess of Wales, shown on British television. It has been argued that this was an important moment in the history of the monarchy in the United Kingdom (Abell and Stokoe, 2001). Some years earlier Diana's husband, Prince Charles, had given a television interview in which he admitted infidelity; and it was widely believed that relations between the couple were frosty. Subsequently a biography of Diana was published by Andrew Morton, which portrayed Diana in a more sympathetic light. This book, and Diana's complicity in its writing, was regarded as a way of getting back at Prince Charles.

During the interview, Bashir raises Diana's motivation for her involvement in the writing of Morton's book. Potter points out that in her responses Diana is managing issues of stake and stake inoculation.

(6.5)   (From Potter, 1997: 151)

```
Bashir:   Did you (.) allow your ↑friends,>your close friends,< to speak to Andrew
          °Morton°
Diana:    Yes I did. Y⌐es I did
Bashir:              L°Why°?
Diana:    I was (.) at the end of my tether (.)
          I was (.) desperate (.)
          >I think I was so fed up with being< (.)
          seen as someone who was a ba:sket case (.)
          because I am a very strong person (.)
          and I know (.) that causes complications (.)
```

<pre>
          in the system (.) that I live in.
          (1) ((Diana smiles and purses lips))
Bashir: How would a book change that.
Diana: I ↑dunno. ((raises eyebrows, looks away))
          Maybe people have a better understanding (.)
          maybe there's a lot of women out there
          who suffer (.) on the same level
          but in a different environment (.)
          who are unable to: (.) stand up for themselves (.)
          because (.) their self esteem is (.) cut in two.
          I dunno ((shakes head))
</pre>

Bashir is questioning Diana's motives for her implicit consent for the book. She acknowledges that she was unhappy with how she felt she had been portrayed, and suggests that the expectations about how members of the Royal Family should conduct themselves clashed with her personality. Bashir then asks her 'How would a book change that.'

At this point, Diana's involvement in the book is a sensitive matter. Its credibility as an accurate account of her mistreatment by the Royal Family would be at issue if it were to become apparent that it was motivated by revenge or spite. Her answer is prefaced by 'I dunno': this portrays Diana's uninterest or lack of concern for the possible impact of the book on her own domestic situation. She then goes on to suggest that the book may help other women who are burdened by expectations and responsibilities, thus portraying altruistic motives for the book. Finally she closes her account with another 'I dunno'.

These 'I dunno' formulations open and close a turn in which Diana has to address her own stake in the production of Morton's book and its anticipated consequences. They allow her to manage the range of potentially unsympathetic inferences: that she was motivated to cause embarrassment for her husband and the Royal Family; that she was driven by revenge, and so on. 'I dunno', then, performs work in talk-in-interaction, and is not a simple representation of knowledge, uncertainty, or any other cognitive state.

With that in mind, we will return to the extract from the interview about personal style and appearance. This comes from a study, conducted by Sue Widdicombe and myself, of the language used by members of youth subcultures during informal interviews about their lifestyle. The initial question in the interview was designed as an indirect attempt to get the respondents to identify themselves in terms of particular subcultural group categories: punk, gothic and so on. (This was because the interviews were initially undertaken as part of a more traditional social psychology project in which it was necessary to establish the respondents' subcultural affiliations without explicitly presenting them with relevant category terms.) On occasions when the respondents described themselves in terms of a subcultural identity, they did so immediately after the interviewer's question, and their turns were fairly minimal in design.

(6.6) (From Widdicombe and Wooffitt, 1995: 81–2)

```
        ((Tape starts))
1  I:   … about your sty:le
2       (0.3)
3  I:   and who you are
4       (0.4)
5  I:   how would you describe yourselves
6  R1:  huhh huhh hhagh punk rockers
7  R2:  punk rockers yeah huhh huhh
```

However, we noted that at the start of interviews, our respondents used a variety of resources to avoid identifying themselves as members of particular subcultures. (For an account why categorical self-identifications were resisted, see Widdicombe and Wooffitt, 1995: 94–107.) It was striking that these resistance strategies were often accompanied by 'I dunno' formulations.

(6.7) (From Widdicombe and Wooffitt, 1995: 96–7)

```
1   I:   can you tell me something about your style and the way
2        you look,
3        (0.7)
4   I:   how would you descri:be yourselves
5        (0.7)
6   R1:  hh
7        (0.7)
8   R1:  I dunno >I hate those sorts of quest⌐ions uhm
9   R2:                                      ⌊yeah horrible
10       isn't it
```

In this extract, for example, prior to the 'I dunno' formulation, there are gaps and a brief exclamation prior to the respondent's first words in the turn. 'I dunno' is produced as a preface to the respondent's statement 'I hate those sorts of questions', which constitutes a complaint about having to provide a characterisation of herself. This is a clear resistance to the (tacit) invitation to provide a self-categorisation in that it topicalises the respondent's objections to precisely that kind of self-report.

In the next extract the second respondent (R2) provides an 'I dunno' formulation on behalf of him and his friend, and then uses another one to preface his claim that his distinctive appearance is a reflection of his own personal taste, rather than a recognisable subcultural style.

(6.8) (2H:F:FP T3SB)

```
8   I:   How would you descri:be the way you look,

         ((some lines omitted))
```

```
14  R1:  a*h huh ┌h
15  R2:          └Er::m:: (.3) we dunn┌o
16  R1:                                └>a good question<
17       (1.3)
18  R2:  ah dunno=ah jus'
19       (0.4)
20  R2:  ah jus dress how I feel like dressin'
```

Finally, in the following extract the respondent eventually acknowledges the relevance of a subcultural identification. However, this is managed very carefully. He does not endorse or provide a self-categorisation; rather, he merely acknowledges that there is a consensus that his appearance would be described in terms of a particular subcultural identification. And, again, we find the turn in which this resistance is accomplished is prefaced by an 'I dunno' formulation.

(6.9)   (1P:M:KHS: T9SA)

```
1   I:  OKAy: can you tell me something about
2       yourself your style and that,
3   R:  er::m
4       (1.2)
5   R:  what sort've thing,
6       (0.4)
7   I:  WEll how would you descri:be it.
8   R:  erh:
9       (1)
10  R:  ah dunno
11      (0.7)
12  R:  most people describe it as punk ah suppose
```

These extracts illustrate three ways in which respondents can resist identifying themselves in subcultural terms: by complaining, 'I dunno >I hate those sorts of questions'; by asserting that their (subculturally implicative) dress and appearance is a reflection of personal preference, 'ah dunno=ah jus'(.4) ah jus' dress how I feel like dressin'; and by portraying the relevant subcultural label as someone else's description, 'ah dunno (.7) most people describe it as punk ah suppose'. 'I dunno' formulations thus seem to be clearly implicated in utterances in which self-identification in terms of subcultural categories is resisted. Perhaps this is not surprising. If, as Potter has argued, 'I dunno' formulations allow speakers to mark a lack of concern for a potentially sensitive object or topic, we might expect them to occur in turns in which speakers actively seek to deny the relevance of particular issues. 'I dunno' works here to allow the speakers to distance themselves from the relevance of particular kinds of self-identification; it is a way of displaying that they have no vested interest in their identities as punks (or whatever), a stance further underlined by the resistance strategies subsequently undertaken in their utterances.

On the basis of these remarks, we can outline areas for future research. First, the use of 'I dunno' does not mark cognitive uncertainty (or whatever); rather it constitutes interactional activity. It works (at least in these data) as a device to attend to sensitive or delicate matters generated in interaction. We can ask then: what other kinds of work does it do, if any? Second, these data suggest that there may be a sequential basis to the use of 'I dunno' which requires more extensive study. Do 'I dunno' formulations cluster in particular kinds of activity sequences? Moreover, in the four extracts discussed in this section, 'I dunno' claims tend to preface other activities such as complaining, accounting, explaining, and so on. Is this structural positioning echoed in the use of 'I dunno' claims in other instances of talk-in-interaction? These suggestions are based on preliminary observations; but they demonstrate the kind of empirical inquiries which are opened up if we treat 'I dunno' formulations – or other reports of ostensibly cognitive events – as activities in interaction, rather than representations of psychological states.

Summary

- Discursive psychology grew out of discourse analytic interest in the ways in which the realm of ostensibly cognitive phenomena were invoked, or their relevance oriented to, in the production of persuasive or factually oriented discourse.
- Discursive psychology treats avowals of cognitive phenomena as activities in interaction, rather than representations of psychological states.
- It has been used to explore, among other topics, naturally occurring conversational rememberings, social identity, attitudes, and formulations of personal knowledge.

The range and varieties of discursive psychology

Discursive psychology rejects the traditional cognitivist paradigm in psychology which treats inner mental processes as the proper topic for empirical research and theorising. From this dominant perspective, discourses of all kinds – talk and texts – are taken simply as expressing or representing in various ways the workings of these inner mental processes. Discursive psychologists, however, treat discourse as the proper topic for research. They take seriously the

> … ethnomethodological injunction to treat (what cognitivists take to be) mental objects as things whose 'reality' is their *invocation* in whatever human activities they appear in – in 'work talk', 'intimate talk' and 'casual talk' as much as in 'scientific talk'. (Condor and Antaki, 1997: 338; original italics)

Potter and Edwards (2003) outline three strands of discursive psychological research. First, there is an attempt to critique traditional approaches, and to offer an alternative in which psychological topics are re-cast as features of verbal and textual activities. So, for example, there is a shift from thinking about 'memory' as a set of storage facilities hardwired into the physiological structures of the brain, towards the study of discourse in which people offer recollections. Second, there is the study of the psychological thesaurus: the ways in which psychological terms are used to perform work in discourse. So, our observations on the use of 'I think' and 'I dunno' would fall into this category. Finally, there is the study of the ways in which discourse is used to manage implied psychological themes. Think about the studies of the organisation of factual or authoritative language that we discussed in the previous chapter. These revealed some of the kinds of devices and resources through which speakers manage others' inferences about their agency, personality, social competence and so on. But these issues are addressed as a feature of routine verbal interaction concerned with other matters, such as the authority and reliability of a witness to a claimed paranormal experience can be established by what seems to be a 'mere' description of the utterances of another witness.

Studies in discursive psychology have dealt with a wide range of topics. In addition to the research on memory formulations outlined in this and earlier chapters, there have been studies of emotion discourse (Edwards, 1999), evaluations of food preferences (Wiggins, 2001; Wiggins et al, 2001), and the talk of sex offenders (Auburn and Lea, 2003) and interaction in police questioning of suspects (Auburn et al, 1999). There has been a sustained critical reappraisal of attribution theory and script theory which takes as its point of departure the observation that formulations of events and causes are produced with respect to interactional or inferential concerns (Edwards, 1994; 1995a; Potter and Edwards, 1990). Finally, there are a number of studies of the ways in which the relevance of characterisations of identity may be established in talk (Antaki and Widdicombe, 1998; Antaki et al, 1996; Edwards, 1991; Nikander, 2002; Widdicombe, 1993; Widdicombe and Wooffitt, 1990, 1995).

What is consistent throughout this body of research is the use of findings from conversation analytic studies of mundane interaction, and the use of some of the methodological steps associated with CA; we will explore this relationship between CA and discursive psychology more fully in a later section. But it is important to note that there are other approaches which are also called discursive psychology which, although sharing many of the broader goals of the kinds of work discussed here, have very different assumptions and methodological procedures. For example, Ian Parker is a critical psychologist who has described his work as a form of discursive psychology (Parker, 1997). His work draws heavily from European social theorists and philosophers, such as Foucault and Derrida, as well as more traditional Marxist analyses of capitalist society. Parker's work is strongly informed by emancipatory concerns: he wants psychology to play a role in understanding and alleviating the production and perpetuation of inequalities in society. Consequently we will discuss his approach in more detail in the next chapter, which deals specifically with critical approaches in the study of language.

Another branch of work known as discursive psychology is associated with Rom Harré. Harré's work is broadly social constructionist (but see Harré, 1979), and thus there are overlaps with the kinds of theoretical positions found in the discursive psychological work we have been concerned with in this chapter (Edwards and Potter, 1992; Potter, 1996a). Harré has been at the forefront of the critique of the cognitive orientation of psychology (1987), and we can illustrate his position by thinking about the concept of the 'self'. He argues that it is no longer reasonable to assume that 'selves' are theoretical mental entities or cognitive schemata (Harré, 1979; Davis and Harré, 1990). Instead he argues that we need to study the discourse through which selves are occasioned and brought into being. In this, Harré draws from Wittgenstein's later philosophy (1953). Wittgenstein argued that the vocabulary of the mind (such as concepts and words referring to the self) is defined by observations of symptoms and not of mental phenomena in themselves. His philosophy emphasised that linguistic discourse is essentially part of an on-going social process: the uses of, and constraints over, the language of the mind and self are social derivatives which arise in human practice. Following this line of philosophy, Harré states that the theoretical mental entities (the will, the self, etc.), which are currently invoked to explain how people behave, should be replaced by a concern to investigate the linguistic procedures through which this mental vocabulary is used in social life (e.g., Harré, 1995; see also his work on 'account analysis', 1997).

It is at this point where Harré departs from the kinds of discursive psychological research discussed in this chapter. This is because he seeks to identify the grammars of expression through which selves (and other mental entities) are brought into being (Harré, 1989). The focus on grammar reflects his interest in the formal and logical properties of the ways in which psychological discourse is used: that is, the pre-conditions of the use of psychological language. The focus on formal and logical structures of language means that investigation of psychological discourse is largely viewed as a conceptual exercise, and not as a task for empirical research. His kind of discursive psychology is an exercise in logical analysis, in which the analyst tries to identify the kinds of conditions in which it makes sense to use particular kinds of psychological discourse (cf. Coulter, 1989; 1999). Moreover, Harré relies on Speech Act Theory by which to investigate these formal grammars of psychological discourse. This encourages inventing examples of discourse as an aid in this form of logical conceptual inquiry (e.g., Harré, 1989). However, as we saw in Chapter 1, the reliance on intuited or made-up examples of discourse is problematic. First, it encourages analytic speculation rather than empirical investigation of actual utterances in real-life situations (Schegloff, 1988b). But it also invariably offers an impoverished view of the detail and complexity of actual language use. It is comparatively easy to address issues such as sentence structure. It is much harder, however, to anticipate the subtle interactional matters which are addressed in language use; and it is even more difficult to try to anticipate the ways in which such issues may be negotiated in the fine detail of utterance design. This is not the approach of the work we discussed earlier, which emphasises empirical investigation of the ways in which the relevance of psychological vocabularies is invoked with respect to specific interactional activities in naturally occurring real-life data.

Harré's work is important because it challenges many of the assumptions which inform not only dominant perspectives in psychology, but also common sense thinking as well. However, because it offers a form of logical or concep-tual analysis, it is less powerful than those discursive psychological studies which develop analytic claims which are grounded in the inspection of real-life data (Potter and Edwards, 2003).

Finally, Billig's rhetorical psychological approach has many features in common with discursive psychology. (Indeed, in some of the literature, rhetor-ical psychology and discursive psychology seemed to be used synonymously, for example, Billig, 2001b; Wiggins, 2001). For example, he rejects the assump-tions that talk merely expresses inner thought or represents the operation of determinant cognitive events. We saw the following quote in the previous chapter, but it is equally appropriate (and useful) here.

> Cognitive psychologists have assumed that thinking is a mysterious process, lying behind outward behaviour. However, the response and counter response of conversation is too quick for it to be the outward manifestation of the 'real' processes of thought. The remarks are the thoughts: one need not search for something extra, as if there is always something lying behind the words, which we should call the 'thought'. (Billig, 2001b: 215)

Billig asks that we focus on discourse because it seems intuitively implausible that the complexity and delicacy of interactional procedures should be gener-ated by corresponding mental processes. Moreover, as rhetorical psychology argues very strongly, discourse is a form of argumentation. While we may not wish to endorse such a narrow view of interaction it has the benefit of draw-ing attention to the way language is itself the site in which we can explore psychological issues such as the causal attributions, the production of recollections, and the relevance of identity.

Discursive psychology and conversation analysis

Consider the studies we discussed to illustrate discursive psychology: the use of 'I think' prefaces to statements or accounts, 'I dunno' (lack of) knowledge claims, and the ways in which recollections can be formulated. It was apparent that there was a strong CA influence. We used data from CA studies, and considered the kinds of inferential matters addressed through descriptions of memories and examined the use of a cognitive vocabulary in specific interactional episodes. There would seem to be clear links between CA and discursive psychology, and in this section we shall explore this relationship in more detail.

It is clear that CA is a major resource for discursive psychology. In a recent review of discursive psychology, Potter (2000) identifies Sacks' work, and the form of analysis he began, as one of the most significant influences in the emergence of post-cognitive psychology. It has provided a cumulative body of knowledge about the organisation of interaction in mundane settings and in institutional contexts. Discursive psychologists have found these to be a valuable resource; for example, it allows them to ground their own analytic claims in the findings from a burgeoning body of research (Edwards, 1995b). For example, Potter and Hepburn are conducting a discursive psychological study of interaction in calls to a child protection helpline. Their analyses draw upon and build from earlier CA studies of mundane telephone interaction, and studies of 'institutional' calls; such as 999/911 calls to emergency services (Potter and Hepburn, 2003). Another feature of Potter and Heburn's study is that it simultaneously addresses research issues in CA and discursive psychology. Thus they analyse the sequential organisation of early turns in calls to the helpline, while at the same time attending to the kinds of psychological business which informs the participants' sequentially organised conduct. Similarly, Wiggin's (2002) study of gustatory 'mmms' – offered as appreciations of food at meal times – is a contribution to the discursive psychological investigation of the interactional organisation of evaluations and opinions, while at the same time contributing to the CA literature on non-lexical particles such as 'mm hm' and 'uh huh' (Jefferson, 1984a; Schegloff, 1981).

While discursive psychologists have developed lines of empirical inquiry which overlap with those in conversation analytic studies, their work has retained a solid constructionist edge, treating discourse as the site in which the relevance and properties of what are traditionally taken to be mental phenomena are constituted and negotiated. Paradoxically, this is in contrast to the work of some conversation analysts who take a much more traditional position on the relationship between cognitive phenomena and socially organised interactional practices. (See, for example, the contributions by Drew, Pomerantz and Heritage in the collection edited by te Molder and Potter, 2005.) The conversation analytic position on the relationship between mental processes and linguistic action can, then, resemble more the perspective common to the tradition of North American communication research (for example, Tracy, 1991).

CA has developed a distinctive methodological procedure and discursive psychologists have often adopted these in their own projects. Indeed, on occasions it would seem that the methodology of discursive psychology is hard to distinguish from that of CA. For example, the following quote comes from

Potter and Edward's (2003) debate with Coulter (1999) about the epistemological and empirical position of discursive psychology.

> Discursive psychology works through collections of instances, the close study of deviant cases and a major focus on participant's orientations. (Potter and Edwards, 2003: 178)

As we have seen in earlier chapters, a distinctive feature of much CA research is that it seeks to identify particular interactional phenomena from close analysis of a collection of instances. CA research also pays special attention to deviant cases in which there is a clear departure from an established pattern; this is because participants' utterances in these deviant cases will display their understanding of the significance of that departure, thereby providing the analyst with a deeper understanding of the normative framework which underpins interaction. And perhaps the key feature which distinguishes CA from other approaches to the study of language is that it is fundamentally concerned to investigate how participants themselves are making sense of on-going interaction. A concern with participants' orientations therefore informs all CA research. It would be possible, then, to replace the words 'Discursive psychology' with 'Conversation analysis' and have an accurate (albeit partial) description of CA methodology.

Perhaps the overlap between CA and discursive psychology is not surprising: there are many CA studies which address concerns which were later to inform discursive psychology, even if this is not an explicit focus of the research. We will consider three examples. In his first lecture, Sacks discussed the following fragment of interaction taken from a corpus of calls to a suicide prevention centre.

(6.10)   (From Sacks, 1992, vol. I: 3)

```
A:  this is Mr. Smith, may I help you
B:  I can't hear you
A:  This is Mr Smith
B:  Smith
```

B's 'I can't hear you' clearly implies that information offered by another speaker – a name – had not registered. This is a cognitive claim about the speaker's state of knowledge. But this is not a simple disclosure of a determinant cognitive reality. Sacks' analysis shows how this turn in this sequence performs delicate interactional work: it is a method by which to avoid giving a name where name giving is expected, without explicitly having to refuse to give a name. In this, there are close parallels with discursive psychological studies of the way in which mental states are invoked with respect to specific interactional tasks.

Heritage (1984b) has studied the use of the particle 'oh' in conversational interaction in a variety of sequentially organised activities, such as informings, repair and displays of understanding. He found that it is used to exhibit that the speaker has undergone a change of state, for example, in response to being informed of some state of affairs. However, he is not making the claim that this particle is a public display of some real change at a cognitive or mental level. As he points out, there are occasions when informings occur but are not marked with 'oh' receipts. For example, in medical consultations and news interviews there are occasions in which one participant informs another, but these kinds of interaction are distinctive because of the *absence* of 'oh' particles. This strongly suggests that its occurrence is constrained by, and oriented to, the interactional contingencies of particular social contexts.

Finally, Goodwin (1987) has studied the interactional basis of an instance of 'forgetting'. His data come from a video and audio recording of a group of friends having dinner. He examines a sequence in which one of the group is reporting on a television programme he has recently watched. While making this report, the speaker seems to forget momentarily the name of the show's host. Instead of treating this ostensible lapse in memory as an indication of a cognitive or psychological aberration, Goodwin investigates the 'forgetting' as a display of 'not remembering', and focuses on its sequential placement to see what kinds of work it performs in that setting. His subsequent analysis reveals that the spate of not remembering allows the speaker to warrant and facilitate the involvement of a co-participant in the telling of a story. It is, therefore, interactionally organised.

These studies are significant because they show that ostensibly psychological phenomena – not being in possession of information, changes in the state of one's knowledge, forgetting a minor detail in a story – are grounded in particular activity sequences. And in this, they suggest a further way in which CA can inform and enrich discursive psychological research.

Conversation analysis is centrally concerned to discover and explicate sequences of utterances: highly patterned ways of talking together in which participants engage in a circumscribed set of interactional and inferential activities. What is particularly useful to discursive psychology is that part of the work of analysing sequences in interaction requires showing how they are interactionally produced: to show how participants' orientation to the requirements of that sequence inform their activities, and in so doing, 'bring off' or realise that sequence collaboratively. The ways in which utterances are designed, then, will embody the participants' tacit understanding of the normative and procedural properties of sequential organisation: that certain activities are appropriately placed in specific positions. The discursive psychological investigation of the embeddedness of cognition in social life may then be enriched by close attention to the ways in which participants can be shown to be orienting to the relevance of, and collaboratively producing, avowals to or invocations of cognitive or psychological phenomena.

To illustrate this, we will examine some features of interaction between members of the public and psychic practitioners: people who claim to have access to paranormally derived knowledge, such as psychic powers, clairvoyance, the ability to discern information from tarot cards, or the power to communicate with the spirit world (Wooffitt, 2000, 2001b).

The sequential organisation of parapsychological cognition: a CA study in discursive psychology

It is well known that members of the public who consult mediums and psychics often believe they have been told information which the psychic could not have known by the use of normal senses. They are convinced that the authenticity and accuracy of paranormal powers have been demonstrated. But what exactly, in this case, constitutes proof of the psychic practitioners' paranormal powers? Psychic practitioners have to demonstrate some form of paranormal *cognition*. A CA-informed discursive psychology would ask then: what are the sequential properties of those episodes associated with ostensibly successful demonstrations of parapsychological cognition? That is, *where* in the structure of interaction in these settings do displays of a parapsychological mind occur?

A routine feature of the psychic practitioners' discourse is the use of questions to initiate topics, or develop on-going topics, which then become, even if only momentarily, the focus for both participants. Moreover, these questions embody or 'hint at' aspects of the sitter's current circumstances, or their future plans, information which should not be available to a stranger such as the psychic. In the extent to which they can establish that these references to ostensibly private matters are correct or accurate, psychic practitioners provide evidence for, and, by implication, demonstrations of, their access to paranormal sources of information. Instances such as these, which, from the psychics' perspective, may be considered 'successes', routinely exhibit a three turn structure (Wooffitt, 2000), as follows:

T1 Psychic: a question embodying a claim about, or knowledge of, the sitter, their circumstances, etc.
T2 Sitter: minimal confirmation/acceptance
T3 Psychic: attribution of now-accepted information to paranormal source.

Consider the following instance which comes from a sitting between a member of the public and a psychic practitioner who is interpreting tarot cards.

(6.11) (Tarot reading) (Discussing S's plans to travel after graduating.)

```
S:  I graduate in June I'm probably going to work until
    about february      -so: jus' (.) any old j┌ob    ┐y'know.
    -RIght okay         └right  ┘
```

```
P:   and are you going to the states,                        T1
     (.)
S:   yeah.                                                    T2
P:   yea:h, c'z e I can see the old ehm:                      T3
     (.)
S:   Hh  ┌huh Hah ˙h        ┐
P:       └statue of         ┘liberty around you,
S:   heh heh h┌e ˙hhh
P:            └there you are, there's contentment for
     the future.
S:   oh go┌od
P:        └who's pregnant around you?                         T1
```

The question 'and are you going to the states' may be heard as displaying the psychic's special knowledge that the sitter is indeed planning to visit the US. Once this has been accepted it is retrospectively cast as having been derived from the tarot cards: the psychic's utterance 'c'z e I can see the old ehm: statue of liberty around you,' portrays her prior turn as a consequence of her paranormal ability to detect from the arrangement of cards a classic iconic representation of the US, and interpret its relevance to the sitter. Moreover, the turn is initiated with a derivation of 'because', thus explicitly establishing that the topic of her prior utterance was generated from the special powers claimed in her subsequent turn.

Once the attributive turn is complete, and the psychic has made a general remark about the sitter's future contentment, she initiates another topic with the question 'who's pregnant around you?' which, should it be accepted by the sitter, would project the relevance of another attributive turn and further demonstration of special powers.

This three turn structure is a routine organisation of psychic sitter interaction in which the psychic elicits affirmative responses from the sitter. For example:

(6.12)   (Medium–sitter interaction)

```
P:   So spirit wants me to do a scan on your bo:dy, talk
     about your health, so I'm going to do that okay? I'm
     going to do this for your health (0.8) Let's see
     what's going on with you. ˙hh number one thing is your
     >mother in spirit please?<                             T1
     (0.2)
S:   Yes                                                    T2
P:   >'cause I have (n-m) y'r mother standing right over    T3
     here,   ˙hh and she said I WANna TAlk to HEr and I want
     to speak to her because hh your mother has very
     lou::d when she comes through. h she speaks with a in
     a very lou:d way a very uhm (.) y'understand
```

```
            very   ┌she has to be
      S:           └ye:s:.
      P:   heard, 'h and like this would not happen today
           without her coming through for you. D'y'┌un'erstand
      S:                                           └'kay
      S:   Ye:s.
```

Extract 6.12 begins with a section from the psychic practitioner's description of how the sitting will proceed. After this initial preamble, he produces a question about the sitter's mother. This has an interesting design in that it could be heard as a genuine question about the sitter's mother, that is, it may be equivalent to 'has your mother passed on or is she still living?'; or it could be heard as a question which seeks confirmation of information already known to the medium. The sitter's minimal response does not disambiguate the prior turn, in that a simple 'yes' could be 'a telling' or 'a confirmation'. The medium's next turn, however, reveals that he is in contact with the spirit of the sitter's mother. Moreover, the psychic prefaces this turn with ''cause'; this establishes that his prior turn was a consequence of, or an upshot of, information or events he is about to disclose in his current turn. This retrospectively characterises his first turn as a question seeking confirmation of information already at hand. Also, it can now be inferred that the knowledge that the sitter's mother has died came from a paranormal source: the spirit of the mother herself.

The display of paranormal cognition, then, is sequentially ordered: it is in the third turn of the sequence where now-accepted claims about the sitter are attributed to a paranormal source, and thus constitute evidence of paranormal cognitive abilities.

There is evidence in this sequence that both sitters and psychics orient to significance of the third turn. For example, the sitters' affirmative responses are predominantly minimal in design and speedily produced, thus facilitating as quickly as possible the onset of the turn in which the now-accepted information is attributed to a paranormal source. But psychics too demonstrate an awareness of the inferential significance of third position attribution. For example, in some instances, psychics do not move to the third turn after the sitter acceptance/confirmation, but instead ask a second, related question, thus temporarily delaying the onset of the third turn.

(6.13) (Medium–sitter interaction)

```
1        P:   hh AHrm I'am also he's talking to me about
2             an anniversary, (.) I don't know why:, (.) but he's
3             mentioning the anniv- an anniversary here. h ah've-
4             some kind of anniversary. ah >d'no (th's)< a death
5             ANniversary,
6             (0.2)
7 T1a    P:   ahr- a passing, an anniversary of a passing,
```

```
 8              (0.2)
 9         P:   would you be aware of ⌈this?   ⌉
10 T2a     S:                          ⌊y:es,  ⌋
11 T1b     P:   okay. and that's his passing is it please?
12 T2      S:   ye:s.
13 T3      P:   because he's talking about his anniversary of
14              his passing.
15         S:   yes.
16         P:   okay?
```

There are two utterances that stand as topic initiating questions: the first, 'would you be aware of (the anniversary of a death)', is met with a minimal acceptance/ confirmation. However, instead of moving to the third turn, the psychic produces another (related) question, 'and that's his passing is it please?', which again receives minimal response. Only then does the psychic move to the third turn in which he identifies the spirit of the sitter's husband as the source of his knowledge of the anniversary. The turn after the sitter's initial response is clearly not an attribution. However, this departure from the sequence is not noted or topicalised by the sitter, as the psychic's next utterance can be heard as recycling the first turn. Indeed, the sitter's second minimal response treats the second question in this way, thus reissuing the slot for the third turn.

The psychic is able to exploit the sitter's orientation to the on-going relevance of the third turn. Note the difference between the two questions: the first suggests that the psychic knows that the sitter 'is aware of' a relevant anniversary; the second, however, implies that the psychic knows the *identity* of the person whose anniversary is being discussed. The consequent attribution of this upgraded proposal in the third turn thus provides a more convincing demonstration of parapsychological powers. It seems that the second, stronger claim may be generated out of the sitter's acceptance/confirmation of an initial, weaker first turn. The psychic is able to produce a second first turn where a third turn attribution might be expected because of the sitter's orientation to the on-going relevance of the third turn.

Why are these sequential considerations significant for discursive psychology? There are two issues. As Potter and Edwards (2003) point out, discursive psychology is concerned to describe participants' orientations to the relevance of psychological states and vocabulary. And one way to expose these orientations is to study how they inform the ways in which turns are designed with respect to the sequence they collaboratively produce. So in this sequence, it is apparent that the minimal second turns are designed to facilitate the speediest possible onset of the third position turn. Moreover, it is clear that the first position questions do not offer a paranormal source for the hinted-at information. These observations allow us to make strong claims about the participants' orientation to the relevance of the (para)psychological activity undertaken in the third sequential position.

More interesting, perhaps, the focus on sequential analysis may generate new topics for discursive psychological research. An understanding of the expectations about actions in sequences, then, allows us to view activities accomplished in the turns as being sequentially implicated by earlier turns. This means that we may investigate not only turns in which a demonstration of the relevance of mind is explicitly produced, but also prior turns, which, in their design, facilitate the possibility of such an activity. The relevance of mental states – even ostensible parapsychological ones – may be empirically investigated as a collaborative concern distributed across turns as an oriented-to property of interactional episodes.

Summary

- There are varieties of discourse analysis. While it is most conventionally associated with the work of Edwards and Potter, the term is also associated with the more conceptual form of analysis offered by Harré, and the more critical approaches offered by Billig and Parker.
- There is considerable methodological overlap between Edwards and Potter's formulation of discursive psychology and conversation analysis; and some early conversation analytic studies explored topics similar to those examined in discursive psychology.
- The conversation analytic focus on the sequential organisation of talk-in-interaction offers a valuable resource for discursive psychologists seeking to identify the socially organised basis of avowals or invocations of mental phenomena.

The relationship between cognitive processes and language use is a complex and controversial issue. Discursive psychology adopts a radical position, in that it treats discourse as the proper object of study for psychology; the brain is simply the biological stuff which underpins complex social activities. This inverts the traditional view in cognitive psychology which sees cognitive structures as the proper object of study, and which regards social conduct as the epiphenomena of these determinate mental processes (Edwards and Potter, 1995). However, it should be stressed that the discursive psychological position is not shared by all language researchers: many still subscribe to the view that it is necessary and profitable to explore links between cognitive processes and communicative competencies. A neat summary of some of these arguments can be found in van Dijk (1996).

7
Critical Approaches to Discourse Analysis

In this chapter we will consider approaches to the analysis of discourse and communication which are markedly different from conversation analysis, discourse analysis and discursive psychology, in terms of both methodology and substantive focus. First, we will discuss critical discourse analysis (CDA), which has its roots in linguistics and sociolinguistics. Then we will assess a form of discourse analysis which emerged as a critical movement (primarily) within European social psychology, and which is influenced by the work of Michel Foucault (among others); this can be termed Foucauldian discourse analysis (FDA) or the analysis of discourses, for reasons which will become clear.

However, if CDA and FDA are so different from CA, why do we include them in this book which so far has focused on the close relationship between CA, discourse analysis and discursive psychology? Both approaches are distinguished and established intellectual traditions. They offer rich and stimulating empirical accounts of the role of language in contemporary society. For these reasons alone it is important to provide a flavour of their theoretical orientations and empirical research, and to map their broader contribution to the study of discourse and interaction. But more important, both critical and Foucauldian discourse analysis present a set of challenges to CA, in that they articulate an alternative approach to the study of interaction. A discussion of critical and Foucauldian discourse analysis allows us to outline some of the key areas of disagreement.

Critical discourse analysis

Critical discourse analysis is associated with researchers such as Norman Fairclough, Teun A. van Dijk and Ruth Wodak. Broadly put, it is concerned to analyse how social and political inequalities are manifest in and reproduced through discourse. In this section I will describe the general methodological and substantive orientation of CDA research. It is important to stress from the outset, however, that there is no one way of doing CDA. Unlike conversation analytic research, which adheres to a distinctive set of methodological principles, research in critical discourse analysis varies in style and focus. These different styles of analysis may reflect the diverse theoretical or philosophical orientations of researchers, or even the traditions of research associated with particular nations (Meyer, 2001; van Dijk, 1993; Wodak, 2001a). Before we address common themes in CDA research, it will be useful briefly to outline differences in the positions of some of the key figures working in this area.

Empirical work from this perspective largely draws upon what van Dijk has called a 'solid "linguistic" basis' (2001: 97), in that it often examines topics such as sentence structure, verb tense, syntax, lexical choice, the internal coherence of discourse, and so on. Unlike other approaches to discourse, critical discourse analysis extends its analytic focus to examine broader features of the production and consumption of discourse. So, for example, Fairclough adopts a broadly Marxist perspective on social conflict which emphasises the importance of the means of production. For him, the task of CDA is to identify how inequalities and conflicts which arise from the capitalist mode of production are manifest in discourse (Fairclough, 1989, 1995). Van Dijk is distinctive because he gives special attention to the role of cognition in the understanding and interpretation of texts and discourse practices. He argues that we need to understand the role of social cognitions and representations – ways of thinking about the world which emerge from social activities – in order to understand how wider inequalities inform particular discursive or interpretative acts. Cognition is thus the theoretical interface between discourse and dominance (van Dijk, 1993, 1996, 2001). In his (1993) account of CDA, van Dijk gives an example of why it is so important to focus on social cognition in an illustrative example of how racism may inform verbal interaction between a white and a black person. The production of 'discourse structures that signal underlying bias' (van Dijk, 1993: 262), such as impoliteness, or the use of derogatory vocabulary, will be a consequence of the 'activation' of attitudes and mental constructs. (See also van Dijk, 1991, for an account of the importance of social cognition in studying racist aspects of newspaper reporting.) By contrast, Wodak emphasises the importance of taking into account the wider context of discourse. For her, context has four levels: the actual or immediate use of language or text; the relationship between utterances, texts, discourses and genres; the extra-linguistic sociological and institutional context of discourse; and the sociopolitical and historical contexts. Her research seeks to identify the operation of power and dominance in discourse across these four contextual levels (Wodak, 2001b).

Despite the clear differences in research styles, all critical discourse analysts try to explore the role of discourse in the production and reproduction of power relations within social structures. In particular, they focus on the ways in which discourse sustains and legitimises social inequalities. In this, CDA begins with a clear political agenda.

The emancipatory goal of CDA

Critical discourse analysis adopts an overt political stance, in terms of both the kinds of topics it studies and the role it sees for the results of research. It sets out to reveal the 'role of discourse in the (re)production and challenge of dominance' (van Dijk, 1993: 249). Moreover, critical discourse analysts want to understand the role of 'structures, strategies or other properties of text, talk, verbal interaction or communicative events' (van Dijk, 1993: 250) in establishing and maintaining power relations between different groups in society (Fairclough, 1989).

However, it is argued that it is not sufficient simply to document the broad discourse processes which sustain power relations: analysis should be motivated by a clear political intent.

> What is distinctive about CDA is both that it intervenes on the side of dominated and oppressed groups and against dominating groups, and that it openly declares the emancipatory interests that motivate it. (Fairclough and Wodak, 1997: 259)

There is a moral imperative informing empirical research: critical discourse analysts should take an explicit sociopolitical stance, within both the academic community and wider society. This means that theoretical approaches and the topics of empirical inquiry should be motivated by the underlying concern to identify injustices in the structure of society and to seek to ameliorate the conditions of those groups who suffer from them. The objective is, then, social change through critical analysis. Moreover, the analytic focus is deliberately skewed. While it is acknowledged that asymmetries of power, status and opportunity can be resisted in various ways, the prime concern is to expose and explore the top-down processes of domination. How language can be mobilised to resist inequalities and asymmetries of power is relatively unexamined.

Texts, ideology, discourse and power

In critical discourse analysis, empirical research focuses on the interrelationships between discourse and wider social structures. The analysis of texts is central to this task. In everyday use, a text would be taken to refer to a written document, such as a letter, a film script or this book. But in critical discourse analysis (and, as we shall see, in Foucauldian discourse analysis) 'text' has a more complex meaning: it can refer to a speech or spoken discourse, written documents, visual images, or some combination of these three. Texts are regarded as multi-semiotic because many forms of representation may be combined in their construction. Take the example of a televised advertisement, in which spoken language, written words, visual images, music and special sound effects may all be used to portray a product, each of which adds layers of meaning and contributes to the sense or force of the advert. To obtain a rounded understanding of the production of meaning in texts it is thus necessary to extend the focus of analysis to include these kinds of non-linguistic representations. It is argued that these 'textural' properties of texts must be included in analysis because they reflect broader cultural and social influences which in turn make them 'extraordinarily sensitive indicators of sociocultural processes, relations and change' (Fairclough, 1995: 2).

The concept of ideology is crucial in CDA. Ideologies are taken to be organised sets of beliefs which mobilise practices and viewpoints which sustain inequalities across society. Ideologies thus serve to protect the interests of powerful groups. They perform this function in subtle ways because they inform how we come to interpret the world around as: ideologies ensure that certain events, ways of acting and relationships come to be regarded as legitimate or appropriate. For example, in recent history, it is not hard to find instances of discriminatory social and legislative practices which are premised on the assumptions that heterosexuality is the 'natural' sexual orientation, or that women are 'naturally' more suited to child rearing and home making.

Discourse and its texts are viewed as embodying ideological assumptions. (A useful discussion of the relationship between discourse and texts can be found in Wodak, 2001b.) Thus the ways in which we talk and write about the world reflect wider ideological pressures and, ultimately, particular constellations of power relations. Discourse, then, is the site of power.

Fairclough (1989) has identified two aspects of the relationship between language and power. First there is power *behind* language. This points to the ways in which powerful groups can determine aspects of language. For example, he argues that the standardisation of English pronunciation reflected the interests and influence of a merchant class which emerged in the southeast of England during the latter part of feudal society. They were able to define a particular way of speaking – *their* way – as *the* way of pronouncing English. This had important ramifications in Great Britain, the effects of which are still observable today. The very notion of a 'regional' accent to refer to non-standardised forms of speech assumes that standardised forms of pronunciation were somehow unconnected to any specific part of the country, thus masking the disproportionate influence and power of a particular group with a clear geographical base. It also established a benchmark by which other accents could be regarded as inferior. This is evident in many ways: for example, it is only in the past two or three decades that people with non-standardised accents have presented television programmes broadcast nationally in the UK. This in turn meant that people from outside the southeast of England were at a disadvantage in those social and work relationships and job interviews which tend to be conducted in middle-class London accents.

Second, Fairclough identifies various ways in which power can work *in* language. In face-to-face or telephone interaction there are constraints on the nature and extent of participation. There are constraints on content (what is said or done); constraints on the kinds of interpersonal relationships people enter when they engage in talk; and constraints on subject positions (the kinds of participatory roles which people can occupy in their discourse). In interaction between friends, these constraints may be flexible and relaxed, but in more formal encounters, a different set of assumptions become relevant. In doctor–patient consultations, for example, it is likely that the patient will describe symptoms and the doctor will ask questions, offer a diagnosis and, if necessary, suggest a course of medical treatment. It is unlikely that either party will deviate from these normatively prescribed participatory roles without good reason.

An illustrative study in CDA: racism and political discourse

The analysis of texts can involve a complex series of interpretative procedures; in his account of the principles of CDA, van Dijk (1993) illustrates the various ways in which texts may be interrogated by analysing the transcript of a political speech.

During the mid-1980s, a school headteacher from Bradford (which has a large Asian population) wrote some controversial articles on multi-cultural education for predominantly right-wing journals and newspapers. Many Asian parents with children at the school complained that these writings were racist and potentially inflamatory. The headteacher's case became a national issue: some argued for his sacking; others defended his right to free speech, and indeed claimed his articles were a welcome contribution to debates about race relations in the UK more generally. The text van Dijk examines is the transcript of a speech made in support of the teacher by a Conservative Member of the British Parliament to the House of Commons. (The transcript comes from Hansard, the official record of all debates in the House of Commons.)

(7.1) (From van Dijk, 1993: 269–70)

Mr. Marcus Fox (Shipley): This Adjournment debate is concerned with Mr. Ray Honeyford, the headmaster of Drummond Road Middle School, Bradford. This matter has become a national issue – not from Mr. Honeyford's choice. Its consequences go well beyond the issue of race relations, or, indeed, of education. They strike at the very root of our democracy and what we cherish in this House above all – the freedom of speech.

One man writing an article in a small-circulation publication has brought down a holocaust on his head. To my mind, this was a breath of fresh air in the polluted area of race relations ....

Who are Mr. Honeyford's detractors? Who are the people who have persecuted him? They have one thing in common – they are all on the Left of

British politics. The Marxists and the Trots are here in full force. We only have to look at their tactics, and all the signs are there. Without a shred of evidence, Mr. Honeyford has been vilified as a racist. Innuendos and lies have been the order of the day. He has been criticised continuously through the media, yet most of the time he has been barred from defending himself and denied the right to answer those allegations by order of the education authority. The mob has taken to the streets to harass him out of his job ....

The race relations bullies may have got their way so far, but the silent majority of decent people have had enough. ... The withdrawal of the right to free speech from this one man could have enormous consequences and the totalitarian forces ranged against him will have succeeded. (Hansard, 16 April 1985, cols 233–6)

In keeping with critical discourse analysis' attempt to show how discourse enacts and reproduces the power of dominant groups, van Dijk seeks to reveal the ways in which this speech, although ostensibly moderate in its tone and in the nature of its arguments, discredits anti-racist arguments, and thereby perpetuates racism. The analysis ranges over the following 'discourse dimensions' (van Dijk, 1993: 270).

First, van Dijk examines how features of the broader context in which the speech was made lend it authority and power. So there is a matter of *access*: not everyone can make speeches to the House of Commons; we might therefore infer that Fox's speech conveys important sentiments which merit consideration. Then there is the matter of *setting*: the House of Commons is adorned with symbols of the power of government, and is part of the Palace of Westminster, the home of the British Parliament, often referred to as the 'Mother of Democracies', all of which further establishes the authority of Fox's speech. And there is *genre*: Fox's speech is part of a parliamentary debate, a speech event to which only a select few can contribute. The extra-linguistic factors serve to signal the import of the speech, and thereby establish the validity of the critique of the anti-racists' arguments.

He then begins to consider the discourse dimensions associated with the speech itself. Thus he considers the *communicative acts and social meanings* in the speech: for example, he notes that Fox associates the anti-racists with with 'Marxists and Trots'; as there is an anti-communist consensus in British politics, this association undermines the anti-racists' position. He also examines the *participant positions and roles*, by which he means the kinds of identities relevant to the interpretation of the speech. So, Fox is a member of the Conservative (right-wing) party (then in government), and also white, male and a member of the middle class. Fox is clearly a member of a dominant group in society, which in turn explains why he is attacking the left, or is hostile to resistance from less powerful groups, such as anti-racists, or members of ethnic minorities from predominantly working-class areas. By examining the *speech acts* in Fox's speech, van Dijk is able to identify the range of assertions which are offered, and to speculate upon their effect on various audiences. So he notes that while Fox's opponents in the House of Commons may expose the falsehoods and bias in the account, pointing out, for example, that Honeyford's opponents were not pre-dominantly Marxists or 'Trots', members of the public outside parliament may not be aware of these inaccuracies and distortions. This in turn indicates the importance of the relationship between speech acts and the subsequent dis-semination of the speech in which they were made.

Van Dijk then turns to *macrosemantics: topics*, by which he means the way in which the debate had been formulated. Thus he points out that Fox claims that the debate is concerned with Mr Ray Honeyford, and raises issues to do with freedom of speech. By harnessing this particular case to the issue of the right to freedom of speech – to which no one would object – Fox cleverly slants the terms of the debate in favour of his position. But the topic of the debate could have been formulated very differently, for example, as a debate about Mr Ray Honeyford and his disparaging articles about Asian students in multi-cultural education, which would, in all likelihood, have led to a very different kind of debate. When he examines *superstructures: text schemata*, van Dijk unpicks the argumentative propositions and moves Fox makes. So, for example, he shows how Fox builds an implicit contrast between Honeyford's action (he wrote an article for a 'small circulation publication') and the response ('a holocaust on his head'). This depicts the response as unwarranted and unfair. In a section on *local meaning and coherence*, van Dijk examines a variety of linguistic features: specificity (which events/groups are explicitly described?); perspective (what is the speaker's position on the events being reported?); implicitness (how, and to what degree, do sentences imply events and actions which support the speaker's case?); and coherence (how can the text be organised to reproduce ideologically laden assumptions?).

Fox's style is examined in terms of various linguistic and grammatical fea-tures. For example, Fox employs a distinctive lexical style, referring in some places to technical terms associated with the conduct of business in British politics, such as 'Adjournment debate'. In other places he uses more vivid language: he characterises Honeyford's opponents as a 'mob' or as 'Trots'. These lexical choices serve to emphasise Fox's importance as a senior political figure (not everyone can participate in an Adjournment debate) while undermining the credibility of those groups resisting the exercise of power by dominant groups. Finally, van Dijk considers the *rhetoric* of Fox's speech. Thus he points to the use of rhetorical questions ('Who are Mr. Honeyford's detractors?'); examines contrasts between a positively formulated 'us' and a negatively formulated 'them' ('the majority of *decent* people' and 'race relations *bullies*'), and outlines the inferential impacts of metaphors used to depict the issues in the controversy ('a breath of fresh air in the polluted area of race relations').

This discussion of van Dijk's analysis is not offered as a model which is followed by all discourse analysts; as I have stressed earlier, there are different styles of critical discourse analytic research. However, it provides an excellent illustration of analytic goals and empirical procedures which would be familiar to much critical discourse analysis. First, there is the attempt to analyse the data to reveal how minority or relatively powerless groups in society are disadvantaged by discourse. Thus Fox's speech is assessed as a vehicle which perpetuates racism by undermining the arguments of people who are protesting against anti-racist writings. The object of the analysis is to reveal how discourse achieves this effect. Of course, there is no claim that Fox is deliberately using language this way; or even that Fox himself holds racist opinions. Indeed, his personal beliefs are irrelevant: the focus of the analysis is on the way that language as social structure works across a range of discourse dimensions in favour of dominant and powerful groups. Second, it is clear that van Dijk has not simply examined the words Fox used, but has also considered the implications of the context in which they were used. Fox is speaking to the House of Commons; this signals in many ways that his words have authority and importance. In this the analysis seeks to establish a link between the political effect of discourse and the wider social structures and practices from which it emerges and which it seeks to preserve. Finally, the analysis emphasises that the overall inferential impact of the text – and its subsequent political import – emerges from the interrelationship of its organisation across various discourse dimensions. Critical discourse analysts seek to identify ways in which discourse (re)produces inequalities and dominance in the broader web of discourse, texts, contexts, non-discursive practices and wider social structures (Fairclough, 1992; van Dijk, 1993; see also the collection in Wodak and Meyer, 2001).

Critical discourse analysis and conversation analysis

A consequence of the broad emancipatory goals of critical discourse analysis is that it rejects certain methodological procedures and assumptions adopted by conversation analysts.

In critical discourse analyses, and as we shall see, other kinds of critical approaches, discourse, including talk-in-interaction, is analysed as a reflection of wider structural and social inequalities. This means that the analyst comes to the data with preconceptions as to what might be relevant, what the key issues are and so on. So for example, in rhetorical psychology, as it is assumed that discourse is broadly argumentative and rhetorically organised, the analyst seeks to identify the argumentative threads and rhetorical stances in the data at hand (for example, Billig, 1997).

In CA, however, analysis is not directed by the kinds of issues which motivate other forms of social analysis. It is not in the first instance theoretically committed to identifying injustices, and analyses are not presented as a contribution to the emancipation of specific social groups, or the solution of particular social problems. Neither does it begin with a conception of what kind of thing discourse is. CA is concerned to discover how people's own interpretations of on-going talk inform their subsequent contributions to the turn-by-turn unfolding of interaction. It is argued that interpreting participants' conduct in terms of the analysts' theoretical or political concerns obscures and diminishes the importance of the communicative competencies which people are using as they organise their talk collaboratively (Schegloff, 1991, 1997). This is an issue to which we shall return in later chapters; for present purposes, we need only note one upshot of CA's distinctive perspective.

In CA it is taken that analytic claims about interaction should be demonstrably relevant to the participants. So, if the analyst is claiming that, in a particular sequence of turns, participants are performing certain kinds of activities, then it is necessary to show how, in the design of their turns, they display their tacit understanding that that is the interactional business to which they are contributing. Thus one criterion for the relevance of analytic claims – if not *the* criterion – is that we can identify the participants' orientation to those activities the analyst is claiming to have identified.

However, this is where a tension between CA and critical discourse analysis emerges. In CDA, the analyst examines discourse as a reflection of wider structural and ideological forces. It is argued that although participants may not display an orientation to these influences, they nonetheless shape and give meaning to the production of discourse. This means that

> [c]ertain categories which have been of key importance in the analysis of social structure will of course do badly on [CA's] criteria for analytical relevance, including social class, power … and ideology. [Critical discourse analysis] by contrast requires such categories. (Fairclough, 1995: 11)

Thus analytic categories which do not have a manifest consequence for the participants might still be important. Fairclough offers the example of mixed gender job interviews. Gender may not emerge as an explicit issue for the participants, but it still may be relevant in other ways, shaping the background expectations and interpretations which underpin the encounter and its outcomes.

Summary

- Critical discourse analysis examines the role of discourse in the (re)production of social inequalities.
- It is argued that analysis should have an emancipatory goal: to uncover how discourse disadvantages minority or relatively powerless groups.
- It draws from linguistic analysis, and tries to link linguistic features to wider contexts of social, political and economic structures.
- Critical discourse analysis is critical of conversation analytic methodology, arguing that to fully understand how language works it is necessary to draw from wider social and political contexts.

Foucauldian discourse analysis/the analysis of discourses

So far in this book we have been using 'discourse' to refer to language use generally, including everyday talk-in-interaction studied in conversation analysis. But in Foucauldian discourse analysis the term 'discourse' has a more technical and theoretically grounded meaning. Parker provides a neat definition: a discourse is 'a system of statements which constructs an object' (Parker, 1989: 61). We will unpack the implications of this definition later; but for now, we can say that the task of Foucauldian discourse analysis is the *analysis of discourses*. This is a very different enterprise from the fine-grained investigation of talk and texts undertaken in discourse analysis and discursive psychology. In the rest of this discussion, the terms 'Foucauldian discourse analysis' (FDA) and 'the analysis of discourses' will be used interchangeably.

This analytic approach is associated with the work of researchers such as Ian Parker, Erica Burman and Wendy Hollway. Although it has come to be known as *Foucauldian* discourse analysis (Willig, 2001a), or the analysis of *discourses*, which is a term widely associated with Foucault's writings, it draws from many theoretical sources. Burman (1996) cites four main intellectual influences. First, there is the kind of historical analyses offered by Foucault. Broadly, he tried to identify the regulative or ideological underpinnings of dominant discourses: vocabularies which constrain the way in which we think about and act in the world. Second, she cites the work of Derrida, who argued that dominant ways of categorising the world inevitably rely on suppressed or hidden oppositional conceptions. He urged the deconstruction of texts to reveal the latent oppositional alternatives on which dominant perspectives depend. Third, a significant strand of FDA draws ideas from psychoanalysis to investigate how notions of subjectivity are implicated in personal and institutional arrangements. Finally, there is a critical historical perspective on the ideological and political context in which psychology emerged as an academic and clinical discipline. Consequently, work within this tradition is varied in both method and theoretical approach. Again, though, we are concerned primarily to describe common themes within this broad research tradition. We start by focusing on the nature of the critical thrust of Foucauldian discourse analysis.

The critical thrust of Foucauldian discourse analysis: discourses, emancipation and academic psychology

Like critical discourse analysts, workers in the Foucauldian tradition begin with clear political intent. For example, Parker (1990) argues that language is structured to reflect power relations and inequalities in society. Discourses are taken to be systems of meanings which reflect real power relations, and which in turn are a consequence of the material and economic infrastructure of society. For Parker, then, discourses support some institutions in society, and have ideological effects. This link between discourse and wider social structure 'means that discourse analysts must draw on other theoretical work which uncovers the material basis of oppression (capitalism, colonialism, patriarchy)' (Parker, 1992: 40). In this, Parker is arguing for a Marxist perspective on the relationship between discourse, dominance and wider social and institutional practices. In this sense, there is considerable overlap between the goals and approaches of Foucauldian and critical discourse analysis.

However, Foucauldian discourse analysis did not emerge solely as a response to social and political inequalities; at least in part it developed from a critical engagement with the academic discipline of psychology and psychological practices. Indeed, its origins can be traced back to what has come to be known as the 'crisis' in psychology during the latter part of the twentieth century (Parker, 1989, 1992). During this time some psychologists in Europe and the United States became increasingly influenced by ideas from other disciplines. Sociology provided two major influences: first, the concept of ideology, and all its ramifications for understanding political and social life, and second, the emergence of social constructionism, which argued for the social basis of all knowledge claims. From philosophy, Wittgenstein and Austin showed that ordinary language use is rooted in social practices, and not determined by linguistic rules. And post-structuralist and postmodern perspectives emerging in European continental philosophy provided new ways of thinking about psychology and the adequacy of its claim to be able to furnish scientific statements about mental processes. These influences focused attention on perceived deficiencies within psychology, such as its lack of concern for language, power and the perpetuation of social inequalities, and its failure to take account of the historical and ideological context of its practices and scientific claims. Energised by exposure to these kinds of ideas, many psychologists began to question the positivistic and empiricist orientation of the discipline. They started to do psychological work which tried to take account of the wider political context of psychological and social life, while at the same time exploring the ideological orientations which informed the way psychology as a discipline went about doing its work (for contemporary examples, see Billig *et al*, 1988; Burman *et al*, 1996; Burman and Parker, 1993a; Parker, 1989; Soyland, 1994; Wetherell and Potter, 1992; see also, Rose, 1989).

Consequently, when Foucauldian discourse analysts state that research should have a political orientation, their arguments are framed within the context of the critique of academic psychology, particularly its failure to realise the political implications of its own history and methodological practices. Thus Burman and Parker claim that analysis which does not function as a critique of contemporary social arrangements amounts to no more than 'traditional positivist methods masquerading as discourse analysis' (Burman and Parker, 1993b: 11). And Parker states that we must be careful not to let 'an analytic sensitivity to discourse become just another thoughtless empirical technique' (Parker, 1992: 123).

Discourses and texts

Parker offers these examples to illustrate how single discourses might work.

> Three unlikely examples ... to illustrate the operation of single discourses: if you say 'my head hurts so I must be ill', you will be employing a medical discourse; if you say 'my head hurts so I cannot really want to go to that party', you will be employing some sort of psychodynamic discourse; and if you say 'my head hurts but not in the way that yours does when you are trying it on in the way women do', you will be employing a sort of sexist discourse. (Parker, 1994: 94)

Discourses have two important effects. First, they constrain how we might participate in social life because they furnish subject positions. A subject position is 'a part allocated to a person by the use of a story' (Stenner, 1993: 114). Thus Foucauldian discourse analysts 'study texts ... to show how ... discourses facilitate and limit, enable and constrain what can be said (by whom, where, when)' (Parker, 1992: xiii). Second, discourses construct objects: entities or processes which acquire an objective status through the use of particular vocabularies. (For a more developed discussion, see Parker, 1990.)

Together, the availability of subject positions and the construction of objects by discourses has a regulatory orientation. Cameron *et al* (1992) provide a nice example. They observe that in recent years some new, ostensibly scientific claims have been made about the behaviour of women. 'Pre-menstrual syndrome' has been cited as an explanation for some acts of women's aggression; and that drinking alcohol during pregnancy has led to a range of medical problems for the newborn child. These have come to be known as 'foetal alcohol syndrome'. Although these terms are presented as objective and value-free, they constitute a form of social control over women in that they provide a vocabulary by which to position women as particular kinds of beings: at the mercy of biology, or morally responsible agents during pregnancy. The vocabularies we have for describing the world bring into play a range of expectations and constraints. These medical discourses about women tie into wider discourses which perpetuate sexism. Dominant discourses thus privilege ways of seeing and acting in the world which legitimate the power of specific groups.

Discourses are said to 'inhabit' texts; they are 'carried out or actualized in or by means of texts' (Marin, 1983, quoted in Parker, 1992: 7). As in critical discourse analysis, in FDA texts are not simply written documents, but are 'delimited tissues of meaning reproduced in any form that can be given an interpretative gloss' (Parker, 1992: 6). This means that anything can be analysed as a text: recordings of ordinary conversations, shopping receipts, the packaging of domestic goods, speeches, songs, official government reports, wedding vows, the scripts for television dramas, advertisements and so on.

Parker (1994) illustrates the ways in which discourses inform and shape everyday or mundane texts. He chooses as his text the wording on the cardboard packet in which a brand of toothpaste is sold. He describes a lengthy series of methodological steps, so we will here only summarise his main procedures. An initial step is to identify systematically objects that appear in the text. A useful guide is to look for nouns. Parker identifies these on the toothpaste packaging (among others): 'night', 'breakfast', 'head', 'intake', 'advice', and '0.8% Sodium Monofluorphosphate'. Similarly it is necessary to identify the kinds of people who are represented in the text: 'professionals', 'children', 'parents', and so on. These nouns and categories of person can now be interrogated to reveal the underlying discourses in the text, and to explore how the rules of the discourse allocate differential rights and responsibilities among agents identified within that discourse. So, for example, how does the organisation of the text allocate tasks and status between categories of individuals which are mentioned? This process allows us to isolate the different versions of the social world which coexist in the text, and to identify the rules of behaviour which these versions imply: that it is inappropriate to question the advice of professionals; or that parents are responsible for implementing and monitoring their children's hygiene regime, and so on.

Parker identifies four discourses which inhabit the toothpaste packaging. There is a rationalist discourse (the text appeals to the importance of following procedures for daily dental care, and requires judgements about the use of the product, and recognition of the authority of health care professionals). There is evidence of a familial discourse (in that ownership of 'your' child is implicated in supervision, care and the daily events connected to dental hygiene); he locates a developmental–educational discourse (in the emphasis upon the importance of teaching the child good dental care habits), and finally he describes a medical discourse (in which the use of the product is linked to hygiene and the ingestion of specific chemicals). Parker argues that these discourses constitute and reaffirm a set of normative expectations about 'appropriate' or 'natural' ways of categorising human beings, the relationship between these categories of people, and moral expectations about behaviour attendant upon those categorisations and relationships.

Foucauldian discourse analysis and conversation analysis

For many, the top-down approach to the study of language which is concerned with power, ideology, discourses, texts and subject positions is incompatible with bottom-up approaches which draw more from a conversation analytic approach and focus on organisation of interactional activities conducted through talk (for example, see Schegloff, 1997, on critical discourse analysis, and Widdicombe and Wooffitt, 1995, on Foucauldian discourse analysis). However, in a series of publications, Nigel Edley and Margaret Wetherell argue that it is not only fruitful to try to merge these perspectives, but necessary if we are to establish a satisfactory account of the organisation of everyday language use.

The context of their work is recent debate about masculinity: what it is, what it means, how it shapes the experience of being a man, how it reflects wider social practices, and so on. Edley and Wetherell observe that empirical and theoretical post-structuralist contributions have tended to provide global or sweeping characterisations of masculinity and male identity; they argue that such accounts need to be grounded in the 'actual interactional and discursive practices of men in mundane life' (Edley and Wetherell, 1997: 204). They acknowledge that conversation analysis is important in that it offers both a set of findings about the organisation of talk-in-interaction and a set of method-ological resources for research on interactional practices. However, they are concerned that some of its methodological prescriptions are too narrow and restrictive. Wetherell (1998) argues that CA's concern to furnish a technical analysis of interaction is limited as it means that the analyst has to ignore the broader historical and cultural context in which any particular interaction occurs. Moreover, she rejects the argument in conversation analysis that analytic claims must be grounded by reference to the demonstrable activities or orien-tations of the participants. In this she is echoing the argument from critical discourse analysis that some analytic categories, such as class, power and gender, may be relevant to participants' conduct but in ways which are not detected by conversation analytic methods. This is an important criticism of conversa-tion analytic methodology and it has stimulated considerable debate; we will consider this issue in more detail in the next chapter.

Edley and Wetherell (1997, 1999) analysed transcripts of recordings of interviews with groups of young men (17 and 18 years of age) attending the sixth form of a single-sexed independent school in the UK. Discussions were loosely structured around topics such as sexuality, images of men in popular culture, feminism and social change. Their analysis explored the following themes. In line with CA they were keen to examine the action orientation of utterances in which masculinity or male identities were invoked or oriented to. However, they argued that to understand these interactional moves, it was necessary to interpret the stances adopted by their respondents as subject positions. In this way, they were trying to forge together an appreciation of the way that particular viewpoints or positions are occasioned phenomena – that is, generated out of the contingencies of interaction – but which at the same time resonate with values and meanings from the wider discourses which constrain and shape gender relations in society.

An illustrative study in FDA: bullying

Hepburn (1997) offers an analysis of bullying from the perspective of Foucauldian discourse analysis. She analysed verbal accounts of bullying pro-duced by teachers from an English secondary school (for 11–18 year olds). This research was not designed to explore traditional or conventional expla-nations of bullying, such as those looking to account for it in terms of individual personalities or psychological traits. Rather, she was interested in the kinds of resources which informed teachers' discourse about bullying, and through which bullying as a social object and interpersonal practice were constituted and constructed.

Although Hepburn's research overlaps with some features of critical discourse analysis (1997: 29), it was predominantly informed by postmodern and post-structuralist thinking associated with the work of Foucault and Derrida. From Foucault she takes the idea that discourses shape and constitute our identities, and legitimate certain kinds of relationships between those identities, thus locking people into particular kinds of social arrangements. From Derrida, she develops the idea that common sense ways of thinking about the world inevitably rest upon and are informed by alternative or opposing ideas. This is a starkly simplistic account of Hepburn's discussion of Derrida; but as his writings are so complex, any lengthy account of them or their relevance to Hepburn's project might detract from the main thrust of her work. (Potter, 1996a, attempts to unpack some of the complexities of Derrida's writings.) All that we need to take with us for the following discussion is Hepburn's argument that Derrida's writings offer a critical perspective on the assumption that rational action stems primarily from the individual. This is central to her case for the analysis of discourses through which bullying is constituted.

She argues that teachers' interview talk about their experiences of bullying, and the problem of bullying more generally, is informed by a humanist discourse. This humanistic discourse encourages us to explain what people *do* in terms of what they *are*. Consider the following extract from Hepburn's paper.

(7.2) (From Hepburn, 1997: 35–6. 'T3' is the teacher, 'I' is the interviewer; this is a simplified version of transcript provided by Hepburn.)

```
T3:   1   … but even then you do have people, who for whatever reason know fine
      2   what's right and what's wrong, or who are people who have family and
      3   friends who care very much for them who … for one reason or another
      4   become a bully, and so there is still, again people still have to understand
      5   that they are personally responsible for their actions
I:    6   yeah, so, it's not just about knowing what's right and wrong it's about
      7   also believing that you are responsible for, er upholding these sort of-
T3:   8   -absolutely, yes, if people think, if people turn round and say 'it's not my
      9   fault because of this, this and this in my background', OK these things are
     10   factors in your background (I: mm) but at the end of the day there are
     11   other people who've had the same background …
```

There are several interesting features in this passage. As Hepburn notes, the teacher's account reproduces a discourse of personal responsibility which creates a reflective, knowing self. Thus children 'know fine what's right and what's wrong', and therefore they understand that *they* are responsible for their own actions. The teacher also addresses an explanation for bullying. It is often claimed that background is in some way causally implicated in bullying. This is reflected in the teacher's formulation of a hypothetical excuse: 'people turn round and say "it's not my fault because of this, this and this in my background"'. But this account is dismissed: 'at the end of the day there are other people who've had the same background …'. The way the teacher raises this hypothetical account and finds it wanting places responsibility for bullying solely on the individual.

Hepburn claims that

> What this talk is doing, therefore, is warranting the blaming and ultimately the punishment of individuals … we get a focus on the individual as the rational decision maker, who must turn the gaze of authority inwards, and take responsibility for her actions, see her 'self' as the source of the problem. (Hepburn, 1997: 36)

Through analysis of a series of accounts, Hepburn identifies the dimensions of the humanistic discourse through which teachers constitute bullying, its perpetrators and its victims. She argues that this humanistic discourse leads into circular reasoning. There is a tendency to identify the characteristics of bullies and their victims, and then to explain instances of bullying in terms of those characteristics: thus 'this child exhibits the characteristics of a victim; this is why she is attacked'. She argues that the humanistic discourse confuses our understanding of bullying because it simply directs us to look at the psychological make-up of bullies and their victims. And as she points out, just as this discourse is available to teachers, so it is available to pupils: their understanding of the dilemmas of childhood and adolescence, and the interpersonal tensions which accompany education – the context in which acts of aggression arise – are shaped by precisely the same kind of circular reasoning. Hepburn argues that although this is understandable, it is actually unhelpful. It is understandable because this kind of explanation reflects the position advocated within academic psychology, and which has a powerful influence over common sense thinking: that the root cause of social behaviour – and its attendant problems – is the individual and her psychological make-up. It is unhelpful, however, because such acts of aggression are invariably rooted in, and a response to, wider moral and political relations. Consequently, she argues that until bullying is interpreted in terms of how 'we construct what it is to be human, and the effects that these constructions can have on the way we relate to each other' (Hepburn, 1997: 29) the true explanations for bullying – and, more important, its remedies – will remain elusive.

How does Hepburn's analysis reflect the broader approach of Foucauldian discourse analysis? There are three points of convergence. First, the research is motivated to understand and offer a solution to a social problem in which there are dominant and disadvantaged groups: bullies and their victims. In this, the research meets Burman and Parker's (1993b) arguments that Foucauldian discourse analysis should critique contemporary social arrangements. Second, Hepburn offers an oblique challenge to the claims and power of academic psychology. A central plank of her argument is that all concerned parties – teachers, parents, pupils and education administrators – rely on a form of reasoning which identifies the individual as a rational decision maker who must take responsibility for his or her bullying (and, incidentally, for his or her status as a 'victim'). This reflects psychology's focus on the individual and relative lack of concern for wider political and social processes. Her main argument is that this interpretative framework will be ultimately unhelpful because it directs the attention of those who wish to tackle bullying away from the real problems, which are the broader ways in which we construct the boundaries of appropriate social relationships. Hepburn is thus contributing to Foucauldian discourse analysis' critique of psychology's powerful hold over common sense thinking and the actions of policy makers, and its focus on the individual as a cognising root of social behaviour. Finally, Hepburn seeks to identify the discourses which inform her interviewees' accounts, and to show how these have wider political and social ramifications. Her argument is that the teachers' talk is shaped by a humanistic discourse which emphasises self-responsibility; and that this discourse constitutes the 'problem of bullying' as a particular kind of social object requiring a particular type of response. Her analytic method thus illustrates Parker's claim that 'discourses facilitate and limit, enable and constrain what can be said (by whom, where, when)' (Parker, 1992: xiii).

FDA, discourse analysis and discursive psychology

What is the relationship between the kind of work described here as Foucauldian discourse analysis, and the analytic approach which emerged from Gilbert and Mulkay's study of scientific discourse and which was developed subsequently in social psychology by Potter and Wetherell? It is not uncommon to find the title 'discourse analysis' used to encompass both kinds of work (Coyle, 2000; Parker, 1994). There are broad similarities, such as the critical stance towards traditional psychological research methods. But the differences, though sometimes subtle, are significant (Potter *et al*, 1990; Widdicombe and Wooffitt, 1995). In this section we will consider the relationship between discourse analysis, discursive psychology and Foucauldian discourse analysis. However, to make the text less cumbersome, we shall for the purpose of this discussion treat discursive psychology as a part of discourse analysis.

Willig (2001b) summarises the difference between DA and FDA. (But note: although she is here referring to discursive psychology (DP), her points apply equally as well as to discourse analysis.)

> DP is primarily concerned with *how* people *use* discursive resources in order to achieve interpersonal objectives in social interaction. FDA focuses upon *what kind* of objects and subjects are constituted through discourse *and what kinds* of ways-of-being these objects and subjects make available to people. (Willig, 2001b: 91; original italics)

Willig argues that discourse analysis shows how participants attend to interactional tasks in their talk, and identifies the kinds of resources they use. In Foucauldian discourse analysis, the focus moves up from the fine-grained conduct of interaction to broader theoretical issues such as subjectivity, self-hood and power relations. Moreover, each approach has a different understanding of agency. In discourse analysis, speakers are active agents, because they can select from available repertoires to accomplish specific communicative tasks. In FDA, however, discourses have agency, because they constitute the objects which populate social life, and make available subject positions which constrain individual participation.

Do the terms 'interpretative repertoires' and 'discourses' refer to the same kind of thing? Potter (1996b) makes the following distinction. Repertoires are variable resources which can be used in a range of settings. In addition they can be selectively drawn upon and reworked according to the interpersonal context. Thus '[p]articipants will often draw on a number of different repertoires, flitting between them as they construct the sense of a particular phenomenon or as they perform different actions' (Potter, 1996b: 131). In this, repertoires are flexible resources managed at local, interactional levels. The concept of a discourse, by contrast, has a monolithic quality. Potter *et al* (1990) argue that in FDA discourses are viewed as great ideologically laden forces which bear down on human affairs and determine the boundaries, objects and vocabularies of social existences. The concept is deployed to illuminate the ideological supports for power relations; it leads the analyst to investigate language practices – texts – as bearers of discourses. As such, the concept does not provide the necessary methodological resources to develop an analysis of the way language is actually used as part of everyday social practices. For this reason, they argue that there is a clear distinction between discourses and repertoires.

What is apparent is that there is a distinction between top-down and bottom-up kinds of analysis (Wetherell, 1998). Foucauldian discourse analysis is an example of a top-down perspective: analysis is directed at broader historical, political and ideological issues; moreover, analysts draw on concepts such as discourses and their relations to texts to show how forms of social organisation are regulated, thereby perpetuating inequalities and injustices. By contrast, discourse analysis is a bottom-up approach. The goal of analysis is to describe the organisation of actual language practices, unencumbered in the first instance by theoretically derived characterisations of their import or nature.

Foucauldian discourse analysis and critical discourse analysis

It will be useful briefly to use Hepburn's and van Dijk's analyses as stepping stones to broader discussion of the relationship between Foucauldian and critical discourse analysis.

In many respects, Foucauldian discourse analysis is similar to critical discourse analysis. There is in both cases a clear engagement with broadly political or ideological issues. It is assumed in many studies that there is a material basis to forms of oppression, such as racism and sexism; and that ideological forces work to sustain inequalities and protect the interests of powerful groups within society. And although FDA focuses more on regulative practices rather than overt oppression, there are leading researchers in both traditions who subscribe to a classic Marxist analysis of how the capitalist mode of production determines social relations.

In both CDA and FDA there is an assumption that analysts *should* be motivated in their work to make political interventions, or to expose the ideological effects of language use. Indeed, some researchers in this tradition argue that there is no point trying to do analysis without this overtly political goal (Burman and Parker, 1993b). It is clear that both Hepburn and van Dijk explicitly 'take sides' on their respective issues. Hepburn seeks to advance our understanding of bullying so that, eventually, more effective preventive measures can be developed. In this, her research begins with the assumption that bullying is a serious social problem, and not, for example, merely a routine part of the trials and tribulations of growing up which all children go through, and which can, ultimately, be 'character building'. Similarly, van Dijk takes it that Fox's speech, although ostensibly in support of a laudable principle, freedom of speech, did in fact work to perpetuate racism and the dominance of a powerful, white middle-class elite. There is no consideration of, for example, the possibility that the teacher's writings were a reasoned response to actual problems of multi-cultural education based on professional experience, and that the Asian parents' misgivings were unwarranted or exaggerated. Finally, in both FDA and CDA, empirical work focuses on texts: objects, events or processes which are imbued with meaning and interpretation. Van Dijk's data come from a written document: an official record of verbal interaction in the House of Commons. However, this is examined to reveal the ways in which anti-racist arguments are discredited. Hepburn's data are interviews she conducted with teachers. In this sense they are not texts in the everyday use of the word. But once transcribed and committed to paper or to computer, these interactional moments are transformed into texts. In Foucauldian discourse analysis texts are examined to expose the discourse(s) which inhabit them, and to reveal their ideological and regulative orientation (Parker, 1994). Hepburn examines her texts in precisely this way: she identifies the humanistic discourse which informs her texts, and shows its wider social and political impact by revealing how it informs teachers' and pupils' understanding of bullying.

But in other respects, there are clear differences. The main difference is in the focus of analysis. Hepurn seeks to identify discourses and their agency in perpetuating a social problem. These are treated as relatively autonomous and independent entities. For example, there is no attempt to tie their content or agency to particular social structures, nor is the account of their importance linked to the specific context in which they are used, an interview between teachers and a social psychologist. Van Dijk's analysis, on the other hand, develops more fine-grained examination of the linguistic features of his data, and offers an interpretation of these in terms of a sharply delineated social and political context. Thus the setting in which the speech was made – a debate in the House of Commons, with all the signals of authority and prestige that bestows – frames and shapes his analysis of linguistic features such as lexical choice, syntax, coherence and so on.

There are important differences in the way that scholars from each tradition conceptualise the nature and importance of ideology. Fairclough (1992) locates the study of ideology as a central concern for critical discourse analysis. In recent years, however, the concept of ideology has become contested. For example, Foucauldian scholars are suspicious of the kind of ideological studies found in traditional Marxist writings because they presuppose that there is one position that is not ideological: the author's. So, instead of trying to say what happened to whom and why (as Marxist theorists have done), and instead of trying to propose another version of the history of events (but this time the 'correct' one), Foucault shifts the focus of attention to the study of the kinds of vantage points which people have adopted in their studies. He argues that it is more important to see how it is that the what, whom and why have been constituted in discourse (Wetherell and Potter, 1992). Thus a concern with ideology is replaced by attempts to show how power is exercised in technologies (discourses, social practices, institutions, and so on) which structure social relations. In this view, the exercise of power is not linked to particular social classes, but is a ubiquitous property of social arrangements. Fairclough is suspicious of such moves to revise the concept of ideology. He argues that if it is to be used to explore domination and power, it is necessary to show how ideology works to support class-based interests through its links to the material infrastructure of society. He therefore seeks to preserve a more traditional conception of ideology and its role in shaping social life.

Another tension between these two approaches concerns the issue of cognition. One characteristic of Foucauldian discourse analysis is a critique of the traditional view of cognition and its determinate role in social behaviour. As in research in discursive psychology and rhetorical psychology, Foucauldian discourse analysts do not treat discourse as a simple representation of determinate cognitive processes. This marks a clear departure from the position in critical discourse analysis, where a more traditional view of cognition and its importance in understanding discourse processes is adopted.

Summary

- Foucauldian discourse analysis tries to understand how language perpetuates social inequalities.
- It primarily studies the ways in which discourses inform and shape our understanding of the world and social and political relationships.

- It examines texts and the discourses which are said to inhabit them.
- Foucauldian discourse analysts are critical of the cognitivist orientations and experimental methods of contemporary academic psychology. They are also critical of conversation analysis and discourse analysis.

Although there are some important differences, critical and Foucauldian discourse analysis share many theoretical and methodological assumptions. They are both concerned to explore how language/discourse works to produce wider social inequalities and sustain the power and influence of dominant groups. It is argued that it is necessary to look at the relationship between language use and its broader structural, political and institutional contexts. In this sense, the empirical analyses of both CDA and FDA are theoretically driven: what is studied, and how it is studied, are shaped by a political and emancipatory agenda. These theoretical and empirical assumptions call into question some of the substantive focus and methodological practices which inform conversation analytic work (and some forms of discourse analysis, such as discursive psychology). For example, analysts working in these traditions have argued that CA's strict focus on the management of fine-grained interactional practices has meant that it has not addressed those topics which should be of central concern to social scientific accounts of interaction and discourse, such as the effect on interaction of asymmetries in the relative power or status of the participants; or the role of gender in shaping the form and content of male–female communication, and so on. Moreover, there have been criticisms of CA's methodology. CA attempts to build analytic claims which are grounded in the observable activities of the participants themselves. Both critical and Foucauldian discourse analysts would argue that to develop a full account of the use of language it is necessary to include in the analysis those extra-linguistic, contextual factors which may inform the participants' conduct, such as culture, context, personality, and shared histories, even if their relevance cannot be demonstrated by reference to participants' actual conduct.

The last two chapters will deal specifically with some of these methodological and substantive issues.

8
Methodological Disputes: How Should We Analyse Talk?

There have been many criticisms of conversation analysis. These tend to cluster into two broad types. The first set of critical objections revolves around the argument that CA either does not, or cannot, address the kinds of topics which are central to traditional sociological inquiry: for example, the analysis of conflict, the manifestation of power and inequality in social relationship and mobilisation of disadvantage based on gender, ethnicity or class. The second broad argument is that the methodological procedures of conversation analysis are in some key respects deficient: that it fails to take account of the essentially argumentative nature of everyday discourse, focusing instead on the management of interpersonal harmony and accord; or that its focus on the 'technical' aspects of the sequential organisation of turn-taking means that it cannot address the wider historical, cultural and political contexts and meanings which are invoked by and reflected in the kinds of words and phrases we use in everyday communication.

Some of these methodological disagreements came into sharp focus in a series of published debates between Emanuel Schegloff, Margaret Wetherell and Michael Billig in the late 1990s. These exchanges were prompted by an article by Schegloff (1997), in which he discusses some points of divergence between the focus of conversation analysis and research in critical discourse analysis. He begins by noting that any spate of talk-in-interaction will have a sense for its participants; and that this sense – their understanding of what-is-going-on-right-here-right-now – is, at least to some degree, displayed in the design of successive contributions to that interaction. CA seeks to describe the social organisation of these endogenous interpretative processes. Consequently, conversation analytic accounts of social action are grounded in close description of participants' activities, and which are demonstrably relevant to the participants themselves as they conduct those activities. Schegloff argued that theoretically oriented approaches, such as critical discourse analysis, are in danger of imposing an interpretation of interaction which reflects the analysts' theoretical or political orientations, and which in turn systematically obscures analysis of what is actually relevant to the participants themselves. To illustrate, he examines a fragment of data from a telephone conversation between a man and a woman, in which there are occasions when the man begins to speak while the women is currently speaking. While it would be a simple matter to interpret these occasions as interruptions which reflect wider asymmetries of power and status between men and women, Schegloff urges caution. He goes on to show that the moments of overlapping speech are not interruptive, but flow from the sequential implications of a particular type of socially organised activity: offering and responding to assessments. It is this matter – the production of successive assessments – to which the participants' conduct is oriented, not their gender identities. Schegloff states 'an account that would treat this brief exchange as but another exemplar of gendered discourse ... would have missed what it was demonstrably about *in the first instance – for the parties*' (Schegloff, 1997: 178; original italics). And he asks: 'Can compelling critical discourse analysis sacrifice that?' (ibid).

Schegloff's paper stimulated two very different kinds of responses. Billig (1999a, 1999b) offered a critique of CA which reflected his interest in the power of rhetoric and the argumentative nature of everyday discourse. He argued that CA's terminology and account of its practices actually obscure the conflictual and argumentative character of talk through which power and ideologies are mobilised and influence our lives. Wetherell (1998) offered an alternative kind of critique. She acknowledges that theoretically motivated analyses of discourse often result in loose and ungrounded analytic claims, and she welcomes the rigorous description of the coordination of interactional activities offered by conversation analysis. Nonetheless, she argues that the exclusive focus on the details of interaction fails to provide a full and complete appreciation of the organisation of talk. Wetherell argues that to provide a rounded account it is necessary to draw from post-structuralist approaches and explore the role of the broader discourses which inhabit talk, and to examine how participants orient to and negotiate the relevance of various subject positions made available by those discourses in the routine turn-by-turn unfolding of interaction.

In this and the next chapter we will be examining these methodological and substantive criticisms. In Chapter 9 we will be assessing the argument that CA offers no analysis of how talk reflects or instantiates wider relations of dominance between groups in society, and is therefore incapable of making a contribution to the study of the differential exercise of power. But in this chapter we examine the criticisms that CA's distinctive methodology needs to be supplemented by a deeper appreciation of the argumentative or ideologically charged context in which talk occurs. In each section we will use the arguments by Billig and Wetherell in their debate with Schegloff as a way of introducing broader critical objections to CA.

The rhetoric of conversation analysis and the argumentative nature of everyday communication

Billig (1999a, 1999b) examines CA's 'rhetoric': its account of its own practices which is taken for granted by its practitioners. Specifically, he notes that in CA research there is an attempt to avoid interpreting talk-in-interaction in terms of established social scientific theories; instead, according to Billig's reading, the goal of analysis is to examine the participants' verbal conduct in their own terms. This reflects the fundamental position in CA that analysis should begin without any a priori assumptions about the data at hand, but should seek to discover the order that is realised through participants' communicative competencies, and which in turn should be demonstrably relevant to the participants. However, Billig argues that this account is misleading, as it does not accurately depict the way CA researchers conduct their analyses. For example, Billig juxtaposes CA's recommendation to examine talk-in-interaction in the participants' own terms, with its actual practice of offering technical accounts of verbal activities – in terms of 'paired action sequences', 'repair', 'preference', and so on – which certainly do not reflect the participants' 'own terms'.

Billig also objects to the way that, in the conversation analytic literature, terms like 'participants' or 'members' are used to refer to the people whose talk constitutes the data for research. He argues that through the use of this terminology CA unquestioningly assumes a particular kind of social order: one in which all people have equal status in the interactions which are being analysed. This means that CA is not atheoretical, as it claims, but actually embodies a distinctive ideological view of social order. Moreover, the assumption of an equal participatory status which is conveyed in the conversation analytic literature is controversial, in that it masks wider social injustices, such as inequalities, oppression and asymmetries in power and advantage. The rhetorical constitution of CA as a form of academic research reinforces and reproduces this assumption of equal participatory status and equality, in that it emphasises the orderly organisation of social activities and the preference for maintaining interpersonal harmony. Thus the rhetoric of conversation analysis – how it constitutes itself as an academic discipline in textbooks and research papers – promotes an overly optimistic view of social life. In this sense, Billig argues, it is politically naive.

In his (1999a) paper, Billig offers a disturbing example of the ultimate consequence of what he considers to be CA's political naivety. Having criticised the way that CA primarily focuses on the technical organisation of talk as the product of 'participants' with equal participatory status, he suggests

> It raises the possibility that ... CA might be problematic if straightforwardly applied to episodes in which power is directly, overtly and even brutally exercised. One might consider how analysts could describe speakers in situations of rape, bullying or racist abuse. One might imagine that the talk, in the course of a rape ... had been recorded and transcribed. One can imagine the rapist threatening and verbally abusing the victim, who in turn pleads ... how should their talk be analysed?
>
> No doubt the typical organizational properties could be investigated. One might presume that, as the rapist threatens and the victim pleads, they would share the same organization system for alternating their turns. Perhaps, they might even show other features, such as 'repairs', 'second assessments', 'WH

questions', and so. [sic] The analyst could show how the two speakers orientate to each other. The analyst might describe them as 'co-participants' in the conversation, or even as 'members' sharing the same practices.

All of this would indicate something had gone seriously awry. The conventional terminology of the 'participatory rhetoric' would assume that victims participate in their suffering. In what sense are victims 'co-participants' in talk which abuses them? Attention to what abuser and victim share in common, in terms of the organization of talk, would seem to miss the point. The analyst would be 'disattending' to the very matters which upset the assumption of an ordered participatory world. To imply that CA *must* disattend to such a matter … is to say something about the limitations of an orthodox CA and its implicitly uncritical theory of the social world. (Billig, 1999a: 554–5; original italics)

For Billig, this exposes CA's fundamental analytic impotence when confronted with incompatibility with inequalities and sometimes brutal acts of oppression. But is this a fair criticism? Is it based on an accurate understanding of conversation analysis?

Schegloff's response begins by making an important point: that Billig's criticisms seem to be directed at a version of conversation analysis which does not chime with his (Schegloff's) experience of the work. As he states, 'I could probably find things to take issue with in 75 per cent of Billig's sentences' (Schegloff, 1999a: 559). This would suggest that Billig's interpretation of CA is – at least – idiosyncratic. And in support of Schegloff's observations, I think it is uncontroversial to suggest that the *vast majority* of scholars who use conversation analytic techniques would find that Billig's characterisation of its approach and assumptions does not capture their practical experiences.

Schegloff addresses specific points raised in Billig's critique, such as Billig's claim the CA is disingenuous when it claims to study participants' verbal activities in their own terms, but then actually offers descriptions of those activities in formal, technical terms. Schegloff points out, though, that CA does not analyse interaction in the participant's own *terms*; but it does seek to offer accounts of action which are warranted by reference to the ways in which participants display what *they* take to be relevant to their on-going interaction. In his interruption/assessment example, discussed earlier, Schegloff's argument that the participants' overlapping contributions are a product of the wider social organisation of successive assessments does not require either party to state explicitly 'I am now doing an assessment'; it is enough to show that in *their conduct* – in the way that their turns are designed – they display that the requirement of providing successive assessments is what is relevant to their contributions (Schegloff, 1999a: 570, fn 8).

And what of Billig's hypothetical conversation analysis of the turn-taking during a rape? Schegloff makes several points, and we can only summarise some of them here. First, he disputes Billig's interpretation of CA's stance towards the participatory status of the interactants. Schegloff observes that the 'rosey-eyed equalitarian optimism' (1999a: 563) Billig attributes to CA does not accord with accounts of CA in key sources in the literature. He cites the seminal Sacks *et al* (1974) analysis of the organisation of turn-taking, which is the infrastructure of interpersonal action. This is one of *the* papers in conversation analysis. Schegloff observes that in this paper he and his colleagues explicitly acknowledge and explore the way that the turn-taking system permits of biases in the way rights, obligations and opportunities to talk are differentially allocated amongst participants. Second, he argues that the account of interaction offered by Sacks *et al* (1974) is one 'that does not *presume* an equalitarian society, [but] it *allows* for one' (Schegloff, 1999a: 564). Thus when Billig objects to CA's analysis of the orderly production of interaction and the orientation to the production of interpersonal harmony, he seems to be misconstruing a series of empirical findings about the properties of talk with some form of theoretical directive or licence to investigate *only* those communicative competencies through which order and intelligibility are produced.

Finally, Schegloff elegantly outlines what CA might actually be able to contribute to an understanding of physical brutality in gender relations.

> Rape, abuse, battering, etc., do not exist in some other world, or in some special sector of this world. They are intricated into the texture of everyday life for those who live with them. How else are we to understand their explosive emergence where they happen if not by examining ordinary interaction with tools appropriate to it, and seeing how they can lead to such outcomes ... If interaction is produced within a matrix of turns organized into sequences, etc., and if it is from those that motives and intensions are inferred, identities made relevant, stances embodied and interpreted, etc, how else – when confronted by the record of singular episodes – are we to understand their genesis and course, how else try to understand what an unwilling participant can do to manage that course to safer outcomes, how else try to understand how others might intervene to detoxify those settings? (Schegloff, 1999a: 561–2)

The point is this: in a world in which violent acts are perpetrated, and categories of individuals are systematically oppressed and hurt, it is necessary to use whatever tools are at our disposal to offer an account of those acts, so better to understand their emergence and shape, and on the basis of which to seek more effective remedial interventions. Conversation analysis can offer an account of the interactional contours out of which particular violent episodes arise. It is difficult to understand how this is *not* useful, or *not* important, as a contribution to a sophisticated and rounded understanding of the lived experience of physical or verbal abuse and oppression.

Rhetorical psychology and conversation analytic methodology

Billig is not entirely unsympathetic to conversation analysis; indeed, he claims that he used CA to study interview data in which members of the public talk about the Royal Family (Billig, 1992); he acknowledges its value in revealing the complexity of social interaction (1991: 15; 1997: 41; 1999a: 544); and he draws from CA in his study of the concept of repression in Freudian psychoanalysis (Billig, 1999c). Moreover, a cursory examination of introductory accounts of rhetorical psychology might suggest that there is some degree of overlap between its methodological stances and those associated with conversation analysis. Indeed, Billig seems to offer support for conversation analysis, in that he recommends that procedures associated with CA research be adopted in rhetorical psychology. For example, in his (1997) account, Billig argues that to understand the significance of a turn in interaction it is helpful to see how its recipient responds to it (1997: 41). This clearly mirrors the focus in conversation analysis on people's own interpretation of on-going interaction as revealed in turn-by-turn unfolding of conversation.

Billig also stresses the importance of transcription, and this is another feature on which rhetorical psychology seems to be in agreement with conversation analysis. In his introduction to rhetorical psychology he states,

> ... the transcripts should contain as much accurate information as possible about the talk. Care should also be taken over the transcripts, because, for most practical purposes, the transcripts provide the material for the analysis. (Billig, 1997: 46–7)

Detailed transcription *per se* is not exclusively associated with CA: technical and painstaking transcription is common in more linguistic studies of language and communication. But in the social sciences, talk tends to be reproduced orthographically; thus Billig's plea for careful transcription is, therefore, surely informed by CA's distinctive attempt to capture the detail of verbal interaction. Moreover, Billig adopts the increasingly common convention in discourse analysis and recommends the transcription system used in conversation analysis. He even cites the appendix in Potter and Wetherell (1987) in which they list the symbols they have used in their text; this, in turn, is a version of the Jefferson system outlined in some detail in Atkinson and Heritage's collection of CA studies (Atkinson and Heritage, 1984: ix–xvi).

However, a closer examination of some of these methodological alignments reveals that they mask some sharp disagreements. For example, take Billig's claim that to understand the significance of a turn in interaction it is helpful to see how its recipient responds to it. He offers this argument in his discussion of artificial data, which is a clear departure from CA's rigorous insistence of naturally occurring interaction. More important, he argues that next turn analysis is useful because it exposes 'the layers of meaning' of an utterance (Billig, 1997: 41). But in CA research this procedure is routinely used to ground claims about how a next speaker interpreted the *action* accomplished by a prior turn. In this sense, a methodological procedure associated with conversation analysis has been recruited to the service of rhetorical psychology in such a way that its conventional purpose and import has been significantly changed.

Further departures from CA methodology become apparent when we consider Billlig's (1997) call for careful transcription, and his recommendation of the symbols conventionally employed in conversation analysis. When Billig actually describes the symbols he is using in his illustrative examples, it is apparent that his transcription practices depart radically from those found in the CA literature. For example, he says that he uses three dots ' ... ' to indicate interruption (Billig, 1997: 46). The implication is, then, that this is the meaning of the use of dots as outlined in the Jefferson system. But it is not: in CA transcriptions, the use of dots does not mean 'interruption', but has a much more technical and specialised function. In the transcription of video data (a truly daunting task), a row of dots is used in conjunction with other symbols to indicate the transitional moment when a person orients their gaze to another participant (Atkinson and Heritage, 1984: xiv). Thus Billig argues for the use of CA transcription techniques which are becoming standard in discourse analysis, while at the same time offering without comment a new definition of one of those symbols. This is, at least, confusing.

But more important, his claim that three dots – or indeed any symbol – can indicate 'interruption' is problematic. CA tries to avoid characterising interactional events with 'common sense' or 'vernacular' terms which impute motive, intent or significance to the participants. This is because, broadly, CA embodies the ethnomethodological claim that it is the participants' understanding of what is happening that is important, not what the analysts think is happening. Consequently, value-laden terms like 'interruption' are avoided. Moreover, as Jefferson (1983, 1986) has shown, on close inspection, much overlapping talk which appears interruptive is in fact closely coordinated with the occurrence of transition relevance places. It is an orderly phenomenon entirely misidentified by the term 'interruption'.

Finally, if we actually consider the example Billig uses to illustrate the use of the three dots, and, by implication, to indicate some form of interactional event vernacularly described as interruption, we find there is little evidence for anything which could possibly be called interruptive, even if we wanted to. His data come from a recording of a family discussion about the Royal Family. At this stage in the discussion the family members are engaged in a fairly lighthearted dispute about the name of a female singer who sang at a Royal wedding.

(8.1)   (From Billig, 1997: 51)

Mother:	I didn't say Kiki Dee
Daughter:	You did ...
Mother:	I didn't Kiki la er er ever such a foreign name
Daughter:	Elaine Paige sang in the Church
Mother:	She didn't (laughs)

Unless Billig has failed to transcribe the daughter's utterance beyond 'you did' (which would render his plea for the importance of careful transcription a little hollow), then we must assume that, at the end of 'did', she had arrived at the completion of the first turn construction unit in that utterance. And, as we saw in the discussion of turn-taking in Chapter 2, this is precisely the point at which turn-transfer is routinely initiated. Mother's subsequent rejection that she had said 'Kiki Dee' is launched right at the place where we would expect to see turn-transition attempted. It is not interruptive; it is not even in overlap. It is an instance of the kind of precision-timed turn-transition which is *routine* in mundane interaction. A cursory inspection of Billig's own data, then, suggests he has mistaken a mundane feature of the turn exchange system for something more interactionally problematic for the participants. This claim is not supported by the data.

These are not trivial matters. If we are to take seriously the study of discourse we need to be careful to attend to the detail of our data. Talk-in-interaction is complex. That complexity is not random or irrelevant. It is an integral dimension of the way humans engage in a primordial activity: interaction with other humans. This is true of spontaneous conversation between friends, work-related talk in an office, or a family discussion initiated for the purposes of a social science research project.

Because CA explores verbal interaction at a level of detail rarely found in the social sciences, it is often misinterpreted as just another form of micro-sociology; one focused exclusively on, for example, the significance of minor gaps in talk, or the inferential or interactional consequences of words cut off in mid-production. Indeed, Billig provides an example of this misinterpretation. Of the relationship between discourse analysis and CA, Billig writes 'discourse analysts have adapted some of the techniques of "conversational [sic] analysis", which micro-sociologists have developed for examining the intricacy of daily interactions' (Billig, 1997: 41). But this is not accurate. As is clear from Sacks' published lectures, or any of the serious introductions to CA, Sacks' overall concern was to develop a new form of naturalistic observational sociology that could handle in formal ways the details of actual conduct (see, for example, Heritage, 1984a; Hutchby and Wooffitt, 1998; Sacks, 1992; Schegloff, 1992a; ten Have, 1999). In this, his work had a broad compass: the nature of sociology as a discipline, and the development of an empirical method of analysis that laid bare the interpretative foundations of order and intelligibility. Tape-recorded conversational materials (and other interactional data) were selected for analysis because they offered a number of analytically convenient properties. As Sacks said in one of his lectures:

> It was not from any large interest or from some theoretical formulation of what should be studied that I started with tape recorded conversation, but simply because I could get my hands on it and I could study it again and again, and also, consequentially, because others could look at what I had studied and make of it what they could, if, for example, they wanted to be able to disagree with me. (Sacks, 1984a: 26)

Moreover, the findings from conversation analysis, while indeed generated from detailed analysis of the intricacies of interaction, reveal consistent and highly patterned interactional phenomena. As Heritage and Atkinson point out, these are *structures* of social actions (Heritage and Atkinson, 1984). The goal of analysis is not solely the explication of micro-interactional practices (although, of course, that is accomplished at a hitherto unimagined level of sophistication and detail), but the discovery of the broader structures of sense-making that constitute 'the procedural infrastructure of interaction' (Schegloff, 1992b: 1338). To identify CA as a tool for the analysis of micro-interactions obscures its primary focus on generic properties of intelligibility, structure and order, and constitutes a serious misunderstanding of its objectives.

Rhetorical psychology and argumentation

From the perspective of rhetorical psychology, discourse is primarily argumentative, consisting of a variety of oppositional and ideological positions which inform everyday reasoning about the world. This is important because it marks a distinction between conversation analysis and those forms of discourse analysis which are focused on ideological or rhetorical struggles.

> Unlike conversation analysis, discourse analysis regards social life as being characterised by conflicts of various kinds. As such, much discourse is involved in establishing one version of the world in the face of competing versions. (Gill, 1996: 143)

This position also has implications for CA studies of talk-in-interaction, in that it proposes that interaction is, at a fundamental level, informed by the argumentative character of everyday discourse. On the basis of this, rhetorical psychologists are critical of CA's focus on the structure of interaction, rather than the content of talk, as this means that, inevitably, it is incapable of attending to the significant social issues – class, power, gender, and so on – which are the focus of people's argumentative discourse (Billig, 1991: 16–18).

It is useful to consider these criticisms, because it allows us to anticipate many of the arguments which will be rehearsed more fully in the next chapter. Let us consider the claim that CA's focus on the 'technical' aspects of interaction means that it cannot handle conflict or competition in talk.

There are, however, numerous conversation analytic studies of the technical or sequential basis of 'contested' or argumentative communication. For example, CA studies of the televised interview in 1988 between then Vice-President George Bush and the CBS news presenter Dan Rather exposed the sequentially ordered basis for the breakdown in normal interviewing conventions, and the subsequent fractious tone of the interview (Schegloff, 1988/9). Similarly, Whalen *et al* (1988) analysed the breakdown in communication in a 911 call for emergency medical assistance and they focused on the sequential basis of the participants' increasing frustration and anger. In an analysis of a call to a talk radio programme,

Schegloff (1984) was able to show how an ambiguity which led to some antagonistic exchanges between host and caller was rooted in routine sequential organisations. And more recently Dersley and Wootton have examined interaction in arguments, focusing on the sequential organisation of complaints (2000), and the sequential characteristics which precede one party unilaterally walking out of an argument (2001). Finally, Pomerantz's (1986) analysis of extreme case formulations focuses explicitly on resources by which accounts and reports can be assembled so that they anticipate and address the potential alternative versions of sceptical responses. What these and many other studies show is that our understanding of the emergence and shape of contested and argumentative interaction is clearly *enriched* by attention to the 'technical' or sequential organisation of interaction.

Moreover, rhetorical psychology's overriding emphasis on the argumentative basis of talk has two unhelpful consequences. First, it predisposes the analyst to seek an argumentative basis for the way people talk, when a more economical account may emerge when we consider the kind of subtle interactional tasks which can be addressed through alternative formulations (Wooffitt, 1992: 17–18). Second, merely stating that discourse may be directed to alternative formulations does not in itself provide access to the detailed practices involved in the construction of descriptions or reports.

Research on everyday conversational interaction, and studies of the organisation of factual discourse, have begun to reveal some of the ways in which speakers are able to design their utterances to counter potential or actual alternative versions of events. This constructive work can occur in the fine detail of the design of descriptions. However, this level of complexity becomes harder to study if analysis begins with a gross characterisation of talk as broadly argumentative. This is because it establishes from the start what it is that might be analytically interesting, inviting the analyst only to observe what is 'already known' about discourse, and obscuring the detailed rhetorical or argumentative resources people actually use, and to which rhetorical psychologists seek to draw attention.

Summary

- The rhetorical psychological critique of CA focuses on its claimed inability to address brutality and acts of oppression, and its (implicit) naive and overly optimistic social theory.
- However, this critique is based on a misreading of CA's methodological practices and empirical orientations.
- The claim that discourse is essentially argumentative imposes an unnecessarily restricting focus for research, thus leading analytic attention away from more mundane interactional practices in everyday communication, and, paradoxically, away from the subtle argumentative and persuasive resources which are used in building controversial or contested accounts.

Discourses and subject positions

Wetherell's (1998) critique of conversation analysis is an important contribution to methodological debates about how to analyse talk because she is genuinely sympathetic to many features of CA's methodology, and appreciates that it has made an important contribution to the study of language use. With Jonathan Potter, for example, she was responsible for the development of discourse analysis in social psychology (Potter and Wetherell, 1987), and their critiques of the experimentalist and cognitivist orientations in social psychological research drew from conversation analytic findings and its focus on the action orientation of language use. Her critiques are therefore borne out of a serious engagement with CA and what she takes to be its strengths and limitations.

During the 1990s Wetherell and her colleague Nigel Edley were engaged in a study of the construction of masculine identities. Part of this research entailed interviews with young men in the sixth form (16–18 years old) of a single-sex school in the UK. These interviews (conducted by Edley) covered topics such as the young men's daily lives, their expectations about their future lives and careers, and their relationships with young women.

Wetherell's argument begins by noting that at the time of writing, discourse analytic research in social psychology was polarised. There were top-down approaches, which were informed by post-structuralist or Foucauldian writings. These tended to analyse data to explore the manifestation of power and inequalities through the influence of discourses, and the subject positions they made available. By contrast, bottom-up approaches drew more from ethnomethodology and, in particular, conversation analysis. Researchers in this tradition studied social psychological phenomena, such as social identity, through the analysis of talk-in-interaction. However, Wetherell was dissatisfied with this polarisation as she argued that each approach offered an incomplete account of the construction of identity, and, therefore, the most fruitful way forward was via some integration of the two perspectives. To this end she suggested that post-structuralist approaches could benefit from CA's strict attention to the detail of talk-in-interaction (see also Edley and Wetherell, 1999). Echoing Schegloff's (1997) critique of critical discourse analysis, she argued that theoretically informed scholars tended to offer cursory analyses of their data, on the basis of which they were advancing claims about the operation of discourse and subject positions. Consequently, it was hard to develop a sophisticated and detailed account of the way discourses impacted on everyday conduct.

However, the main critical thrust of her paper – and explicitly in response to Schegloff's (1997) argument – was that CA studies of talk-in-interaction need to be complemented and informed by the notion of agency and discourse found in post-structuralist writings such as those of Laclau and Mouffe (1987). In particular, she says that the 'technical' (Wetherell, 1998: 394) analysis of interaction offered by CA is incomplete as it fails to take account of 'the social agent as constituted by an ensemble of "subject positions" ... constructed by a diversity of discourses' (Mouffe, 1992: 372; cited in Wetherell, 1998: 393). Moreover,

> The 'identity' of such a multiple and contradictory subject is therefore always contingent and precarious, temporarily fixed at the intersection of those subject positions and dependent on specific forms of identification. ... We have to approach [the social agent] as a plurality, dependent on the various subject positions through which it is constituted within various discursive formations. (Mouffe, 1992: 372; cited in Wetherell, 1998: 393–4)

For Wetherell then, analysis of the young men's identities could not be divorced from consideration of the discourses which provided the subject positions through which those identities are produced. Moreover, she argues that it is necessary to explore the ideological orientations of those discourses to understand fully the way in which they, and the subject positions they make available, resonate with and reproduce group interests and wider relations of dominance and power. As these are unlikely to be displayed in participants' conduct, CA's argument that analytic claims must be warranted by reference to participants' conduct is unhelpful. CA's technical analysis must therefore be supplemented by consideration of the cultural and political implications of the discourses invoked and subject positions thereby established.

To illustrate Wetherell's analysis we will look at her observations on a section of the data from her paper. This comes from an interview conducted by Nigel Edley (identified in the transcript as 'N') and three young men, anonymised here as Phil ('PH'), Paul ('PA') and Aaron ('A'). The topic of discussion is the morality of Aaron's conduct during a weekend in which he had sexual encounters with four young women. Prior to this extract, Phil and Aaron have collaboratively constructed the 'story' of Aaron's weekend. The extract starts at the point at which the interviewer asks the other interviewee, Paul, for his opinion of Aaron's activities.

(8.2)   (From Wetherell, 1998: 408)

```
116   N:    Right: (.) okay (0.2) what do you think Paul?
117         (0.3)
118   PA:   Did you =
119   PH:   = Are you ap┌palled?                                       ┐
120   PA:              └When you ┘·hh no (.) s┌when you went out      │
121   N:                                      └Not appalled?          ┘
122   PA:   I jus I'll tell you in a minute when you went out
123   N:    hh  ┌hhh  ┐
124   ?        └hhhh ┘
125   PA:   When you went out on that Friday (.) evening you were
126         out on the pull yeah?=
127   A:    =No
128   PA:   This (.) you were not?=
```

```
129   A:    =Just out┌as a group┐
130   PH:            └Just out  ┘as a group of friends
131   PA:   On the Saturday you were out on the pull?
132   PH:   No
```

Wetherell is interested in Paul's description of Aaron's activities as 'out on the pull'. She notes that this seems to work as an accusation that Aaron was callously promiscuous. Aaron deals with this by adopting a variety of subject positions: he was not intending to have a series of sexual encounters; he was just 'lucky'; he was drunk; his encounters with the young women were entirely consensual, and so on. Wetherell notes that in this extract, and indeed throughout the interview, Aaron's subject positions – his identities – become topicalised, ascribed, resisted, negotiated and so on. Moreover, she argues that CA's focus on the detailed, technical organisation of these exchanges exposes the interactional basis for the appearance and contestation of these subject positions. But knowledge of the interactional organisation through which these identities become salient is insufficient to provide a complete account of their relevance and import. For this it is necessary to identify the wider discourses and repertoires from which they are drawn. In these exchanges Wetherell argues that the participants are drawing on the repertoire of male sexual performance as achievement, a repertoire around the disinhibiting effects of alcohol, and a repertoire concerning the ethics of sexual conduct characterised by notions of reciprocity and commitment. These repertoires 'are the common sense which organizes accountability and serve as a back-cloth for the realization of locally managed positions in social interaction … and from which … accusations and justifications can be launched' (Wetherell, 1998: 400–1).

To summarise, then, what are Wetherell's criticisms of CA's methodology? There are a number of interrelated arguments. It is claimed that CA's focus on the turn-by-turn unfolding of interaction is too narrow, and unnecessarily inhibits the analyst from taking account of the broader political and social context in which talk occurs. And many other discourse researchers have objected to CA's argument that it is necessary to ground analytic claims by reference to close description of the participants' conduct. It is suggested that there are influences on social interaction – class, gender, ethnicity – which have important consequences for the relationships manifest in and accomplished through talk, but which resist the kind of empirical demonstration required by CA (Fairclough, 1992, 1995; van Dijk, 1993). Furthermore, it is argued that language is not a neutral representation of reality but a value-laden way of making sense of the world. When we use language we are inevitably trading in the kinds of sentiments and social relationships which are reflected by, and embedded in, the history of the linguistic forms we adopt. Our words thus resonate with a set of meanings and relevances which are not limited to the immediate interactional context. For these reasons, some Foucauldian discourse analysts prefer to view even interactional data as a form of text, as this characterisation foregrounds the larger historical, cultural and political threads that weave through and give meaning and shape to our conduct (Coyle, 2000;

Parker, 1988). Finally, Wetherell argues that it is necessary to analyse the discourses, repertoires and ideologies which inform our talk. This is because discourses (and repertoires and ideologies) are constitutive. They construct objects: entities or processes which acquire an objective status through the use of particular vocabularies (Edley, 2001; Edley and Wetherell, 1999). Moreover, discourses provide subject positions which circumscribe the range of identities and relationships available to individuals. On the basis of this view of communication, it is argued that CA's attempt to ground analytic claims solely by reference to what can be demonstrated empirically leads to an impoverished and politically etiolated view of social life (Wetherell, 1998).

So how powerful are these arguments? Do conversation analytic studies need to be supplemented by a consideration of discourses and the subject positions they make available? Do these broadly post-structuralist positions provide greater insight into the ways in which talk-in-interaction is organised than that offered by CA? One way to address these questions is to examine the methodological value of the alternatives on offer. So: does the analysis of discourses offer a coherent analytic framework for the analysis of verbal communication? Does this analytic framework advance our understanding of talk-in-interaction? Does it offer more accurate or more revealing accounts of social interaction than those currently offered in conversation analysis?

In the following sections, I will outline a number of what seem to me to be serious problems with the analytic style of Foucauldian and critical discourse analysis, and the use of concept of 'discourses' (and repertoires) in empirical analysis. In this discussion I will be drawing from Schegloff's methodologically oriented papers on critical discourse analysis and his debates with his critics. But I will also be rehearsing some issues raised earlier in methodological discussions of these and related issues (Potter *et al*, 1990; Widdicombe, 1995; Widdicombe and Wooffitt, 1995). In what follows I focus my arguments on the claims made for the analysis of discourses; but many of these remarks are relevant also to the analysis of repertoires and ideologies, terms which are often used by scholars broadly sympathetic to forms of analysis influenced by post-structuralist writings (for example, see Edley, 2001).

The interactional vacuum in the analysis of discourses and their subject positions

Although critical and Foucauldian discourse analysts study 'texts', in many cases these texts turn out to be interview data: accounts, stories, narratives and anecdotes produced during informal interviews. For example, many of the contributors to collections edited by Burman *et al* (1996), Burman and Parker (1993a) and Wilkinson and Kitzinger (1995) analyse some form of interview data; and Edley and Wetherell's study of young men's identities also uses interview data (1999; Edley, 2001). However, it is common to find that analysts pay little attention to the fact that the research interview is a period of *social interaction*, conducted primarily through language (Wetherell's 1998 paper being a notable exception). Nor is there any consideration of the ways in which the outcomes of an interview – the data recorded on tape – may have been influenced by the interactional practices of the interviewer and respondent. Admittedly, interview interaction is more formal and constrained than everyday conversation. There may be a restricted range of activities undertaken by participants, and in many kinds of interview one participant sets the agenda as to what is talked about. But this is a form of interaction, nonetheless. This means that the way an utterance is produced will in some way reflect the producer's understanding of the prior turn. A turn in an interview will exhibit design features which show how it is connected to the on-going stream of interaction.

Conversation analytic studies of interaction in research interviews, or interviews in work-related settings, have consistently shown that the participants' conduct attends to requirements of the setting. For example, in doctor–patient consultation the turn-taking system common to everyday interaction may be temporarily suspended to facilitate the doctor's diagnostic work (Heath, 1992). In televised news interviews, turn design will reveal how the participants orient to each other's setting-relevant identities as interviewer or interviewee (Heritage and Greatbatch, 1991). And studies of interaction in social science research interviews have revealed how participants' utterances are shaped by, and oriented to, their tacit understanding of expectations attendant upon asking and answering questions in semi-formal environments (Suchman and Jordan, 1990; Widdicombe and Wooffitt, 1995; Wooffitt and Widdicombe, forthcoming).

However, it is a noticeable tendency in Foucauldian and critical discourse analytic studies of interview data to focus on the respondents' turns as if they were discrete speech events isolated from the stream of social interaction in which they were produced. Analytic attention is thus focused squarely on the respondents' turns. This may seem a reasonable procedure; after all, it is the respondents' experiences the analysis seeks to explore. But conversation analytic research repeatedly shows that turns at talk are invariably connected in significant ways to prior turns. Turns in interaction are designed with respect to the activities performed by prior turns. This is true of talk in interviews as it is of everyday interaction.

To illustrate, consider a phenomenon identified by Heritage and Watson (1979) in their study of the ways in which news interviewers formulate the gist, upshot or relevance of the interviewee's utterances in subsequent questions. The following extract is taken from a face-to-face interview with a winner of a 'Slimmer of the Year' competition, which was broadcast on the radio.

(8.3) (From Heritage and Watson, 1979: 132. IE = interviewee;
         IR = interviewer.)

```
1  IE:   You have a shell that for so long
2        protects you but sometimes
```

```
 3         things creep through the shell
 4         and then you become really aware
 5         of how awful you feel. I never
 6         ever felt my age or looked my age
 7         I was always older – people took me
 8         for older. And when I was at college
 9         I think I looked a matronly fifty.
10         And I was completely alone one weekend
11         and I got to this stage where I
12         almost jumped in the river.
13         I just felt life wasn't worth it any
14         more – it hadn't anything to offer
15         and if this was living
16         I'd had enough.
17   IR:   You really were prepared to commit
18         suicide because you were
19         a big fatty
20   IE:   Yes because I – I just didn't
21         see anything in life that I had
22         to look forward to ....
```

Heritage and Watson show that the interviewer's phrase 'a big fatty' preserves the essential aspects of the interviewee's prior utterances – her weight problem. But it also transforms that topic. The phrase 'a big fatty' trivialises the speaker's obesity. This in turn establishes an inauspicious sequential context for the speaker. Either she can try to redress the trivialisation accomplished by 'a big fatty', and risk appearing pedantic or self-important, or she can expand upon her suicidal feelings knowing that they may be heard by the radio audience as an unwarranted response to what is now constituted as a trivial problem. And in this sense, the interviewer's question and the speaker's response are *interactionally generated objects*.

The danger is this: analysing utterances with an eye to identifying the discourses (or subject positions, or repertoires) which they are said to embody invites the analyst to diasattend to the interactional circumstances in which – and *for* which – those utterances were originally produced. It is as if utterances were produced in an interactional vacuum, untainted by the contingencies of the turn-by-turn unfolding of talk out of which they were generated.

Let us take a concrete example, and examine some of the data Wetherell used in her (1998) argument that CA needs to be supplemented by a concern with discourses and subject positions. In her analysis of data from an interview between Nigel Edley and the young men, reproduced earlier, Wetherell examines the use of the phrase 'out on the pull'.

```
125   PA:   When you went out on that Friday (.) evening you were
126         out on the pull yeah?=
```

She argues that this phrase is part of an accusation that Aaron, the person whose behaviour was so described, was intent on being promiscuous, and did not care about the feelings of the young women with whom he might have sexual relations. She argues that this in turn establishes the relevance of a particular subject position for Aaron which is troubling, in that it portrays him in a negative light. He rebuts this ascription by drawing on different subject positions (lucky, drunk, and so on). Wetherell argues that each of the subject positions mobilised by, or in response to, 'out on the pull' draw from culturally available repertoires relevant to the morality of sexual activity (Wetherell, 1998: 399). Analytically, then, in this post-structuralist account, much rests on the analyst's assumption that 'out on the pull' has a certain meaning, or inferential force, largely independent of the context of its use, because of its embeddedness in wider cultural understandings about the morality of young people's – especially young males' – heterosexual activity.

It is tempting to rely on intuitions about the broader cultural resonances of a phrase like 'out on the pull', especially if they derive from, and reaffirm, a pre-existing, theoretically driven, political or moral perspective. And, of course, it is easy to imagine occasions in which that phrase might be used euphemistically to characterise actions which are morally reprehensible, and thereby form part of an accusation. However, it is just as easy to imagine its use as a simple description of the intentions for an evening out; or as a form of tease, for example, as a way of imputing a (mildly deviant) ulterior motive for taking just a little too much effort over one's appearance or dress when there is no expectation of meeting members of the opposite sex (see Drew, 1987, for an analysis of the interactional organisation of teasing). And there is good evidence that figures of speech like 'out on the pull' cluster in particular sequential positions, and perform specific interactional functions (Drew and Holt, 1988, 1998), properties which could not be intuited from a decontextualised assessment of their wider cultural or ideological meanings. The point is that it is imperative to investigate the interactional context in which a phrase is used to get a sense of what it is doing.

So what is the interactional context in which Paul uses the phrase 'out on the pull'? Here is the relevant strip of talk.

```
116   N:    Right: (.) okay (0.2) what do you think Paul?
117         (0.3)
118   PA:   Did you=
119   PH:   =Are you ap┌palled?                                          ┐
120   PA:             └When you ┘hh no (.) s┌when you went out
121   N:                                    └Not appalled?               ┘
122   PA:   I jus I'll tell you in a minute when you went out
123   N:    hh ┌hhh ┐
124   ?       └hhhh┘
125   PA:   When you went out on that Friday (.) evening you were
126         out on the pull yeah?=
```

Prior to this sequence, Aaron and Phil have been talking about the morality of Aaron's sexual exploits. In the first turn in the extract, the interviewer asks another interviewee for his thoughts on the matter. As the current topic of the interview is the morality of Aaron's actions, the question 'what do you think Paul?' is hearable as an invitation to address that topic. Paul's response begins with 'Did you'. Although we do not have the benefit of video evidence showing Paul turn to face Aaron, we can feel confident that this turn was addressed to him, and not Phil or the interviewer (besides, some turns later, Paul eventually launches a question to Aaron in which 'did you' is the turn initial component). In which case, this turn projects an interesting course of action: he is not answering the question, but (in all likelihood) building another question for Aaron. However, after Paul's 'Did you' he in turn is asked another question by Phil, 'Are you appalled'. Paul temporarily abandons his turn, and begins speaking again in overlap with Phil's production of the word 'appalled'.

'Are you appalled' is a turn designed with exquisite precision to discomfort Paul. Structurally it comes after Paul has started a turn which is legitimately his to take: the interviewer has issued a first part of a paired question–answer action sequence, and has identified its recipient by the use of a name. Phil's utterance 'Are you appalled' does not come in the vicinity of a transition relevance place where turn-transfer may legitimately be initiated; it cuts right over Paul's on-going turn. This is not to say that Phil is simply interrupting Paul in a random manner. Some features of this extract resemble what Jefferson has called interjacent overlap (Jefferson, 1986: 159), which has orderly properties. But it is a clear display that Phil is explicitly not aligning with the trajectory of the utterance Paul is trying to build.

The simple production of the first part of an adjacency pair does not necessarily legislate that the second part will follow immediately. Before the provision of the expected second part there may be *insertion sequences* (Schegloff, 1972a), often composed of embedded and nested question–answer adjacency pairs, during which matters relevant to the first part are addressed before the second part is produced. Thus one obtains patterns which take the following form.

(8.4)   (Taken from Sacks, 1992, Vol II: 546–7; start of telephone conversation)

Gene:	Is Maggie there.	Q1
Lana:	˙hh Uh who is calling,	Q2
Gene:	Uh, this's Gene:. Novaki.	A2
Lana:	Uh just a mom'nt	A1

Paul's response is being built as a question; and it can be heard, therefore, not as an attempt to avoid answering the question, but as the first part of an insertion sequence designed to address matters *prior to* the production of an answer. Now look to see what Phil's 'Are you appalled' does in this context. Phil's utterance offers a candidate answer; and it is offered as soon as it becomes apparent that Paul is not in the first instance doing 'answering'. Earlier it was noted that Phil's overlapping turn has the character of interjacent overlap. This is a method by which a speaker can initiate a turn the relevance of which may be jeopardised by the on-going talk (Jefferson, 1986). What Phil's intervention does, then, is to propose that right at that moment Paul *should be* offering an answer; and that if an answer is not offered right at that moment, the opportunity or likelihood of an answer is diminished. In this, Phil's question to Paul subtly transforms the interactional landscape. Prior to 'Are you appalled', Paul's 'Did you' was at least hearable as the onset of an insertion sequence as *a preliminary to* an answer; but Phil's intervention proposes that an answer should be forthcoming, and in this sequential context Paul's current turn is hearable as an *evasion of* an answer.

Also, consider the inferential impact of 'Are you appalled' as a candidate answer. Phil could have selected any kind of response to attribute to Paul. His selection of 'appalled' indexes a moral response (which has been topicalised earlier in the interview). Moreover, it offers an *extreme* moral response; this is not, for example, merely disapproval. Finally, given the range of candidate answers which Phil could have offered at that point, this selection is hearable as one fitted to what is known about Paul: that he is the kind of person likely to have taken an extremely negative view of Aaron's conduct. However, up to this point in the interview, Aaron, Phil and the interviewer have handled the topic of Aaron's sexual adventures in a fairly lighthearted and casual manner. Consequently, the question 'Are you appalled' establishes a discrepancy between the seriousness of the incidents under discussion and the extreme nature of Paul's (likely) reaction. And this in turn transforms the inferential relevances in play, in that it raises the possibility that Paul's response (whatever it transpires to be) may be heard as unwarranted or exaggerated.

Phil's question thus establishes an inauspicious interactional and inferential environment for Paul and the turn he is trying to build. And there is evidence – intrinsic to the data – that Paul himself is sensitive to the inferential implications of Phil's question. Note that Phil's 'Are you' is produced in the clear of any other talk. There is good reason to assume that Paul heard that Phil was embarking on a question. Paul begins to speak, re-starting his turn, this time with 'When you'. However, 'When you' is produced in overlap with all but the first sounds of 'appalled'. Having re-started his turn knowing that Phil was asking him a question, Paul subsequently abandons it at the first possible point after the word 'appalled' – the point at which it becomes clear what kind of question Phil was asking and the kind of action it was accomplishing. Paul immediately produces a minimal and unequivocal 'no' before trying again to launch his response to the interviewer's question.

The point is this: Wetherell argues that this particular use of the phrase 'out on the pull' has an accusatory orientation because of its claimed wider cultural, historical and ideological resonances. A CA re-analysis reveals that the turn which (eventually) ends with the phrase 'out on the pull' is sequentially implicated in and generated out of what is demonstrably a sceptical – perhaps even hostile – interactional context. Thus what Wetherell interprets to be a turn which *initiates* a hostile environment, transpires to be a turn which is itself *responsive* to the collaborative production of an inferentially sensitive moment in the interview.

And what kind of response does it initiate? In this sequence, the co-participants – including the interviewer – have topicalised and made accountable what they anticipate will be Paul's extreme and negative evaluation of Aaron's activities. CA and DA studies indicate that in this context, a particular kind of next activity becomes highly relevant. The person whose position or claims have been made accountable will seek to establish or reaffirm the warrant for holding that position or making those claims. This is precisely what Paul does: he directs a question to Aaron which focuses on his *intentions* on the night in question, immediately raising the issue of morality and appropriate conduct. Paul's turn, then, is not an accusation which draws on ideologically laden meanings associated with a figure of speech; it is a defensive utterance, in that it seeks to initiate a sequence of turns in which he can establish the grounds for his own moral position to a demonstrably sceptical audience. And in the same way that Phil's 'Are you appalled' achieved its demonstrable character as an aggressive turn by virtue of its precise sequential placement, so too does Paul's turn achieve its character as an aggressively designed defensive response by virtue of *its* location in the unfolding trajectory of the encounter. This use of the figure of speech 'out on the pull', then, will *not* be heard as a mild tease, *nor* a joke, *nor* a simple description of a night's activities; but *because of its sequential context*, it will be hearable as seeking to establish that Aaron's behaviour was extreme, and extremely bad. On this occasion, the inferential force of 'out on the pull', then, comes not from culture or history or ideology, but from its use as a component of a turn which performs a particular kind of activity in a specific sequential location.

There are other features of this fragment which are likely to be significant. First, and as Schegloff (1998) pointed out in his response to Wetherell's (1998) plea for the fusion of CA and post-structuralist analyses, there is no account of the fact that this is *interview talk* initiated by a researcher (and a relative stranger to the group) for the purposes of an academic research project. There is a substantial literature in CA which shows that the organisation of talk in non-conversational or work-related settings is shaped by the participants' tacit understanding of the tasks and identities relevant to those settings. But there is no analytic consideration of the way that the respondents' talk may be organised with respect to, and constitute the relevance for them, of these contextual factors. This means that details of the talk which may be consequential for the subsequent trajectory of the interaction may be overlooked. To illustrate, look at the interviewer's utterance in line 121.

```
119   PH:   = Are you ap┌palled?
120   PA:             └When you ┘'hh no (.) s┌when you went out ┐
121   N:                         └Not appalled?         ┘
```

The interviewer's 'Not appalled?' actively aligns him with Phil's hostile question; and it also has the consequence of ensuring that the topic of 'Paul's extreme response' is kept alive just at the point that Paul has completed a stark rebuttal that he was appalled. Remember, this is the researcher who has asked this question: an adult stranger, with academic credentials, in a semi-formal research interview with adolescent boys, occasioned by him specifically to explore fairly sensitive matters, participating in such a way as to perpetuate and reinvigorate an inauspicious interactional environment for one of the respondents. It is difficult to imagine how this cannot have had a bearing on the subsequent interaction; yet there is no attempt to track its outcomes.

But there are other interesting features of these few lines which would need to be explored in further detail to provide a rounded account of the interactional activities in which the participants are engaged and to which they are oriented: the way that Phil and Nigel's collaborative efforts seem temporarily to sidetrack Paul into beginning some form of declaration ('I jus-') which is jettisoned in favour of a promise about future disclosures (line 122); the (sceptical?) laughter from the interviewer (again) and another unidentified interviewee in response to Paul's prior contortions (lines 123 and 124); and so on.

The point is that without detailed analysis of the interactional context and its relevance to the participants' conduct, it is hard to assess analytic claims about the kind of work an utterance is doing and its significance in the unfolding interaction, let alone arguments about the subject positions or discourses which it is claimed to represent. It is at least possible that the very nature of the talk reflects mundane interactional contingencies involved in conducting research interviews rather than the influence of discourses and subject positions. The identification of discourses and subject positions as the *explanation* for the organisation of the talk forecloses precisely the kind of detailed analytic work required for an empirical investigation of these possibilities.

To summarise: talk-in-interaction is social action. When examining talk-in-interaction it is important to take account of what is being done with the talk. As we have seen, the kind of interactional business people address through their talk is consequential for the design and shape of the things people say. Interactional considerations have an impact on the very composition of the utterances people produce, utterances which in turn become texts for analysts' empirical endeavours. Talk is social action produced in the first instance for specific co-participating others, and is designed to attend to interactional and interpersonal matter relevant to the parties' immediate 'here-and-now' concerns as interaction unfolds.

In social research interviews, both inteviewers' and respondents' utterances will be action-oriented, and it is necessary to incorporate this in subsequent analysis. Respondent utterances which are identified as bearing the imprint of a discourse will have been interactionally generated; their shape, content and design will to some degree inevitably reflect the interactional contingencies for which they were designed. Utterances may exhibit particular properties not because they convey some form of meaningful information which the analyst can identify and interpret in terms of the operation of discourses, or other theoretical concerns, but because they have been designed to perform sequentially relevant actions. Those features of the respondent's talk which are initially taken to be evidence of a discourse, then, may be more intimately tied to immediate sequential and interactional context in which that talk was produced.

The dangers of discourses and repertoires

In this section I want to examine more broadly the nature of discourses, and their role in empirical analysis, as indicated in the methodological writings of researchers who work in the Foucauldian or post-structuralist traditions and related critical approaches.

The analysis of discourses offers an impoverished view of human conduct   As we have seen throughout this book, conversation analytic studies have revealed that talk-in-interaction is extraordinarily intricate. People attend to and manage their verbal activities at a hitherto unimagined level of detail. In the world exposed and explored in conversation analysis, human social interaction is a living tapestry of complex and sophisticated activities, the micro-sociological accomplishment of which is informed by socially organised webs of normative and interpretative practices.

Discourse studies which seek to identify the operation of discourses and repertoires invariably offer a much more shallow image of human conduct. We have already seen in earlier sections that the attempt to identify discourses (or repertoires) invites the analyst to disattend to the interactional frameworks in which such discourses, etc., are claimed to be present. But there is a more direct indication of the impoverished view of human conduct fostered by Foucauldian discourse analysis and related critical approaches.

In their analysis of the way scientists characterise a debate in biochemistry, Gilbert and Mulkay found the use of *two* repertoires: the empiricist repertoire, in which scientific knowledge claims are depicted as the consequence of proper scientific procedures; and the contingent repertoire, in which the validity of scientific claims were interpreted in terms of the social factors, such as the scientists' biography, friendships or personality (Gilbert and Mulkay, 1984). Billig's account of the methodology of rhetorical and discursive psychology (which he treats as related approaches) illustrates some methodological steps by discussing some of his work on how members of the public talk about the Royal Family in research interviews. Specifically he discussed how the respondents formulated the importance of history in their reflections on the Royal Family. Following from the broader argument in rhetorical psychology that discourse is inherently oppositonal, Billig claims that the interviewees' talk is constructed around *two* competing narratives: History as National Decline, in which contemporary attitudes to the Royals, or their own actions, are interpreted as indicating falling standards of public behaviour; and History as National Progress, in which contemporary attitudes to the Royals, and hereditary privilege more generally, are seen as an advance on earlier expectations of servility and unquestioning deference (Billig, 1997: 49–50). And in his account of the analysis of repertoires in discourse analysis, Edley draws on interview data collected as part of his and Wetherell's project on masculine identities. He illustrates the analysis of repertoires by considering interview data in which the topic of (men's) discussion was feminism. In these data, Edley identifies *two* repertoires: in the first, feminists are depicted as 'simply wanting equality'; and in the second, more negative repertoire, feminists' appearance, sexual orientation and hostile attitudes to men were invoked (Edley, 2001: 201).

Of course, not all studies which focus on discourses and repertoires find only two. Hollway (1995) reports how in her earlier work on sexuality she identified three discourses; Phillips and Jørgensen illustrate Laclau and Mouffe's post-structuralist position by examining data from an interview with young people about environmental issues, and find three discourses (Phillips and Jørgensen, 2002: 166–7); Edley and Wetherell (1999) identify three discursive strategies in their analysis of young men's talk about their imagined futures; and Parker's (1994) introductory account of the analysis of discourses finds four discourses, although these are not generated from an analysis of interactional data, but are found to inhabit the packaging for a tube of toothpaste.

But there is clear pattern emerging here. In the analysis of interview data informed by a focus on discourse or repertoires, participants' conduct seems to be organised around a highly limited set of interactional and interpretative relevances; in many cases, only two: this or that discourse; this or that repertoire. Given the complexity of the organisation of social interaction revealed in conversation analytic studies – the discovery of which is acknowledged even by critics of CA – one is forced to ask: is this really all there is to say about those stretches of talk in which these repertoires or discourses were said to have some influence? Is that *it*? It seems unlikely. A more likely explanation is that the very nature of the analytic enterprise – the analysis of discourses and repertoires, and the exploration of theoretically derived positions on the oppositional or contested nature of social life – establishes at the outset a set of expectations about what might be uncovered in whatever data the analyst might be examining.

Discourses and the slide to ascriptivism   In our critical assessment of Foucauldian discourse analysis, Widdicombe and I noted how empirical claims routinely lapsed into a form of ascriptivism. We described ascriptivism and its dangers in the following way: it involves

> … imputing a discourse to texts (or bits of speech and writing) without explicating the basis for that imputation. Consequently, empirical analyses tend to gloss the social functions of language use, rather than describing them. (Widdicombe and Wooffitt, 1995: 62)

To illustrate why this important, we can discuss Widdicombe's (1995) paper on the relationship between identity, politics and talk. In this paper, she considers Gavey's (1989) study of interview talk about sexuality, and re-examines some data in which Gavey claims to have identified the mobilisation of various discourses. It is worth reproducing Gavey's data and then Widdicombe's subsequent reassessment in full.

(8.5)   (From Gavey, 1989: 469. 'I' is the interviewer, 'Sue' is the inteviewee, and this is Gavey's transcription. Cited in Widdicombe, 1995: 108–9.)

```
36   I: What, if any, were some of the initial consequences of this event?
     (gap of half a line)
37   Sue: Um (pause) Well, he must have gone away with a fairly disillusioned
     attitude towards sex as far
38   as his first encounter had gone. I um felt depressed about the
     whole incident. I didn't like it. I hadn't
39   wanted it, and I'd simply done it because I didn't want (pause) I
     seemed to have sex a lot at that time
40   because I didn't want to hurt someone's feelings. As though I was
     strong and they were not. Um, and I
41   know my feeling in those days was that sexual activity by itself isn't
     important, it was how I felt about
42   someone that made it important or not important. I still feel that way a
     bit. You know, it's (pause)
43   although I've been study with one person for many years it's (pause)
     sex without the love is just (pause) it's
44   no different from wiping your bottom after you've gone to the toilet,
     or brushing your hair. It's a physical
45   act. It's an enjoyable one, um, well it can be an enjoyable one.
```

These are Widdicombe's observations on Gavey's analysis of this extract.

> The reader is informed that the discourse of permissive sexuality can be found on lines 39, 41, and 43 to 45, and that within this discourse Sue is positioned as a liberated woman. Lines 37 and 39 to 40 illustrate the male sexual needs discourse, through which is constituted her identity as a person who is responsive to male needs. But what exactly is it about the words or phrases found on these lines that substantiates the claim that they are informed by or illustrate particular discourses? Without some indication of the empirical grounding of these discourses, there is little to inspire confidence that Sue's experiences are permeated with these discourses. Indeed, the primary warrant for the identification of these discourses lies not in the analysis of the account, but through Gavey's reference to Hollway's (1984, 1989) prior identification of their existence. But Hollway (1984: 231) simply tells us that she delineated three discourses through a combination of her own knowledge and what was suggested by the data; we are not given access to how exactly the data suggested these discourses. The reader is left

all the more in the dark since 'I don't want to hurt someone's feelings' (line 40) does not seem to be entirely synonymous with satisfying men's need to have sex; yet this statement is the most obvious candidate for the male sexual needs discourse which we are assured is located on line 40 ... it seems that the ways discourses are manifested in talk are less important than the political claims which can be made having ascribed discourses to a piece of text. (Widdicombe, 1995: 109)

Numerous problems spring from the 'analytic rush' (Widdicombe, 1995: 108) to impute the presence and relevance of discourses to people's utterances. First, as the quote from Widdicombe illustrates, analytic claims about the presence of discourses may be advanced without clear explication of how the relevant data support those claims. Second, there is no attempt to trace how the interview as a form of social interaction impacts upon the those utterances which are deemed to bear the imprint of discourses. A third issue is this: are empirical claims *descriptions* of some real discursive processes, or are they *attributions* which merely reflect the analyst's theoretical perspective, and which are motivated by a desire to interpret the world in terms of the analysts' theoretical or political orientation? (This point is also made by Kitzinger, 2000a, in her analysis of strategies by which idioms can be resisted.) As long as analysts in the Foucauldian and critical traditions continue to resist grounding empirical claims by reference to close description of participants' actual conduct, then analysis is at risk of a slide into ascription, and the subsequent 'discovery' of discourses or repertoires which does not illuminate the subtle organisation of talk-in-interaction, but which merely reflects the theoretical perspective of the analyst and the immediate concerns of their project.

Identifying discourses   Much is claimed about the importance of investigating the influence of discourses in people's talk. But how do we go about identifying discourses? What is it about a stretch of talk which indicates the presence of a discourse? Ian Parker is a long-standing advocate of the analyses of discourses as a method in critical social psychology, and in an introductory account of Foucauldian discourse analysis (discussed in the previous chapter), he offers some clues.

> Three unlikely examples may serve to illustrate the operation of single discourses: if you say 'my head hurts so I must be ill', you will be employing a medical discourse; if you say 'my head hurts so I cannot really want to go to that party', you will be employing some sort of psychodynamic discourse; and if you say 'my head hurts but not in the way that yours does when you are trying it on in the way women do', you will be employing a sort of sexist discourse. (Parker, 1994: 94)

What is common to these three hypothetical discourses are the words 'my head hurts', which means that what follows must be the crucial items by which the different discourses are identified. So, as 'my head hurts so I must be ill' is a medical discourse, then we can assume that what is consequential here is the word 'ill'. Thus a single word can identify the presence of a discourse. But as 'my head hurts so I cannot really want to go to that party' is a psychodynamic discourse, then a longer stretch of talk like 'so I cannot really want to go to that party' can also be crucial. And in the final instance, the phrase 'but not in the way that yours does when you are trying it on in the way women do' indicates yet another discourse.

But this illustration captures some significant problems. How do we know which word is crucial in identifying a discourse? For example, with respect to 'my head hurts so I must be ill', what is the warrant for identifying this as a *medical* discourse? Why is it not a 'head discourse'? Or a 'body discourse'? Or a 'pain discourse'? Or a 'possessive discourse'? Or a 'complaining discourse'? Or a 'causal discourse'? Or an 'inference about one's health discourse'? And of course, the problems multiply when we try to understand the warrant for identifying the presence of discourses in larger, more complex stretches of talk.

There seems to be little consistency in the way that the term discourse is used to identify a patterned feature of verbal data or language use more generally. Some discourses seem to index a wide range of meanings and positions, or identify broad dimensions of language use. For example, Burman (1995) refers to general 'discourses of childhood'; and Hepworth and Griffin (1995) write of 'the discourse of femininity'. But in other writings, discourses seem to be more closely derived from inspection of specific features of the data being assessed. Thus in Phillips and Jørgensen (2002: 166–7), the 'cynical, sceptical discourse' is derived from analysis of just a few lines of interview data; similarly Marks (1993) identifies the presence of a 'humanistic therapeutic discourse' from inspection of a series of shorter extracts from a recording of a meeting; and according to Widdicombe (1995), Gavey (1989) finds the 'discourse of permissive sexuality' in particular lines of a transcript.

There is a clear lack of consistency as to what counts as evidence for the presence of discourse: it could be a single world, or a short stretch of talk, or a slightly longer account or narrative. This lack of consistency is problematic: what value is the concept of discourses as an analytic tool if there is no clear method by which to establish the presence of any particular discourse in any specific sequence of talk-in-interaction?

Summary

- The critique of CA from the perspective of Foucauldian discourse analysis centres on CA's claimed reluctance or inability to attend to the implications of broader political, social and historical contexts in which talk occurs.
- However, there is little to suggest that the alternatives on offer, particularly the analytic focus on discourses (and, relatedly, repertoires and subject positions), are coherent or methodologically sound.

- Moreover, the analytic focus on discourses (etc.) systematically encourages a premature rush to ascribe the presence of discourses at the expense of more systematic analysis of the complex interactional organisation of talk.

The rhetorical psychological critique of CA has two main strands. First, there is the claim that CA's own rhetoric is inappropriate and misleading, in that it does not accurately convey what CA researchers actually do; and that in various ways it presents an uncritical and overly optimistic view of everyday social interaction, thereby avoiding and obscuring investigation of oppression and injustices which occur in talk. Second, it is argued that CA's focus on the technical aspects of interaction, such as turn-taking and sequence organisation, is inadequate because it fails to capture the argumentative and oppositional character of everyday discourse. However, both sets of arguments have been found to be weak. The critique of CA's rhetoric is based on an idiosyncratic and occasionally inaccurate reading of CA. Moreover, there are numerous CA studies of the sequential underpinnings of argumentative talk; and CA's attention to the detail of interaction, and its reluctance to engage with data in terms of pre-formed theoretically conceived analytic priorities, means that, compared to those approaches in which analysis is restricted to the level of meaning, it is *better* equipped to expose the resources through which arguments and discursive contests are actually managed.

The Foucauldian or post-structuralist critique of CA claims that its focus on the interactional and sequential organisation of interaction needs to be supplemented by an appreciation of the discourses which inhabit talk and the subject positions which these make available to participants. In this way it will be able to accommodate and take account of the broader historical, cultural and political influences which inform talk, thereby affording a more rounded and satisfactory analysis of the ideological concerns which inform everyday communication. However, there are serious problems with this position, and the concept of discourses more generally. There is little clarity in the literature as to how to identify a discourse; or what constitutes evidence of the presence of a discourse in any stretch of talk. Analyses influenced by Foucauldian discourse analysis, and related approaches which investigate repertoires or the argumentative character of discourse, overwhelmingly tend to identify two or three discourses (or repertoires, or rhetorical positions). Given the sheer complexity of interaction, this consistency suggests that Foucauldian discourse analyses are circumscribed more by the analysts' common theoretical or political positions than the nature of the data. Finally, Foucauldian discourse analyses largely disattend to the detail of talk in favour of the ascription of discourses and subject positions. Indeed, the ascription of discourses and subject positions is often offered without a detailed analysis of the activities of the participants whose conduct is represented in the data. This means that the interactional contexts of utterances are rarely explored; moreover, interactional considerations which have an impact on the very composition of the utterances people produce – utterances which in turn become data for analysts' empirical endeavours – are not adequately explored. And this raises a broader concern with Foucauldian and post-structuralist discourse analyses of talk: that utterances whose design is claimed to bear the imprint of discourses, or reflect the relevance of subject positions, may in fact be shaped by the participants' orientation to interactional contingencies generated out of the turn-by-turn unfolding of talk-in-interaction.

9
Conversation Analysis and Power

Conversation analysis has always had an uneasy relationship with its parent discipline, sociology. This is because its distinctive methodology – specifically its rejection of premature theorising – and its focus on the detailed analysis of the organisation of interaction as a topic in its own right, has led its critics to argue that it fails to address the range of issues traditionally studied by sociologists. Thus it does not try to conceptualise its data in terms of the theoretical stances currently influential in the discipline. Furthermore, it does not try to make links between the micro-phenomena of interaction and what might be called macro-level order, in which relations of power, the role of ideologies and the influence of history and cultural values are said to operate.

This critique has become more pronounced in the past twenty-five years as researchers in other disciplines have become interested in what were once taken to be distinctly sociological concerns. For example, many critical social psychologists have been influenced by the writings of Foucault, Marxism and various other theoretical perspectives, and are now concerned with (broadly) the role of power in contemporary society (amongst other things); and critical discourse analysts, whose primary disciplinary base is linguistics, are researching the relationship between communication and ideologies. As the influence of the 'sociological agenda' (Hutchby, 1999: 85) has spread across related social science disciplines, so the community of scholars for whom CA is perceived to offer an inadequate account of macro-phenomena has grown.

It is untrue, however, to assume that conversation analysts have simply ignored the sociological agenda. To illustrate, in this chapter we will examine three areas of conversation analytic work which forge links between the interactional order and traditional macro social science concerns. In the following sections we will review a study of market traders' sale pitches, the findings from which suggest some forms of social control derive their power from the web of interactional obligations and expectations which inform sales encounters. We will then discuss an analysis of the talk between host and callers in radio talk shows, which examines the operation of power in the normative organisation of turn-taking in institutional settings. And finally we will look at recent attempts by feminist researchers to develop the tools of CA to explore the interactional basis for the production of gendered identities. What becomes apparent is that conversation analysis offers a distinctive perspective on issues of power and social control.

Interaction, social control and the economic order

In the mid-1980s Colin Clark and Trevor Pinch conducted a series of studies of the verbal strategies of market pitchers: traders who sell goods from a stall, usually at open air markets (Clark and Pinch, 1986, 1988; Pinch and Clark, 1986). Drawing from conversation analysis, their approach was to investigate selling as an interactional achievement. They were interested in the communicative techniques by which market pitchers recruited an audience from passing members of the public, kept their attention, and then managed to persuade them to buy the goods on sale. What were the features of the pitchers' sales discourse which ensured it was difficult for members of the audience to walk away without having made a purchase? In this sense, Clark and Pinch were interested in social control: how did the market pitchers use language to control the economic decisions and subsequent purchase actions of their audience?

In their (1988) paper, Clark and Pinch explicitly frame their work in relation to the wider assumption in macro-sociology that micro-sociological approaches, such as conversation analysis, are unable to address concerns relating to power relationships. They argue that,

> [a]lthough power may have been neglected in micro-studies we would claim that there is no reason why micro-analysis *per se* cannot address this topic. Indeed, we hope in this paper to demonstrate one way in which social control is effected and a 'power relationship' constituted…. (Clark and Pinch, 1988: 120)

So, how is a power relationship constituted interactionally in this setting? We will discuss a number of findings from Clark and Pinch's research.

Establishing the value of the goods

One of the main tasks facing a market pitcher is to persuade the audience that the sale price represents good value. One common way by which pitchers achieved this was by building a contrast between the alleged value of the goods and the actual price at which they were being sold. For example, in extract 9.1 the pitcher is selling a large quantity of meat.

(9.1) (From Pinch and Clark, 1986: 172–3. 'P' is the pitcher. In this and extracts 9.2 to 9.4 some features of the original transcription have been changed to make the text more readable.)

P: 'ere I've gotta piece o' braisin' beef 'ere or roastin' beef whatever yuh
want can anybody us that?
(0.5) *[Hands raised in audience.]*
P: 'ere y'are (0.3) quick (0.9) just' ave a look a' that (0.5) not an
ounce o' waste on it look a' that. (.) beautiful (0.4) braisin'
or roastin' beef (0.4)' ere, (0.3) that little lot
twenty one fifty one an' sharp quickly
(0.3)
gimme a tenner fer the lot

Note how the pitcher draws attention to the quality of the meat, then implies that it is worth £21.51; then, after a short gap, he announces the actual sale price, £10, which is considerably less. The sharp contrast between the two prices has many inferential benefits: the audience may feel they are being offered good value for money, and a rare chance to take advantage of such a reduced price. In this way the pitcher is organising a crucial part of his sales pattern around a contrast structure, a device common to many forms of persuasive discourse which is used to manage the actions and inferences of the audience or recipient (Atkinson, 1984a, 1984b; Smith, 1978).

Inverting the normative basis of sales relationships

Clark and Pinch argue that the power relationship between pitcher and audience is also constituted in the way that the language of the pitcher draws upon and inverts conventions associated with everyday sales transactions, such as those which occur in shops (Clark and Pinch, 1988). Consider the following extract: the pitcher has just sold a number of china vases for £2 each. He then tries to persuade his audience to buy the remainder of the vases by stating that he will sell them at less than £2.

(9.2) (From Clark and Pinch, 1988: 121. 'A1', 'A2' etc. are members of the audience directly involved in purchasing goods; 'As' refers to the entire audience at the stall.)

P: 'an' oo's gonna buy the other one an' ah'll make the buggers
cheaper than two quid? Come on?
(1.5)
P: Come on?
(1.7)
P: 'oo's gonna buy the other set?
(1.2)   *[A1 raises hand.]*
P: Lady here.
(1.7)

P: An' 'oo's 'avin' the very very
      [A2 raises hand.]
P: gen'elman there. (0.5) Knock 'em all the profit off
      (0.3) *[BANG]* one ninety-nine an' a 'alf (.) Now then
      'ere y'are.
      [Throws goods down to pitch crew – they are then exchanged for money
      from A1 and A2.]
As: *[Laughs.]*
P: Theh wasn't a lot of -, (0.9), there wasn't a lot of profit on them
      ah'll tell yuh now
As: *[Laughs.]*

Eventually, the pitcher recruits two willing purchasers from his audience and then sells the vases at only half a penny less than the original selling price; this is the smallest reduction possible given the currency denominations at the time. In effect, then, the pitcher has been able to sell two additional vases but for almost exactly the same price as he had originally charged. How has the pitcher achieved this (for him) favourable outcome?

Clark and Pinch use this extract to illustrate how normal conventions associated with sales transactions are flouted in the sales routines of market pitchers. So, in everyday transactions, it is the buyer who initiates transactions, for example, by expressing an intent to purchase, or by taking goods to a till. In market selling it is the pitchers who attempt to initiate a transaction by extolling the quality and value of the goods on offer. In extract 9.2 the pitcher initiates a transaction by announcing the price reduction of the goods on offer. This inducement is packaged in the form of a question: ''an 'oo's gonna buy the other one an' ah'll make the buggers cheaper than two quid?', and subsequent reiterations: 'Come on? (1.5) Come on? (1.7) 'oo's gonna buy the other set?'. This question and its subsequent reiterations works in that it solicits a commitment to purchase from two members of the audience.

In routine sales encounters, customers know the price of the goods before the point of sale; but in extract 9.2 it is clear that the sale price is disclosed after the sale has been agreed. Why would anyone commit to a purchase before they know the price? The two members of the audience show their intent to buy after being informed only that the price will be *less* than £2. But there are grounds to believe that they expect that the price will be considerably lower. Clark and Pinch argue that the audience members' interpretation of the pitcher's offer to sell the vases 'cheaper' is informed by the cultural convention that in these contexts this means a significant price reduction. This expectation is evidenced by the laughter which follows the pitcher's disclosure that the reduction is only half a penny. Moreover, prior to disclosing the actual selling price the pitcher says he will 'Knock 'em all the profit off': that is, sell the goods at cost price. This reinforces the assumption that the subsequent price will be a considerable reduction, and increases the likelihood of a commitment to purchase.

Eventually the pitcher announces the new price and the sale proceeds, despite the fact that the audience members who signalled an intent to purchase did not get the bargain they clearly had expected. But this raises a puzzle: so why buy goods now that they did not want just moments before, and at practically the same price? Why not refuse to go through with the sale? Why not take the pitcher to account for deceiving them as to the nature of the reduction that he intended to make?

First, the purchasers have been required to signal their intent to buy before the announcement of the actual price. Raising their hands thus constitutes 'purchase implicative commitments' (Clark and Pinch, 1988: 125) which act as obligations to carry through the transaction. Second, Clark and Pinch consider the role of humour: the 'joke' that the actual reduction was only half a penny. This joke is clearly at the expense of the two members of the audience who evidently thought they were getting the vase at a price lower than that paid by others just moments before. The laughter is thus predicated on their implied greed, and displays alignment with the pitcher, in that it is he who has artfully orchestrated their purchase at almost the same price. This characterisation of their actions and the laughter it subsequently generates constitutes an environment in which a complaint or refusal to pay would be hard to sustain. The pitcher thus uses humour as a resource in the interactional management of selling goods.

Constituting obligations to buy

In extract 9.1 the pitcher seeks indication of intent to purchase before the actual point of the sale. Through this he is able to generate the relevance of an obligation to buy. Clark and Pinch note that establishing this commitment is an important feature of the market pitcher's sale routine – indeed, they suggest that few routines proceed without an attempt to establish purchase implicative expressions from the audience (1988: 126). This can be managed in subtle ways. In this extract the pitcher is selling sets of pens.

(9.3)   (From Clark and Pinch, 1988: 126)

P: ah won't charge yuh five ninety-five (0.8) ah won't even charge yuh three ninety-five or one ninety-five, (0.3) in fact ah'm not even chargin' look, (0.5) a pound and ten pence for all the five of 'em. (0.4) Now 'oo can use 'em if ah go a bit lower, (0.3) than a pound tenpence? (.) Raise an 'and?
[Many audience members raise hands.]
P: One, (.) two, (.) three, (.) four AH CAN ONLY DO IT FER SO MANY (.) five, six, seven, (.) eight, nine, anybody at the back? (0.3) Ten, (.) eleven. (0.3) Here's what ah'll do with yeh FIRST come first served, (0.4) ALL the five of 'em yeh must have fifteen pounds worth uh pens (0.3) *[CLAP]* ah'll tek a pound the whole jolly lot …
[Sale occurs.]

Eventually he sets the price at a pound, but seeks expressions of interest well before the actual sale occurs. As in the previous extract, here the pitcher asks a question 'Now 'oo can use 'em if ah go a bit lower, (0.3) than a pound ten-pence?', and then explicitly asks for interested parties to raise their hands. But this question is not designed to solicit expressions of intent to buy; ''oo can use 'em if ah go a bit lower,' merely asks the audience to consider their potential attractiveness at an as yet unspecified price. Thus the audience at this stage is asked for expressions of interest in the goods, as opposed to a firm intent to buy. But even merely expressing interest has important consequences, in that it transpires that all those who show interest subsequently end up making a purchase. In this way a non-committal show of interest is ultimately taken by both parties to have an unequivocal 'purchasing-implicative and purchasing-obligative component' (Clark and Pinch, 1988: 127).

But there is another reason why pitchers like to see expressions of interest in the form of raised hands: it allows them to incorporate the audiences' physical responses into their subsequent turns in the on-going sales routine, and in such a way as to maximise the likelihood of mass purchases. Note that in extract 9.3 the pitcher counts all those who have raised arms. However, this extract comes from a video recording which shows the audience. Thus Clark and Pinch are able to report that the pitcher actually counts to a higher number than there are arms in the air. By exaggerating the number engaged in purchase-implicative actions, the pitcher displays his understanding that selling in that context has an imitative element: people are more likely to buy goods if they see others buying them. This is not unique to this extract; it is a common practice among market pitchers. And this strategy seems to work. With respect to this sequence, Clark and Pinch point out that the video data show that people who had not initially raised their hands also subsequently bought the goods.

Clark and Pinch argue that there is a common theme in the routines of market pitchers: it is that they engineer a gap between soliciting interest or intent to buy and the actual sale, or what they call the Sale Relevance Place (SRP). The SRP is invariably that point when the pitcher announces the actual price, and is often accompanied by clapping or banging on the stall. Clark and Pinch argue that this time between expression of interest and the SRP is important for the pitcher. It allows him or her time in which interactionally to constitute what may be initially equivocal expressions of interest into firm commitments to buy. And as we saw in the last extract, it allows them to work on those who have not expressed any interest to buy; for example, by artificially inflating the numbers in the audience engaged in purchase-implicative actions to exploit the others' imitative purchasing impulses. In the final extract from their study, we can observe another technique by which pitchers exploit the delay between the expression of interest and the SRP to engineer a strong likelihood of mass purchases by the audience. In this sequence the pitcher is selling perfumes. During this sale he occasionally breaks from talking to the audience to speak to his assistant, one of the 'pitch crew', here referred to as 'PC'.

(9.4) (From Clark and Pinch, 1988: 128)

P: now 'oo can use (.) all the four of 'em, (0.7) fer the purposes of
    the advertisement, (0.9) theh've got tuh be cleared cheaply an'
    quickly. (0.3) 'oo can use all the four of 'em, (0.5) twenty three
    pounds w'th, (0.4) at less than three fifty raise an 'arm
    [Many audience members raise hands.]
    (0.8)
P: Anyone else? (0.5) now as- (0.3)
    Now listen Rick   ][To PC]
    (0.5)
P: the first eighteen people wi' their 'and in the air, (0.) will yuh
    please step forward. (…) now look
    (0.6)
P: give every one o'these people wi'   ]
    their 'ands up in the air a   ][To PC]
    carrier   ]
    (0.4)
P: Ah'm givin' out eighteen carriers an' that's it

Note that after soliciting expression of interest the pitcher asks his assistant to hand out a carrier to each person with a raised hand. Obviously the implication is that these carriers will be used to hold the goods being sold; acceptance of the carrier thus establishes a strong obligation to see through the sale and make a purchase. But to minimise the likelihood of anyone rejecting the carrier, the pitcher simply instructs his assistant to hand them out. The audience is not offered a choice as to whether they want a carrier or not. This minimises the likelihood of anyone rejecting a carrier, which would constitute a weakening of the obligation eventually to make a purchase.

The pitcher's sales strategy is premised on the assumption that goods do not sell themselves; some discursive intervention is necessary. Clark and Pinch's research shows that the verbal strategies of the market pitchers seem remarkably successful in ensuring that audience members buy the goods on offer. But this is not to say that the audience members are being duped, or that they are acting foolishly. People would not buy the goods unless they were convinced that they were getting value for their money. They can always walk away, and at any moment. Indeed, as Clark and Pinch show, although the audience members may not be as familiar with the practices of market selling as the traders, they are nonetheless active participants in this sales encounter. But the traders do have important resources by which to manage the audience's interpretations of the value of the goods (contrasting the actual price with an alleged value); and to encourage purchase-implicative actions (asking interested parties to raise their hands); and to engender purchase-obligative orientations (handing out bags); and to anticipate and defuse potential hostility from disgruntled customers (the use of humour). These and other interactional resources allow pitchers some control over the purchasing decisions of their audience, and the outcome of their sales patter.

In this sense, Clark and Pinch claim that they have demonstrated a power relationship between the market pitcher and their audience which is the outcome of interactional practices: the ability of one participant to influence the course of action of another through the use of language by invoking and drawing upon normative conventions associated with sales exchanges more generally. This has important implications for those attempts to understand these kinds of economic exchanges (and perhaps other kinds too) which draw upon macro-sociological variables or theories.

> It is not any external attributes (for example class, gender or age) which the pitcher or audience members may or may not share, nor their subject position (pitcher as 'seller' versus audience member as 'buyer'), nor indeed aspects 'inherent' in the goods themselves (for example, their quality) or their selling price which preordains, guarantees or determines that sales success. Rather, we would claim, that it is the manner in which economic exchange can be managed by the pitcher which is the central feature of how this interactional project can be effected, social control accomplished, and how this type of power relation can be constituted. (Clark and Pinch, 1988: 138)

Summary

- Clark and Pinch draw from conversation analysis to investigate selling as an interactional achievement, rather than an economic act based on the value or personal need of goods for sale.
- They show market pitchers' communicative skills by which they are able to manage the expectations, obligations and (potential) hostile responses of the audience.
- They are thus able to explore how the 'economic power' of the pitchers is interactionally generated, collaboratively produced and normatively organised.

Turn-taking and power in institutional settings

In his work on interaction between presenters and callers to radio 'phone in' talk programmes, Ian Hutchby has focused explicitly on the relationship between conversation analysis, control and power (Hutchby, 1992, 1996a, 1996b, 1999). He has argued that CA studies of talk in institutional or work-related settings already offer analyses of features of interaction that lend themselves to interpretation in terms of interpersonal power relations. He notes, for example, that in Drew and Heritage's introduction to their seminal collection of studies of talk at work, institutional interaction is characterised by

> ... role structured, institutionalised, and omnirelevant asymmetries between participants in terms of such matters as differential distribution of knowledge, rights to knowledge, access to conversational resources, and to participation in the interaction. (Drew and Heritage, 1992b: 49)

Hutchby focuses on the use of the word 'asymmetry' in this passage and wonders if its neutral connotations adequately capture the differentials in social power suggested by phrases such as 'rights to act in certain ways' and 'access to conversational resources' (Hutchby, 1999: 89). He goes on to argue that conversation analysts should not be reluctant to consider the extent to which their work captures power relations in the analysis of the organisation of interaction.

This is not to say that Hutchby rejects CA's strong methodological principles: he supports Schegloff's argument that it is risky to assume the operation of power prior to empirical analysis because it invites the analyst to 'discover' power relations in talk wherever she may look. Nor does he assume that social interaction is merely a screen on which are reflected pre-existing power relationships. He argues that 'the sequential structures out of which the differential distributions of resources emerge are not a natural but an *oriented-to* feature of the interaction' (Hutchby, 1999: 90; original italics). We can illustrate his argument by looking at some of his analytic work on interaction on talk radio shows.

In talk radio shows members of the public are invited to ring the studio and talk to the presenter live on air to offer their opinions on the topic(s) of that day's programme. To make the show more interesting to its audience, the hosts may adopt a position of professional scepticism with regard to the caller's opinions, for example, taking an oppositional stance regardless of their own personal views. Hosts thus try to engender some element of confrontation.

Who has the power in these confrontations? Initially, it might seem that the balance of power rests with the callers. Talk radio shows are explicitly advertised as vehicles in which the members of the public can express *their* views and have them broadcast nationally, or to more local communities. Moreover, the caller knows what they are going to say. The presenter may have some idea of the kind of point a next caller might make (callers may have to outline the purpose of the call to an assistant prior to being connected to the host), and the programme may be concerned with a limited range of topics. But the host does not know *exactly* what the caller is going to say. In this sense, the host would seem to be at a disadvantage. Finally, it is a routine feature of talk radio shows that callers get the first chance to offer an opinion. The following extracts come from Hutchby's study of a nationally broadcast talk radio show in the United Kingdom. Note that the host's turn announces the next caller, where they are calling from, and offers a greeting. The callers return the greeting, and then immediately begin to talk about the point they wish to make. (The following discussion draws from Hutchby's extended 1996a account.)

(9.5) (From Hutchby, 1996a: 42; 'H' is the host, 'C' the caller)

```
1  H:  Bob is calling from Ilford. Good morning.
2  C:  ˙hh Good morning Brian. (0.4) ˙hh What I'm phoning
3      up is about the cricket …
```

(9.6) (From Hutchby, 1996a: 43)

```
1  H:  Mill Hill:: i:s where Belinda calls from. Good
       morning.
3  C:  Good morning Brian. ˙hh Erm, re the Sunday
       o:pening I'm just phoning from the point of
       vie:w ˙hh as a:n assistant …
```

Because callers have the 'first go' they are in a position to set the agenda for the subsequent discussion with the host. Moreover, there is an expectation that callers *should* establish the topical agenda in their first turn in the call.

(9.7) (From Hutchby, 1996a: 47)

```
1   H:  Jo:hn next.
2       (.)
3   C:  He=Hello?
4   H:  Hello John in: Marylebone.
5   C:  Er, hello er, your- your people didn't give me
6       any wa:rning er. (.) Okay.⌈˙h
7   H:                            ⌊Well I said hello:
8       you're John now that was the warning now what
9       d'you have to say.
10  C:  Right. Erm (.) i:t's about the dogs …
```

In this extract the caller's first opportunity to make his point comes after the host's introduction 'Jo:hn next.', but instead he merely checks the line. After the host reissues the introduction, the caller offers an account for not moving straight to his topic-initiating turn (lines 5 and 6), which, of course, constitutes another delay in its eventual production, a fact recognised by the host's rather testy encouragement (lines 7 to 9).

It would seem that the callers have some degree of control over the proceedings which is not available to the hosts. However, Hutchby argues that because callers are expected to set the topical agenda they are in fact, paradoxically, in a vulnerable and relatively powerless position. Drawing on earlier CA work on arguments, he argues that those who go second in an argument are in a powerful position because they can oppose an expressed opinion or viewpoint simply by taking it apart. Successful opposition does not require an alternative argument. Consequently, those who go first are in a weaker position, as they may be called upon to defend their argument. In radio talk shows, it is the callers who 'go first' and offer a position or an argument. Hosts 'go second', and thus find it relatively easy to challenge the caller, or to express scepticism; and that as a consequence, callers are forced to adopt a more defensive posture.

Hutchby notes various ways in which hosts can exploit the advantage of going second in talk radio discussions. They can question the relevance of the caller's argument or position in relation to their own agenda by asking questions such as 'So?' or 'What's that got to do with it?'. In the following extract, the caller has been complaining that telethons and unsolicited requests for charitable donations represent a form of psychological blackmail.

(9.8)   (From Hutchby, 1996a: 51)

```
 1  C:  I have got three appeals letters here this week
 2      (0.4) All a:skin' for donations. (0.2) hh Two:
 3      from tho:se that I: always contribute to
 4      anywa:y
 5  H:  Yes?
 6  C:  hh But I expect to get a lot mo:re
 7  H:  So?
 8  C:  h now the point is there is a limi┌t to (   )
 9  H:                                     └What's that got
10      to do- what's that got to do with telethons though
11  C:  hh Because telethons … ((Continues))
```

Hutchby notes that the host's 'So?' (line 7) proposes that the caller's point at that moment is not relevant to her general argument about telethons. This in turn raises doubts about the coherence of her position. Furthermore, it requires the caller to perform a particular kind of defensive next action: to *account* for her prior utterance.

A second strategy available to hosts is to formulate a version of what the caller has just said. In radio talk shows, they can be used 'cooperatively' to offer the caller a gloss of their position to which he or she can assent (Hutchby, 1996a: 53). But they can be used more aggressively to engineer some level of control over the agenda or the topic of the conversation. In the following extract the caller is advancing the argument that charity telethons have negative consequences because they encourage passive altruism, thus fostering a 'separateness' between the viewer and the specific problems which discourages active involvement.

(9.9)   (From Hutchby, 1996a: 54)

```
 1  C:  … but e:r, I- I thing we should be working at
 2      breaking down that separateness I┌think ┐these
 3  H:                                    └Ho:w? ┘
 4      (.)
 5  C:  these telethons actually increase it.
```

```
 6  H:  Well, what you're saying is that charity does.
 7  C:  h Charity do::es, ye⌈::s I mean      ⌉
 8  H:                  ⌊Okay we- so you ⌋'re (.) so
 9          you're going back to that original argument we
10          shouldn't have charity
11  C:  Well, no I um: I wouldn't go that fa:r, what I
12          would like to⌈ see is-
13  H:              ⌊Well how far are you going then.
14  C:  Well I: would- What I would like to see is …
```

The host formulates the caller's position thus: 'Well, what you're saying is that charity does. [increase separateness]' (line 6). Although the caller then offers only a tentative agreement, in that the extended 'does' and 'yes' suggest some element of disagreement, the host builds on his formulation to attribute to the caller an extreme position: that charity *per se* is a bad thing. In this way, the host has been able to hijack the discussion to focus on a more controversial topic. It also places the caller in a disadvantageous position of having to clarify what exactly his argument is, rather than elaborating it, or offering a more forceful defence.

A third strategy available to talk show hosts is to attribute a position to the caller – often using direct or indirect reported speech – but then to challenge that position. This argumentative move often takes the form of a device Hutchby identifies as 'You say X but what about Y?'. The following extract illustrates this, and comes from a programme in which callers were offering their views on proposals to change Sunday trading laws.

(9.10) (From Hutchby, 1996a: 61–2)

```
 1  C:  I think we should (.) er reform the la:w on
 2          Sundays here, (0.3) w- I think people have
 3          the choice if they want to do shopping on a Sunday
 4          (0.4) also, that, (.) i-if shops want to open on a
 5          Sunday th- th- they should be given the choice to
 6          do so
 7  H:  Well as I understand it th:: (.) law (.)
 8          a:s they're discussing it at the moment would allow
 9          shops to open ˙h for six hou:rs ˙hh⌈ e:r   ⌉on a =
10  C:                      ⌊Yes.  ⌋
11  H:  =Sunday.
12  C:  That's righ⌈t
13  H:          ⌊From: midda:y.
14  C:  Y⌈es
15  H:  ⌊They wouldn't be allowed to open befo:re that
16          ˙hh Erm and you talk about erm, (.) the rights of
17          people to: make a choice as to whether they
18          shop or not,  ⌈ on    ⌉ a Sunday,=what about ˙hh the=
19  C:              ⌊Yes,  ⌋
20  H:  =people who may not have a choice a:s to whether
21          they would work on a Sunday.
```

The caller is clearly in favour of extended Sunday trading hours, and argues that there would be benefits for consumers and traders. After a period of talk in which host and caller clarify the nature of the Government's proposals (lines 7 to 14), the host paraphrases part of the caller's argument: 'and you talk about erm, (.) the rights of people to: make a choice as to whether they shop or not, – on – a Sunday' (lines 16 to 18). The caller assents to this formulation, overlapping with part of the host's turn. But the host then goes on to challenge that argument by suggesting that it does not take account of the shopworkers who would be affected by extended trading hours. This device thus allows the host to express scepticism about the caller's point of view.

The 'You say X but what about Y?' device allows the host to make a point with a certain rhetorical flourish. For example, Hutchby notes that in this instance there is a neat symmetry between the two contrastive components of the device: the host challenges the caller's argument by indicating that supporting rights for one group – shoppers – would necessarily restrict the choices of another group – shopworkers.

Hutchby thus argues that hosts are in a relatively powerful position because there is an unequal distribution of argumentative resources. For example, in the opening of calls, callers are expected to offer a point of view in their first turn, which means that hosts necessarily have the argumentative advantage. Moreover, he shows the kinds of resources hosts can use to attack a caller's position without having to advance an alternative argument. Of course, Hutchby's analysis covers a wider range of phenomena than can be discussed here. But running throughout all his analysis is a concern to show how argumentative resources are differentially distributed between host and caller; and how the unequal distribution of these opportunities is embedded in the sequentially organised and oriented-to properties of talk in this setting. In this he has used CA's focus on the interactional organisation of discursive activities to explore topics more commonly associated with critical discourse analysis: the operation of power through language.

In Hutchby's account power is not treated as a 'monolithic feature of talk radio' (1996b: 495) in which the host has power simply by virtue of his or her control over the technology required for radio broadcast. Instead, by focusing on the turn-by-turn development of social actions which constitute talk-in-interaction in this specific work-related setting, he shows that power dynamics are variable and shifting. Moreover, in this view power is contestable: for example, the host can be coerced momentarily into voicing his own opinion, thus allowing the caller to adopt the advantageous position of 'going second' in the argument. Thus there are resources available to the callers by which they can resist the host's argumentative strategies. Consequently, by viewing power in terms of the relationship between turns in interactional sequences, Hutchby argues that CA can be used to show how 'power is a phenomenon brought into play through discourse' (1996b: 494).

Hutchby argues that this view of power is not very different from conceptions of power found in Foucault's more theoretically oriented writings. Foucault

(1977) does not assume that power resides with one group, who can then use it to influence other groups. Instead, he sees power as a set of ever-present possibilities which can be mobilised or resisted by social agents (individuals, groups, and larger collectivities). Moreover, power is embedded in that set of relationships between social agents who may variably exercise or resist power. Foucault thus views power as a set of structured but variable potentials, not a static feature of unchanging relationships between well-defined social groups. This focus on the shifting and contestable relationship between agents in which power can be mobilised and contested chimes with Hutchby's account of power as fluid and sequentially organised argumentative opportunities and resources.

But Hutchby goes on to offer a more challenging argument: that conversation analysis can offer an empirically grounded elaboration of some of Foucault's ideas. For example, Foucault emphasises the role of discourses in power relations; and he argues that the operation of, and resistance to, power relations through discourses does not just occur on a macro-sociological scale across large social formations, but infuses mundane, everyday activities. But as we saw in the last chapter, there are problems with the concept of discourses, not the least of which is that it invites the analyst to disattend to the detail of social interaction – the very environment in which Foucault says power operates. But conversation analysis is directly concerned to describe the subtlety and intricacy of everyday communicative processes. For Hutchby, then, CA offers a way to explore power in the very infrastructure of sociality: the relationship between turns at talk-in-interaction.

Summary

- Hutchby studied the mobilisation of power in the allocation of turn types between the participants in calls to talk radio programmes.
- He identified a number of practices and devices through which the host seeks to maintain an argumentative advantage over the caller.
- His work stands as an illustration of his broader position that conversation analysts should not be reluctant to consider the extent to which their work captures power relations in the analysis of the organisation of interaction.

Gender and sexuality: feminism, language and conversation analysis

So far we have studied how particular researchers have used conversation analysis to explore power in the organisation of interaction in specific settings, such as the market, and the radio talk show. In this final section, however, we will be looking at debates about the use of CA amongst a community of scholars: feminist researchers interested in the relationship between language, gender and sexuality.

According to Kitzinger, 'Feminism is a politics predicated on the belief that women are oppressed' and it has an emancipatory agenda in that it is 'a social movement dedicated to political change' (2000b: 163). Feminist scholars have had a long-standing interest in the ways in which language reproduces or reflects women's disadvantage. They argued that inequality is rife in various institutions and practices within society; and language is no different: the language we have reflects and enforces patriarchal, male power and ensures the subjugation of women as a disadvantaged and marginalised group within society (Lakoff, 1975). Dale Spender's famous book *Man Made Language* (1980), for example, explored the various ways in which the structure, vocabulary and conventional use of English enforced the patriarchal order and perpetuated gender inequalities. Similarly, Kramarae (1981) argued that English language effectively silences women, in that it predominantly reflects men's experiences of and attitudes about the world. There is no vocabulary or conceptual framework through which women can express their distinctive perspectives and life experiences; therefore women become a muted group.

Other approaches focused more on the way in which wider institutional and societal gender inequalities were reflected in differences in women's and men's speech patterns. Thus Fishman (1983) studied tape recordings of naturally occurring interactions in mixed-sex heterosexual couples. She wanted to explore how gendered conversational practices reinforced wider gender asymmetries in power and status. She found that women asked more questions than men, and were more likely to use 'attention beginnings' – phrases such as 'this is interesting' – to preface remarks. Fishman argued that questions and attention beginnings were designed to increase the possibility of a response; thus their predominance in women's speech reflected women's experience of not being treated as an equal conversational partner. Similarly, West and Zimmerman (1983) studied the incidence and organisation of interruptions between men and women, and found, on the whole, that males interrupted the females more than vice versa (but see James and Clarke, 1993, whose overview of interruption research suggests a less clear-cut picture). These kinds of studies thus tried to identify how wider structural gender inequalities were realised in mundane speech practices.

A third perspective on the relationship between language and gender also focused on differences between women's and men's speech, but regarded each communicational style as equally valid. For example, Holmes (1995) examined politeness behaviour: compliments, apologies, and so on. She was primarily interested in the different ways women and men performed these discursive actions. Similarly Tannen (1991) has explored how different conversational styles of men and women can lead to misunderstanding and miscommunication. And West (1995) argued that conversation analysis could be used to expose women's interactional competence, thus acting as a corrective to those perspectives which treated women's communicative abilities as inferior to those of men, or which merely argued for the parity of women's speech skills without actually being able to demonstrate them empirically.

During the 1990s, however, research on gender and language began to move away from an attempt to identify men's and women's conversational styles. Stokoe (2000) and Stokoe and Smithson (2001, 2002) outline in summary the main parameters of this change. It was argued that these approaches rested on an essentialist (and common sense) view of gender, that is, as an identity that is a fixed property of the individual. Thus the categories of 'men' and 'women' were regarded as static entities, and analytic attention focused on the socio-linguistic behaviours with which they were differentially associated. This essentialist position was criticised because it led to research which tended to exaggerate the communicative differences between women and men, rein-force gender stereotypes, and reproduce binary conceptions of gender. Instead, feminist researchers began to develop broadly constructionist approaches, in which gender and gender relations were viewed as being constituted through language and communication. Much of this work was informed by the ethno-methodological approach to facts as social accomplishments realised in mun-dane reasoning practices, particularly Garfinkel's study of Agnes, an intersexed person who, having been raised as a male, had to learn explicitly the otherwise tacit skills required to pass as a female (Garfinkel, 1967). Other work was prompted by more theoretical re-workings of traditional gender categories. For example, Butler (1990) offered a Foucauldian, post-structuralist analysis of gender as performance, in which she argued that gendered identities are dis-cursive and cultural productions. These approaches were anti-foundationalist, in that they did not treat traditional conceptions of gender as givens, but sought to explore how those categories were constructed and reproduced in language. Researchers in this tradition thus began to investigate how gender is *accomplished* in discourse.

A second departure from the traditional study of gender differences in con-versational styles was research in the relationship between language and sex-uality. Again, there is a strong constructionist and anti-essentialist thrust to this work. For example, Edley and Wetherell have tried to draw from conversation analysis and post-structuralist theory to investigate the way that masculine identities are constructed in discourse (1997, 1999). And constructionist per-spectives were brought to bear on the discursive practices through which hetero-sexuality is constituted as a normal or natural state, thereby privileging this one form of sexuality over non-heterosexual orientations, identities and relation-ships (McIlvenny, 2002; Speer and Potter, 2000).

Feminists sympathetic to the anti-essentialist and constructionist position focused on the achievement of gender and sexuality in language use. It is no surprise, therefore, that some researchers sought to utilise the approach meth-ods of conversation analysis, first, to research the interactional basis of gender production, and second, to ground empirical claims about the constitution of gender and sexuality in the detailed analysis of ordinary communication (for example, Hopper and LeBaron, 1998; and see the collection of papers in Fenstermaker and West, 2002). But despite the insights offered by these kinds of studies, some feminist scholars remain sceptical of the relevance of CA for their work.

Kitzinger (2000b) identifies three features of conversation analytic work of which feminists might be wary. But in each case she offers a robust defence of conversation analysis and its potential for feminist research. First, she argues that they might be suspicious of what she calls CA's social theory: its (ethno-methodologically informed) commitment to treating the social order as a contingent and socially accomplished phenomenon. Conversation analysis investigates talk as action; therefore, it offers a way to see how social order is produced through communicative actions in concert. This view of social order is not committed to a particular view of power relations and inequalities. This has led some of CA's critics to argue that it embodies a sociologically neutral view of social order which masks precisely the kind of oppression which feminists wish to expose and challenge (e.g., Billig, 1999a, 1999b).

But Kitzinger argues that CA is not intrinsically incompatible with the analysis of power relations. This is because it focuses directly on the actual details of gender relations conducted through talk in everyday settings. It forces feminists to address exactly how inequalities in interpersonal relations may be manifest and reproduced in the mechanics of interaction, and thereby invites them to question the value of theoretical accounts of gender relations. Moreover, she points out that feminists themselves have advocated greater attention to the detail of everyday life, not less, citing Wise and Stanley's (1987) use of CA to expose the social organisation of an (albeit fictitious) case of sexual harassment. And as we shall see later, CA can tell us a great deal about the play of power and resistance in an instance of real-life interaction which, at the very least, strongly invites characterisation as a form of sexual harassment.

Second, conversation analysis is centrally concerned to identify participants' tacit understanding of the on-going interaction. Consequently, in CA research analytic claims are derived from close description of, and grounded by reference to, the participants' demonstrable orientations. Kitzinger states that this might initially appear to mesh with feminism's goal of exploring and celebrating women's perspectives. But what if there is a discrepancy between the visible orientations of the participants and the feminist researcher's wider political and theoretical commitments? Feminists might argue that just because participants may not display an orientation to, say, patriarchy, does not mean that it is not relevant to the interpretation or wider political significance of their talk. CA's emphasis upon participants' orientations therefore 'raises difficulties for the analyst who "hears" in the data oppressions and power abuses not "oriented" to by the participants' (Kitzinger, 2000b: 169).

However, Kitzinger argues that this is a problem which feminists already encounter: tension always arises when feminists wish to adhere to and privilege women's own perspectives, while at the same time advancing claims about the political or ideological import of discourse in the absence of any indication that that's what is relevant to the participants. CA's particular stance on the importance of grounding analytic claims by reference to participants' orientations thus simply reproduces 'an old problem in a new guise' (2000b: 171). Moreover, she argues that in some places Sacks' lectures illustrate an analytic mentality through which it is possible to investigate how talk resonates with wider political realities in the absence of any overt orientation to those realities on the part of the participants, but in such a way as to remain faithful to conversation analytic injunctions against premature theorising or the simple ascription of political relevance (2000b: 172).

Finally, Kitzinger suggests that feminist scholars may be uneasy with what they perceive as CA's narrow focus on the micro detail of verbal interaction at the expense of an analysis of the wider social and political context. But she argues that this is a false dichotomy. The social and political realities which feminists wish to explore may resonate in both the overt acts of oppression and brutality, but they are also produced through talk. Moreover, conversation analytic studies have repeatedly shown that it is necessary to attend to the detail of the organisation of talk because it is demonstrably consequential to the way participants understand the emergent trajectory of interaction,

> If we want to understand what people are saying to one another, and how they come to say it, and what it means to them, then we, as [feminist] analysts, have to attend to their talk *at the same level of detail that they do*. (Kitzinger, 2000b: 174; original italics)

Kitzinger, then, is optimistic about the potential of conversation analysis for feminist research. In the following sections we will discuss three studies which illustrate the various ways in which CA has been used to inform feminist research, and which suggest that her optimism is well-founded.

Liisa Tainio: conversation analysis and harassment-in-action

Tainio studies a telephone conversation between a 59 year old male – then a recently elected member of the Finnish Parliament – and a 15 year old girl (Tainio, 2003). Tainio reports that it was known the man had been spying on the girl; and the conversation she examines came from the second of two calls to her made by the man. The man was charged and eventually found guilty of the offence of attempting to 'sexually abuse a child'. The recording of the conversation was used as evidence of the man's guilt during the trial; and, as the recording and the transcripts were in the public domain, its contents were widely interpreted as an instance of sexual harassment.

Following Schegloff's (1997) recommendation that critical discourse analysts use CA as a resource, Tainio focused on the sequential organisation of activities in the call. Her goals were to identify the interactional basis of the man's sexual pursuit of the girl and her attempts to resist his suggestions. Moreover, she wanted to consider if 'harassment can be traced interactionally in the mundane procedures of conversation' (2003: 176). To illustrate her analytic focus, we will consider her analysis of the man's strategies in trying to persuade the girl to go for 'a ride' with him. The primary strategy is one of repetition. The following extract comes from that part of the call in which the man first raises the topic of a joint excursion.

(9.11)   (From Tainio, 2003: 176–7; 'MP' [Member of Parliament] is the male caller, 'G' is the female recipient. For presentational purposes, I have reproduced only the English version of the transcript.)

```
043   MP:   I see=are you busy now in the
044         daytime.
045         (0.8)
046   G:    I shall work now I came just
047         from the job,=and then I
048         will go a↑gain,
049         ˙hh⌈     °and >work<°
050   MP:        ⌊Yes.
051         (1.0)
052   MP:   I see: >I see<.=When shall
053         we go for a ride then.
054         (.)
055   G:    ↓What did you say.
056   MP:   When shall we go for a ride
057         (.)
058   G:    Hey listen I don't k°now°hhh
059         (.)
060   MP:   h What?
061         (0.6)
062   MP:   Are you coming with me then.
063         (0.5)
064   MP:   Do⌈you dare to come.
065   G:       ⌊I don't know. hhh
066         (.)
067   MP:   ↓But come along,↓
068         (0.6)
069   G:    Why is ↑that
070   MP:   (We-) well I know why, (.)
071         see I have heard (.)
072         I know (.) I know >much more
073         about you than you think<.
074         (0.7)
075   G:    Is that so.
076   MP:   Ye:s? Yes I a- Absolutely.
```

In this sequence the caller issues, repeats and reformulates his invitation five times (lines 52, 56, 62, 64 and 67). Throughout the call the man reissues the invitation on many more occasions. Tainio observes that prior to this extract, the caller had built several pre-invitations. Preliminary turns, such as pre-invitations, pre-requests and so on, allow participants to deal with potentially delicate matters related to the projected actual request prior to its issue; for example, to discover if an invitation would be appropriate, welcomed or accepted (Schegloff, 1980). In this extract there is one pre-invitation from the caller: 'are you busy now in the daytime.' which clearly orients to possible external restrictions on the girl's time and subsequent availability. Her response does not explicitly address the (implied and projected) invitation, but focuses on factual matters. However, (potential) invitees, faced with a pre-invitation, can indicate likely refusal by demonstrating that they are unable (as opposed to unwilling) to accept the anticipated invitation (Davidson, 1984). In this way 'face' and interpersonal harmony can be maintained. These ostensibly neutral reports therefore tend to be heard as rejection-implicative.

Davidson (1984) has shown that inviters treat reports of an inability to accept as though they imply rejection, and build any subsequent reissue of the invitation to address the grounds of the invitee's implied rejection. In extract 9.11 the caller issues the invitation to go for a ride as though it was an existing mutually agreed arrangement: 'When shall we go for a ride then.' This neatly side-steps the grounds of the implied rejection; and, in a sequential location in which an inviter might infer that any actual overture will be rejected, actually manages to reinvigorate the primary activity with which he is concerned: pressing his invitation to the girl.

Tainio makes some subtle points about the girl's response: '↓What did you say.'. She notes that this is a repair initiator, in that it establishes that there is some interactional 'trouble' with the prior turn (Schegloff *et al*, 1977). The precise nature of the trouble, though, is unclear. The girl's turn could be heard as an outraged exclamation at the caller's proposal, or as asking for a repeat because she did not hear what he had said. The caller's next turn is a straight repeat of his prior turn: he interpreted her repair initiator as indicating that she had not heard.

(In Chapter 1 we reviewed Sacks' discussion of an extract from a call to a suicide prevention agency in which the caller seemed to be having trouble hearing the name of the agency staff member. Sacks argued that the caller's repair initiator (a report of a hearing problem) was strategic and organised in that it allowed the caller not to give a name where that activity would be normatively expected. Although Tainio does not make such a speculative claim, could it be that the caller's hearing of '↓What did you say.' – as inviting a repeat – is similarly strategic? If it were heard as an outraged exclamation, then the caller's projected appropriate next action would be an account, an apology, or some explanatory defence of that infereably transgressive component of the offending turn. Either way, the caller's pursuit of the invitation – and through that, of the girl herself – may have been sidetracked, thus undermining his interactional project, perhaps irretrievably.)

Compare this repair sequence with the one that follows. In line 58 the girl offers a weak refusal of the man's invitation: 'Hey listen I don't k°now° to which the caller responds with 'What?'. Sequentially then, the normatively appropriate next turn is one in which the girl offers the now relevant other-initiated self-repair (Schegloff *et al*, 1977). But she does not, and the next speaker is the caller, who does not pursue the absent self-repair, but prompts for an acceptance in the form of a question 'Are you coming with me then.'. Thus there is interactional asymmetry here: the girl's next turn repair initiation in response to the pursuit of an acceptance generates a repeat of that pursuit; but the caller's next turn repair initiation in response to the girl's weak refusal is treated with silence. Pursuit and resistance are thus managed via differential uptake of sequentially organised options and activities.

Conversation analytic studies have shown repeatedly that silences following requests or invitations are routinely interpreted as indicating refusals or declinings (Davidson, 1984). In extract 9.11 the following occurs:

```
062   MP:   Are you coming with me then.
063         (0.5)
064   MP:   Do -you dare to come.
```

The caller pursues the girl's acceptance of the invitation but this is met with a half second silence. This absence of an immediate response is treated as rejection-implicative, in that the caller presses again for an acceptance, but this time with a different approach, in that the invitation to go for a ride is characterised as a daring proposition, a formulation which seems designed to appeal to a sense of rebellion and adventure stereotypically associated with teenagers.

Analysis of these few turns, then, reveals an interactional basis on which to claim that the caller's pursuit of an acceptance is unwarrantedly insistent, and thereby suspicious in intent; and an insight to the interactionally grounded strategies by which the girl attempts to resist the invitation, and its implied consequences.

Tainio goes on to offer a similarly detailed and insightful account of other aspects of the call: for example, the girl's responses to the invitations; the caller's attempt to establish intimacy and common knowledge (indicated in lines 72 and 73 when he says 'I know >much more about you than you think<.'), and the extent to which this hearably constitutes an element of threat. But underpinning her analysis is an attempt to show how actions which can be heard as a form of harassment (and, indeed, which *did* come to be heard that way by the jury, journalists and the public at large) are predicated on, mobilised in and resisted through mundane practices of interactional organisation. And in this Tainio makes a significant contribution, because she shows that it is possible to develop a conversation analytic account of the infrastructure of sexual harassment.

Celia Kitzinger and Hannah Frith: conversation analysis and anti-date rape campaigns

Kitzinger and Frith (1999) show how findings from conversation analytic studies of ordinary interaction can have significant implications for feminist practice, specifically training in how to refuse men's sexual advances and campaigns to prevent date rape. They note that such training schemes and campaigns encourage women to 'just say no', clearly and unambiguously, when faced with unwelcome sexual overtures. It is well known, though, that many women report that they feel unable or uncomfortable issuing such an unequivocal rejection. Kitzinger notes that accounts for this reluctance in the relevant literature tend to focus on personality (internalisation of stereotypical female gender traits such as passivity and submissiveness), or the anticipated impact on reputation and standing amongst peers (they might be viewed as sexually cold, inexperienced or lesbian), or an exaggerated concern for the ego and emotional well-being of the male, and so on.

However, Kitzinger and Frith point out that simply saying 'no' is hard for anyone, in any context, at any time. Drawing on conversation analytic studies of the organisation of paired action sequences, they note that some first parts of pairs can be followed by one of two second parts: for example, an invitation can be followed by an acceptance or a refusal. Similarly offers can be accepted or declined. It is noticeable, however, that these kinds of possible second parts are not equivalent in that they are produced in very different ways. That is, refusals have different properties to acceptances. Acceptances tend to be immediate, minimal and direct.

(9.12)   (From Davidson, 1984: 116)

```
A:  We:ll, will you help me ┌ou:t
B:                          └I certainly wi:ll
```

As Kitzinger and Frith point out, 'just saying yes' *is* relatively straightforward. But refusals and suchlike are routinely constructed out of a variety of discursive components: delays, prefaces ('well'), palliatives, such as appreciations and apologies, and accounts, justifications and excuses. For example:

(9.13)   (From Atkinson and Drew, 1979: 58)

```
1  B:  Uh if you'd care to come over and
2      visit a little while this morning
3      I'll give you a cup of coffee
4  A:  hehh Well that's awfully sweet of you,
5      I don't think I can make it this morning
6      ·hh uhm I'm running an ad in the paper and and uh I
7      have to stay near the phone.
```

This means that advice to women just to say no in a minimal and direct manner contradicts the normative requirements of the ways in which refusals are actually managed in everyday interaction. It is no surprise, then, that women report some element of difficulty when trying to follow advice which runs against the grain of their communicative competence.

This has clear implications for the ways in which future date rape and sexual refusal campaigns might be organised. It might be more productive, for example, to offer advice which actually meshes with women's tacit interactional knowledge. But Kitzinger and Frith point out another implication of the conversation analytic research on the organisation of refusals: it should not be *necessary* for women to say 'no' to refuse sex. This is because CA studies have shown that men and women tacitly understand that refusals *should be* accomplished via delays, prefaces, palliatives and accounts. A blunt and unadorned 'no' does not figure in normatively produced refusals. This has important implications for our interpretation of men's claims that they did not understand that their female partners were refusing sex. It would suggest that men are being (at best) disingenuous when they claim that, in the absence of an explicit no, they interpreted women's response to their sexual advances as hinting at or suggesting a possibly receptive attitude. Normatively accomplished refusals do not require an explicit 'no'; and as competent members of the same language community with the same communicative skills, men (tacitly) know this too. Kitzinger and Frith's research thus suggests that 'the root of the problem is not that men do not understand sexual refusals, but that they do not like them' (1999: 310).

Susan Speer: conversation analysis, reflexivity and feminist methodology

Speer's (2002) article addresses a key feature of feminist methodology: the idea that research should be respondent centred, and focused on their perspectives and experiences. This entails that the researcher should be careful not to contaminate or colour the respondent's views with their own understandings, thus ensuring a non-hierarchical relationship with the respondent, and one which better reflects the broader emancipatory goals of feminist research. She notes that many feminist researchers use various kinds of stimulus material as prompts to elicit respondents' views and opinions, such as, video clips, photographs, newspaper clippings, vignettes, group exercises and games. Speer herself used pictures during interviews in which she wished to elicit accounts about gender and sexuality. But in addition to their value of stimulus materials, Speer hoped that the use of pictures would allow her to adhere to the broad feminist recommendation that the researcher should minimise any controlling or directive participation in the collection of interview data. Her experience, however, was that the prompts did not seem to work in the way she had anticipated. For example, interviewees sometimes seemed unsure how to respond to the prompts when they were offered; and while they did eventually succeed in eliciting views about gender and sexuality, this was only after some period of clarification and negotiation between herself and research respondents. Paradoxically then, 'my intentions to remove myself as far as possible from the research process, driven as they were by feminist concerns, were undercut by contextual elements associated with the very business of doing research' (Speer, 2002: 787). Using conversation analysis, Speer was able to examine the participants' orientations as the interview progressed on a turn-by-turn basis; and this helped her understand the interactional basis of those occasions in which her own participation became implicated in the interview, and also in the *construction* of the data she was trying (neutrally) to collect.

Speer is not claiming that prompts in particular or interviews in general are biased forms of data collection. As a discourse analyst, she adopts the broadly constructionist perspective that interviews do not provide the researcher with the opportunity to extract a definitive version of the state of affairs being reported on. Rather, interviews are regarded as useful in that they generate the interviewee's interpretative work, embedded in their accounts, which can then be the subject of analysis (Potter and Mulkay, 1985). But as Speer's analysis shows, it is important to know how that interpretative work is interactionally constituted. Conversation analysis provides the tools to identify the organisation and consequences of these key interactional moments.

Finally, Speer makes some remarks on feminists' concerns with reflexivity: the importance of reflecting on the relationship between the researcher and the researched. She points out that although the feminist research literature emphasises the importance of reflexive considerations, it is rare to find sustained treatments of reflexivity in interactional practices. One reason for this is that feminists have been traditionally concerned with broader political realities which resonate in their data, and have tended not to develop more technical forms of analysis through which reflexivity can be investigated. Here, again, Speer suggests conversation analysis can be used to inform feminists' methodological practices, in that it offers precisely the formal analytic resources by which feminists can gain better understanding of 'the realities of their research', and with which they can 'set about analysing the precise interactional contours of the impact they have upon it' (2002: 798).

Summary

- Stimulated by critiques of essentialist perspectives, in recent years many feminist scholars have begun to explore the extent to which conversation analytic techniques and findings can illuminate the contingent and socially accomplished nature of gender and gendered social interaction.
- Studies in this tradition have examined the interactional basis of sexual harassment; a critique of the rhetoric of date rape campaigns based on findings from CA studies of ordinary interaction; and the application of conversation analytic approaches to debates in feminist research methodology.

A commonly held assumption is that CA's concern to offer formal analyses of the sequential organisation of interaction means that it is unable to contribute to our understanding of the exercise of power and oppression; and that the orderliness discovered in conversation analytic research is irrelevant when set alongside matters of such obvious significance. There are three points that need to be made.

First, and quite simply, researchers working in the conversation analytic tradition *have* tried to utilise its methodology to study the features of power in interpersonal relations. The work of Clark and Pinch on selling, and Hutchby on arguments on talk radio, explicitly address how certain kinds of advantage are embedded in and mobilised through interactional practices. Moreover, some feminist researchers, motivated by a clear emancipatory and political intent, have found conversation analysis to be a useful tool in their attempt to chart the extent and form of inequality and oppression; and to refresh the methodological resources through which they can better understand the experiences of oppression.

Second, the study of power is not normally associated with investigation of micro interactional order; Clark, Pinch and Hutchby are unusual in that, while working in the conversation analytic tradition, they have explicitly tried to make links between their studies of interaction and the concern with power and inequality in traditional social sciences. But conversation analytic studies routinely examine the ways in which we initiate and manage alignments or disagreements, negotiate our way through interpersonal friction and forge interactional advantages; but such empirical findings are usually not framed in terms of the traditional sociological agenda. Perhaps mainstream social sciences need to revisit the cumulative findings from CA studies to see what could be learnt about the ways in which interpersonal power struggles inhabit the very weave of interaction.

Third, a CA-informed approach offers a very different treatment of power from those found in more traditional social science literature: it offers an understanding of power relations built upwards from real events, rather than an account deduced from theoretical arguments.

Mainstream sociological and critical approaches are motivated to seek evidence of disadvantage and operation of power. This, of course, increases the likelihood that data will be interpreted in light of theoretically derived expectations. By contrast, CA offers an account of talk-in-interaction which is constrained by and focused on the participants' actual communicative activities, the finesse with which those activities are produced, and the demonstrable significance of those activities for the participants themselves. Conversation analysis can thus offer an account of the operation of power which captures the complexity and sophistication of actual conduct; and one which resonates with the lived reality of the people whose activities we study.

Appendix
Transcription Symbols

The transcription symbols used here are common to conversation analytic research, and were developed by Gail Jefferson. The following symbols are used in the data.

(0.5)	The number in brackets indicates a time gap in tenths of a second.
(.)	A dot enclosed in a bracket indicates pause in the talk less then two tenths of a second.
˙hh	A dot before an 'h' indicates speaker in-breath. The more 'h's, the longer the in-breath.
hh	An 'h' indicates an out-breath. The more 'h's the longer the breath.
(( ))	A description enclosed in a double bracket indicates a non-verbal activity. For example ((*banging sound*))
-	A dash indicates the sharp cut-off of the prior word or sound.
:::	Colons indicate that the speaker has stretched the preceding sound or letter. The more colons the greater the extent of the stretching.
( )	Empty parentheses/brackets indicate the presence of an unclear fragment on the tape.
(guess)	The words within a single bracket indicate the transcriber's best guess at an unclear fragment.
.	A full stop indicates a stopping fall in tone. It does not necessarily indicate the end of a sentence.
Under	Underlined fragments indicate speaker emphasis.
↑↓	Pointed arrows indicate a marked falling or rising intonational shift. They are placed immediately before the onset of the shift.
CAPITALS	With the exception of proper nouns, capital letters indicate a section of speech noticeably louder than that surrounding it.
° °	Degree signs are used to indicate that the talk they encompass is spoken noticeably quieter than the surrounding talk.
Thaght	A 'gh' indicates that word in which it is placed had a guttural pronunciation.
> <	'More than' and 'less than' signs indicate that the talk they encompass was produced noticeably quicker than the surrounding talk.

cont.

= The 'equals' sign indicates contiguous utterances.
[Square brackets between adjacent lines of concurrent speech
] indicate the onset (and end) of a spate of overlapping talk.

A more detailed description of these transcription symbols can be found in Atkinson and Heritage (1984: ix–xvi).

References

Abell, P. 1983. 'Accounts and those accounts called accounts of actions', in G.N. Gilbert and P. Abell (eds) *Accounts and Action*. Gower: Aldershot, 173–82.

Abell, J. and Stokoe, E.H. 2001. 'Broadcasting the royal role: constructing culturally situated identities in the Princess Diana "Panorama" interview', *British Journal of Social Psychology*, 40: 417–53.

Abrams, D. and Hogg, M.A. 1990. 'The context of discourse: let's not throw the baby out with the bathwater', *Philosophical Psychology*, 3(2): 219–25.

Alcock, J.E. 1981. *Parapsychology: Science or Magic?* Oxford and New York: Pergamon Press.

Alcock, J.E. 1987. 'Parapsychology: science of the anomalous or search for the soul?', *Behavioural and Brain Sciences*, 10(4): 553–65.

Antaki, C. (ed.) 1988. *Analysing Everyday Explanation: A Casebook of Methods*. London: Sage.

Antaki, C. and Widdicombe, S. (eds) 1998. *Identities in Talk*. London: Sage.

Antaki, C., Condor, S. and Levine, M. 1996. Social identities in talk: speakers' own orientations', *British Journal of Social Psychology*, 35: 473–92.

Ashmore, M. 1989. *The Reflexive Thesis*. Chicago, IL: University of Chicago Press.

Ashmore, M., Mulkay, M. and Pinch, T. 1989. *Health and Efficiency: A Sociology of Health Economics*. Milton Keynes: Open University Press.

Atkinson, J.M. 1978. *Discovering Suicide: Studies in the Social Organization of Sudden Death*. London: Macmillan.

Atkinson, J.M. 1984a. *Our Master's Voices: The Language and Body Language of Politics*. London: Methuen.

Atkinson, J.M. 1984b. 'Public speaking and audience responses: some techniques for inviting applause', in J.M. Atkinson and J. Heritage (eds) *Structures of Social Action: Studies in Conversation Analysis*. Cambridge: Cambridge University Press, 370–409.

Atkinson, J.M. and Drew, P. 1979. *Order in Court: The Organisation of Verbal Interaction in Judicial Settings*. London: Macmillan.

Atkinson, J.M. and Heritage, J. (eds) 1984. *Structures of Social Action: Studies in Conversation Analysis*. Cambridge: Cambridge University Press.

Auburn, T. and Lea, S. 2003. 'Doing cognitive distortions: discursive psychology analysis of sex offender treatment talk', *British Journal of Social Psychology*, 42: 281–98.

Auburn, T., Lea, S. and Drake, S. 1999. '"It's your opportunity to be truthful": disbelief, mundane reasoning and the investigation of crime', in C. Willig (ed.) *Applied Discourse Analysis: Social and Psychological Interventions*. Buckingham: Open University Press, 44–65.

Austin, J.L. 1962. *How To Do Things With Words*. Oxford: Oxford University Press.

Baker, C.D. 1997. 'Membership categorization and interview accounts', in D. Silverman (ed.) *Qualitative Research: Theory, Method and Practice*. London: Sage, 130–43.

Banister, P., Burman, E., Parker, I., Taylor, M. and Tindall, C. 1994. *Qualitative Methods in Psychology*. Buckinghm: Open University Press.

Barclay, C.R. and DeCooke, P.A. 1988. 'Ordinary everyday memories: some of the things of which selves are made', in U. Neisser and E. Winograd (eds) *Remembering Reconsidered: Ecological and Traditional Approaches to the Study of Memory*. Cambridge and New York: Cambridge University Press, 91–125.

Barthes, R. 1972. *Mythologies*. London: Paladin.

Beattie, G. 1983. *Talk: An Analysis of Speech and Non-Verbal Behaviour in Conversation*. Milton Keynes: Open University Press.

Bell, B.E. and Loftus, E.F. 1989. 'Trivial persuasion in the courtroom: the power of (a few) minor details', *Journal of Personality and Social Psychology*, 56: 669–79.

Berger, P.L. and Luckmann, T. 1966. *The Social Construction of Reality: A Treatise in the Sociology of Knowledge*. Garden City, NY: Doubleday.

Billig, M. 1985. 'Prejudice, categorisation and particularisation: from a perceptual to a rhetorical approach', *European Journal of Social Psychology*, 15: 79–103.

Billig, M. 1987. *Arguing and Thinking: A Rhetorical Approach to Social Psychology*. Cambridge: Cambridge University Press.

Billig, M. 1988. 'Methodology and scholarship in understanding ideological explanation', in C. Antaki (ed.) *Analysing Everyday Explanation: A Casebook of Methods*. London: Sage, 199–215.

Billig, M. 1990. 'Stacking the cards of ideology: the history of the *Sun Souvenir Royal Album*', *Discourse and Society*, 1(1): 17–38.

Billig, M. 1991. *Ideology and Opinions*. London: Sage.

Billig, M. 1992. *Talking of the Royal Family*. London: Routledge.

Billig, M. 1997. 'Rhetorical and discursive analysis: how families talk about the Royal family', in N. Hayes (ed.) *Doing Qualitative Analysis in Psychology*. Hove: Psychology Press, 39–54.

Billig, M. 1999a. 'Whose terms? Whose ordinariness? Rhetoric and ideology in conversation analysis', *Discourse and Society*, 10(4): 543–58.

Billig, M. 1999b. 'Conversation analysis and claims of naivety', *Discourse and Society*, 10(4): 572–6.

Billig, M. 1999c. *Freudian Repression: Conversation Creating the Unconscious*. Cambridge: Cambridge University Press.

Billig, M. 2001a. 'Humour and hatred: the racist jokes of the Ku Klux Klan', *Discourse and Society*, 12: 291–313.

Billig, M. 2001b. 'Discursive, rhetorical and ideological messages', in M. Wetherell, S. Taylor and S.J. Yates (eds) *Discourse Theory and Practice: A Reader*. London and Thousand Oaks, CA: Sage, in association with the Open University, 210–21. (Originally published in C. McGarty and A. Haslam (eds) 1997, *The Message of Social Psychology*. Oxford: Blackwell.)

Billig, M., Condor, S., Edwards, D., Gane, M., Middleton, D. and Radley, A. 1988. *Ideological Dilemmas: A Social Psychology of Everyday Thinking*. London and Thousand Oaks, CA: Sage.

Blisset, M. 1972. *Politics in Science*. Boston: Little, Brown and Co.

Boden, D. and Zimmerman, D.H. (eds) 1991. *Talk and Social Structure: Studies in Ethnomethodology and Conversation Analysis*. Cambridge: Polity Press.

Bostrom, R. and Donohew, L. 1992. 'The case for empiricism: clarifying fundamental issues in communication theory', *Communication Monographs*, 59: 109–28.

Broughton, R. 1991. *Parapsychology: The Controversial Science*. London and Sydney: Rider.

Brown, G. and Yule, G. 1983. *Discourse Analysis*. Cambridge: Cambridge University Press.

Brown, R. 1986. *Social Psychology* (2nd edition). New York: Free Press.

Brown, R. and Kulik, J. 1977. 'Flashbulb memories', *Cognition*, 5: 73–99.

Burman, E. 1995. '"What is it?" Masculinity and femininity in cultural representations of childhood', in S. Wilkinson and C. Kitzinger (eds) *Feminism and Discourse: Psychological Perspective*. London and Thousand Oaks, CA: Sage, 49–67.

Burman, E. 1996. 'Psychology discourse practice: from regulation to resistance', in E. Burman, G. Aitken, P. Aldred, R. Allwood, T. Billington, B. Goldberg, A. Gordo-Lopez, C. Heenan, D. Marks and S. Warner, *Psychology Discourse Practice: From Regulation to Resistance*. London: Taylor & Francis, 1–14.

Burman, E. and Parker, I. (eds) 1993a. *Discourse Analytic Research: Repertoires and Readings of Texts in Action*. London: Routledge.

Burman, E. and Parker, I. 1993b. 'Introduction – discourse analysis: the turn to the text', in E. Burman and I. Parker (eds) *Discourse Analytic Research: Repertoires and Readings of Texts in Action*. London: Routledge, 1–13.

Burman, E., Aitken, G., Aldred, P., Allwood, R., Billington, T., Goldberg, B., Gordo-Lopez, A., Heenan, C., Marks, D. and Warner, S. 1996. *Psychology Discourse Practice: From Regulation to Resistance*. London: Taylor & Francis.

Burningham, K.A. and Cooper, G. 1998. 'Misconstructing constructionism', in A. Gijswijt, F. Buttel, P. Dickens, R. Dunlap, A. Mul and G. Spaargaren (eds) *Social Theory and the Environment*. Amsterdam: SISWO, University of Amsterdam, 19–31.

Burr, V. 1995. *An Introduction to Social Constructionism*. London and New York: Routledge.

Butler, J. 1990. 'Performative acts and gender constitution: an essay in phenomenology and feminist theory', in S.-E. Case (ed.) *Performing Feminisms: Feminist Critical Theory and Theatre*. Baltimore, MD: The Johns Hopkins University Press, 270–82.

Button, G. 1987. 'Moving out of closings', in G. Button and J.R.E. Lee (eds) *Talk and Social Organisation*. Clevedon: Multilingual Matters, 101–51.

Button, G. and Lee, J.R.E. (eds) 1987. *Talk and Social Organisation*. Clevedon and Philadelphia: Multilingual Matters.

Button, G., Drew, P. and Heritage, J. (eds) 1986. *Human Studies*, 9 nos. 2–3. (Special Edition on Interaction and Language Use.)

Cameron, D. (ed.) 1990. *The Feminist Critique of Language*. London: Routledge.

Cameron, D., Frazer, E., Harvey, P., Rampton, M.B.H. and Richardson, K. 1992. *Researching Language: Issues of Power and Method*. London: Routledge.

Chomsky, N. 1965. *Aspects of the Theory of Syntax*. Cambridge, MA: MIT Press.

Clark, C. and Pinch, T. 1986. 'Getting an edge: how market pitchers manufacture an audience of consumers', presented to the conference 'Erving Goffman: An Inter-disciplinary Appreciation', York University, UK, 8–11 July.

Clark, C. and Pinch, T. 1988. 'Micro-sociology and micro-economics', in N. Fielding (ed.) *Actions and Structure: Research Methods and Social Theory*. London: Sage, 117–41.

Clayman, S.E. and Maynard, D.W. 1995. 'Ethnomethodology and conversation analysis', in P. ten Have and G. Psathas (eds) *Situated Order: Studies in the Social Organization of Talk and Embodied Activities*. Washington, DC: University Press of America, 1–30.

Clayman, S.E. and Whalen, J. 1988/9. 'When the medium becomes the message: the case of the Rather–Bush encounter', *Research on Language and Social Interaction*, 22: 241–72.

Collins, H.M. 1992. *Changing Order: Replication and Induction in Scientific Practice*. (2nd edition.) Chicago and London: University of Chicago Press.

Collins, H.M. and Pinch, T.J. 1982. *Frames of Meaning: The Social Construction of Extraordinary Science*. London: Routledge and Kegan Paul.

Collins, Shorter English Dictionary. 1993. Glasgow: HarperCollins.

Condor, S. and Antaki, C. 1997. 'Social cognition and discourse', in T.A. van Dijk (ed.) *Discourse as Structure and Process*. London: Sage, 320–47.

Conway, M. (ed.) 1992. 'Developments and debates in the study of human memory', Special Issue of *The Psychologist*, 5: 439–55.

Conway, M. 1995. *Flashbulb Memories*. Hove: Lawrence Erlbaum Associates.

Coulter, J. 1979. *The Social Construction of Mind: Studies in Ethnomethodology and Linguistic Philosophy*. London: Macmillan.

Coulter, J. 1989. *Mind in Action*. Oxford: Polity.

Coulter, J. 1999. 'Discourse and mind', *Human Studies*, 22: 165–81.

Coulthard, M. 1977. *An Introduction to Discourse Analysis*. London: Longman.

Coulthard, M. and Montgomery, M. (eds) 1981. *Studies in Discourse Analysis*. London: Routledge and Kegan Paul.

Coyle, A. 2000. 'Discourse analysis', in G.M. Breakwell, S. Hammond and C. Fife-Schaw (eds) *Research Methods in Psychology* (2nd edition). London: Sage.

Crane, D. 1972. *Invisible Colleges*. Chicago, IL: University of Chicago Press.

Davidson, J. 1984. 'Subsequent versions of invitations, offers, requests, and proposals dealing with potential or actual rejection', in J.M. Atkinson and J. Heritage (eds) *Structures of Social Action: Studies in Conversation Analysis*. Cambridge: Cambridge University Press, 102–28.

Davis, B. and Harré, R. 1990. 'Positioning: The discursive production of selves', *Journal for the Theory of Social Behaviour*, 20: 43–63.

Dersley, I. and Wootton, A.J. 2000. 'Complaint sequences within an antagonistic argument', *Research on Language and Social Interaction*, 33(4): 375–406.

Dersley, I. and Wootton, A.J. 2001. 'In the heat of the sequence: interactional features preceding walkouts from argumentative talk', *Language in Society*, 30(4): 611–38.

Drew, P. 1984. '"Speakers" reportings in invitation sequences', in J.M. Atkinson and J. Heritage (eds) *Structures of Social Action: Studies in Conversation Analysis*. Cambridge: Cambridge University Press, 129–51.

Drew, P. 1987. 'Po-faced receipts of teases', *Linguistics*, 25(1): 219–53.

Drew, P. 1989. 'Recalling someone from the past', in D. Roger and P. Bull (eds) *Conversation: An Interdisciplinary Perspective*. Clevedon and Philadelphia: Multilingual Matters, 96–115.

Drew, P. 1994. 'Conversation analysis', *The Encyclopaedia of Language and Linguistics, Two volumes*. Pergamon Press and Aberdeen University Press, 2: 749–54.

Drew, P. 2005. 'Is confusion a state of mind?', in H. te Molder and J. Potter (eds) *Talk and Cognition: Discourse, Mind and Social Interaction*. Cambridge: Cambridge University Press, 161–83.

Drew, P. and Heritage, J. 1992a. *Talk At Work: Interaction in Institutional Settings*. Cambridge: Cambridge University Press.

Drew, P. and Heritage, J. 1992b. 'Analyzing talk at work: an introduction', in P. Drew and J. Heritage (eds) *Talk At Work: Interaction in Institutional Settings*. Cambridge: Cambridge University Press, 3–65.

Drew, P. and Holt, E. 1988. 'Complainable matters: the use of idiomatic expressions in making complaints', *Social Problems*, 35: 398–417.

Drew, P. and Holt, E. 1998. 'Figures of speech: idiomatic expressions and the management of topic transition in conversation', *Language and Society*, 27(4): 495–522.

Drew, P. and Sorjonen, M.-L. 1997. 'Institutional dialogue', in T.A. van Dijk (ed.) *Discourse as Social Interaction*. London and Thousand Oaks, CA: Sage, 92–118.

Dreyfus, H.L. and Rabinow, P. 1982. *Michel Foucault: Beyond Structuralism and Hermeneutics*. London: Harvester Wheatsheaf.

Duranti, A. and Goodwin, C. (eds) 1992. *Rethinking Context: Language as an Interactive Phenomenon*. Cambridge: Cambridge University Press.

Edge, H.L., Morris, R.L., Palmer, J. and Rush, J.H. 1986. *Foundations of Parapsychology: Exploring the Boundaries of Human Capability*. Boston: Routledge and Kegan Paul.

Edley, N. 2001. 'Analysing masculinity: interpretative repertoires, ideological dilemmas and subject positions', in M. Wetherell, S. Taylor and S. Yates (eds) *Discourse as Data: A Guide for Analysis*. London: Sage, in association with the Open University, 189–228.

Edley, N. and Wetherell, M. 1997. 'Jockeying for position: the construction of masculine identities', *Discourse and Society*, 8: 203–17.

Edley, N. and Wetherell, M. 1999. 'Imagined futures: young men's talk about fatherhood and domestic life', *British Journal of Social Psychology*, 38: 181–94.

Edwards, D. 1991. 'Categories are for talking: on the cognitive and discursive bases of categorisation', *Theory and Psychology*, 1(4): 515–42.

Edwards, D. 1994. 'Script formulations: a study of event descriptions in conversation', *Journal of Language and Social Psychology*, 13(3): 211–47.

Edwards, D. 1995a. 'Two to tango: script formulations, dispositions and rhetorical symmetry in relationship troubles talk', *Research on Language and Social Interaction*, 28(4): 319–50.

Edwards, D. 1995b. 'Sacks and psychology: an essay review of Harvey Sacks', *Lectures on Conversation*', *Theory and Psychology*, 5(4): 579–96.

Edwards, D. 1997. *Discourse and Cognition*. London: Sage.

Edwards, D. 1999. 'Emotion discourse', *Culture and Psychology*, 5(3): 271–91.

Edwards, D. 2000. 'Extreme case formulations: softeners, investment and doing nonliteral', *Research on Language and Social Interaction*, 33(4): 347–73.

Edwards, D. and Middleton, D. 1986. 'Joint remembering: constructing an account of shared experience through conversational discourse', *Discourse Processes*, 9: 423–59.

Edwards, D. and Middleton, D. 1987. 'Conversation and remembering: Bartlett revisited', *Applied Cognitive Psychology*, 1: 77–92.

Edwards, D. and Middleton, D. 1988. 'Conversational remembering and family relationships: how children learn to remember', *Journal of Social and Personal Relationships*, 5: 3–25.

Edwards, D. and Potter, J. 1992. *Discursive Psychology*. London and Thousand Oaks, CA: Sage.

Edwards, D. and Potter, J. 1995. 'Attribution', in R. Harré and P. Stearns (eds) *Discursive Psychology in Practice*. London and Thousand Oaks, CA: Sage, 87–119.

Fairclough, N. 1989. *Language and Power*. Harlow: Longman.

Fairclough, N. 1992. *Discourse and Social Change*. Cambridge: Polity Press.

Fairclough, N. 1995. *Critical Discourse Analysis: The Critical Study of Language*. Harlow: Longman.

Fairclough, N. and Wodak, R. 1997. 'Critical discourse analysis', in T. van Dijk (ed.) *Discourse Studies: A Multidisciplinary Introduction*. Volume 2. London: Sage, 258–84.

Fenstermaker, S. and West, C. (eds) 2002. *Doing Gender, Doing Difference: Inequality, Power and Institutional Change*. New York: Routledge.

Fishman, P. 1983. 'Interaction: the work women do', in B. Thorne, C. Kramarae and N. Henley (eds) *Language, Gender and Society*. Rowley, MA: Newbury, 89–101.

Foucault, M. 1970. *The Order of Things: An Archaeology of the Human Sciences*. London: Tavistock.

Foucault, M. 1977. *Power/Knowledge*. Hemel Hempstead: Harvester.

Garfinkel, H. 1967. *Studies in Ethnomethodology*. Englewood Cliffs, NJ: Prentice Hall.

Gavey, N. 1989. 'Feminist post-structuralism and discourse analysis: contributions to feminist psychology', *Psychology of Women's Quarterly*, 13: 459–75.

Gellner, E. 1975. 'Ethnomethodology: the re-enchantment industry or the Californian way of subjectivity', *Philosophy of the Social Sciences*, 5: 431–50.

Gilbert, G.N. 1993. *Analysing Tabular Data: Loglinear and Logistic Models for Social Researchers*. London: UCL Press.

Gilbert, G.N. 1994. *Simulating Societies: The Computer Simulation of Social Phenomena*. London: UCL Press.

Gilbert, G.N. and Abell, P. (eds) 1983. *Accounts and Action*. Aldershot: Gower.

Gilbert, G.N. and Mulkay, M.J. 1984. *Opening Pandora's Box: A Sociological Analysis of Scientists' Discourse*. Cambridge: Cambridge University Press.

Gill, R. 1996. 'Discourse analysis: practical implementation', in J.T.E. Richardson (ed.) *Handbook of Qualitative Research Methods for Psychology and the Social Sciences*. Hove: The British Psychological Society, 141–56.

Glaser, B.G. and Strauss, A.L. 1967. *The Discovery of Grounded Theory: Strategies for Qualitative Research*. Chicago, IL: Aldine.

Goffman, E. 1959. *The Presentation of Self in Everyday Life*. New York: Doubleday.

Goffman, E. 1981. 'Footing', in E. Goffman (ed.) *Forms of Talk*. Oxford: Blackwell, 124–59.

Goodwin, C. 1987. 'Forgetfulness as an interactive resource', *Social Psychology Quarterly*, 50: 115–30.

Gurney, E., Myers, F.W.H. and Podmore, F. 1886. *Phantasms of the Living*. London: Trubner (two volumes).

Hagstrom, W. 1965. *The Scientific Community*. New York: Basic Books.

Halfpenny, P. 1988. 'Talking of talking, writing of writing: some reflections on Gilbert and Mulkay's discourse analysis', *Social Studies of Science*, 18: 169–82.

Halliday, M.A.K. 1978. *Language as Social Semiotic*. London: Edward Arnold.

Hammersley, M. 2003a. 'Conversation analysis and discourse analysis: methods or paradigms?', *Discourse and Society*, 14(6): 751–81.

Hammersley, M. 2003b. 'Doing the fine thing: a rejoinder to Jonathan Potter', *Discourse and Society*, 14(6): 795–8.

Hammersley, M. 2003c. 'The impracticality of scepticism: a further response to Potter', *Discourse and Society*, 14(6): 803–4.

Hanlon, J. 1974. 'Uri Geller and Science', *New Scientist*, 17 October: 170–85.

Harré, R. 1979. *Social Being: A Theory for Social Psychology*. Oxford: Basil Blackwell.

Harré, R. 1987. 'Enlarging the paradigm', *New Ideas in Psychology*, 5: 3–12.

Harré, R. 1989. 'Language games and texts of identity', in J. Shotter and K.J. Gergen (eds) *Texts of Identity*. London: Sage, 20–35.

Harré, R. 1995. 'Agentive discourse', in R. Harré and P. Stearns (eds) *Discursive Psychology in Practice*. London and Thousand Oaks, CA: Sage, 120–36.

Harré, R. 1997. 'An outline of the main methods for social psychology', in N. Hayes (ed.) *Doing Qualitative Analysis in Psychology*. Hove: Psychology Press, 17–37.

Hayes, N. (ed.) 1997. *Doing Qualitative Analysis in Psychology*. Hove: Psychology Press.

Hayes, N. 2000. *Foundations of Psychology* (3rd edition). London: Thomson Learning.

Heath, C. 1992. 'The delivery and reception of diagnosis in general-practice consultation', in P. Drew and J. Heritage (eds) *Talk At Work: Interaction in Institutional Settings*. Cambridge: Cambridge University Press: 235–67.

Hepburn, A. 1997. 'Teachers and secondary school bullying: a postmodern discourse analysis', *Discourse and Society*, 8: 27–48.

Hepburn, A. 2003. *An Introduction to Critical Social Psychology*. London and Thousand Oaks, CA: Sage.

Hepworth, J. and Griffin, C. 1995. 'Conflicting opinions? "Anorexia Nervosa", medicine and feminism', in S. Wilkinson and C. Kitzinger (eds) *Feminism and Discourse: Psychological Perspectives*. London and Thousand Oaks, CA: Sage, 68–85.

Heritage, J. 1978. 'Aspects of the flexibilities of language use', *Sociology*, 12(1): 79–104.

Heritage, J. 1984a. *Garfinkel and Ethnomethodology*. Cambridge: Polity Press.

Heritage, J. 1984b. 'A change of state token and aspects of its sequential placement', in J.M. Atkinson and J. Heritage (eds) *Structures of Social Action: Studies in Conversation Analysis*. Cambridge: Cambridge University Press, 299–345.

Heritage, J. 1997. 'Conversation analysis and institutional talk: analysing data', in D. Silverman (ed.) *Qualitative Research: Theory, Method and Practice*. London and Thousand Oaks, CA: Sage.

Heritage, J. 2001. 'Goffman, Garfinkel and conversation analysis', in M. Wetherell, S. Taylor and S. Yates (eds) *Discourse Theory and Practice*. London: Sage, in association with the Open University, 47–56.

Heritage, J. 2005. 'Meaning, intention and strategy: resources and constraints on the interpretation of talk-in-interaction', in H. te Molder and J. Potter (eds) *Talk and*

Cognition: Discourse, Mind and Social Interaction. Cambridge: Cambridge University Press, 184–202.

Heritage, J. and Atkinson, J.M. 1984. 'Introduction', in J.M. Atkinson and J. Heritage (eds) *Structures of Social Action: Studies in Conversation Analysis.* Cambridge: Cambridge University Press, 1–15.

Heritage, J. and Greatbatch, D. 1986. 'Generating applause: a study of rhetoric and response at party political conferences', *American Journal of Sociology,* 92(1): 110–57.

Heritage, J. and Greatbatch, D. 1991. 'On the institutional character of institutional talk: the case of news interviews', in D. Boden and D.H. Zimmerman (eds) *Talk and Social Structure: Studies in Ethnomethodology and Conversation Analysis.* Berkeley, CA: University of California Press, 93–137.

Heritage, J. and Watson, D.R. 1979. 'Formulations as conversational objects', in G. Psathas (ed.) *Everyday Language: Studies in Ethnomethodology.* New York: Irvington, 123–62.

Hollway, W. 1984. 'Gender difference and the production of subjectivity', in J. Henriques, W. Hollway, C. Urwin, C. Venn and V. Walkerdine, *Changing the Subject: Psychology, Social Relations and Subjectivity.* London: Methuen.

Hollway, W. 1989. *Subjectivity and Method in Psychology: Gender, Meaning and Science.* London: Sage.

Hollway, W. 1995. 'Feminist discourses and women's heterosexual desire', in S. Wilkinson and C. Kitzinger (eds) *Feminism and Discourse: Psychological Perspectives.* London and Thousand Oaks: Sage, 86–105.

Holmes, J. 1995. *Women, Men and Politeness.* London and New York: Longman.

Holt, E. 1996. 'Reporting on talk: the use of direct reported speech in conversation', *Research on Language and Social Interaction,* 29(3): 219–45.

Honorton, C. 1993. 'Rhetoric over substance: the impoverished state of scepticism', *Journal of Parapsychology,* 57: 191–214.

Hopper, R. and LeBaron, C. 1998. 'How gender creeps into talk', *Research on Language and Social Interaction,* 31: 59–74.

Horton-Salway, M. 2001. 'The construction of M.E.: the discursive action model', in M. Wetherell, S. Taylor and S. Yates (eds) *Discourse as Data: A Guide for Analysis.* London: Sage, in association with the Open University, 147–88.

Hutchby, I. 1992. 'The pursuit of controversy: routine skepticism in talk on talk radio', *Sociology,* 26: 673–94.

Hutchby, I. 1996a. *Confrontation Talk: Arguments, Asymmetries and Power on Talk Radio.* Malwah, NJ: Lawrence Erlbaum.

Hutchby, I. 1996b. 'Power in discourse: the case of arguments on a British talk radio show', *Discourse and Society,* 7: 481–97.

Hutchby, I. 1999. 'Beyond agnosticism? Conversation analysis and the sociological agenda', *Research on Language and Social Interaction,* 23(1&2): 85–93.

Hutchby, I. and Wooffitt, R. 1998. *Conversation Analysis: Principles, Practices and Applications.* Oxford: Polity Press.

Irwin, H.J. 1999. *An Introduction to Parapsychology* (3rd edition). Jefferson, NC, and London: McFarland.

James, D. and Clarke, S. 1993. 'Women, men and interruptions: a critical review', in D. Tannen (ed.) *Gender and Conversational Interaction.* New York: Oxford University Press.

Jaworski, A. and Coupland, N. 1999. *The Discourse Reader.* London and New York: Routledge.

Jayyusi, L. 1991. 'The equivocal text and the objective world: an ethnomethodological analysis of a news report', *Continuum: The Australian Journal of Media & Culture,* 5 (1).

Jefferson, G. 1983. 'Notes on some orderliness of overlap onset', *Tilburg Papers in Language and Literature No. 28*. Department of Linguistics, Tilburg University.

Jefferson, G. 1984a. 'Notes on the systematic deployment of the acknowledgement tokens "yeah" and "hm mm"', *Papers in Linguistics*, 1(7): 197–206.

Jefferson, G. 1984b. '"At first I thought": a normalizing device for extraordinary events', unpublished manuscript, Katholieke Hogeschool Tilburg.

Jefferson, G. 1986. 'Notes on "latency" in overlap', *Human Studies*, 9: 153–83.

Jefferson, G. 1987. 'On exposed and embedded correction in conversation', in G. Button and J.R.E. Lee (eds) *Talk and Social Organisation*. Clevedon: Multilingual Matters, 86–100.

Jefferson, G. 1990. 'List construction as a task and resource', in G. Psathas (ed.) *Interaction Competence*. Washington, DC: University Press of America, 63–92.

Jefferson, G., Sacks, H. and Schegloff, E.A. 1987. 'Notes on laughter in pursuit of intimacy', in G. Button and J.R.E. Lee (eds) *Talk and Social Organisation*. Clevedon and Philadelphia: Multilingual Matters, 152–205.

Jodelet, D. 1991. *Madness and Social Representations*. London. Harvester Wheatsheaf.

Kelly, H.H. 1967. 'Attribution theory in social psychology', in D. Levine (ed.) *Nebraska Symposium on Motivation*. Lincoln, NE: University of Nebraska Press, 15: 192–238.

Kitzinger, C. 1987. *The Social Construction of Lesbianism*. London: Sage.

Kitzinger, C. 2000a. 'How to resist an idiom', *Research on Language and Social Interaction*, 33(2): 121–54.

Kitzinger, C. 2000b. 'Doing feminist conversation analysis', *Feminism and Psychology*, 10(2): 163–93.

Kitzinger, C. and Frith, H. 1999. '"Just say no?" The use of conversation analysis in developing a feminist perspective on sexual refusal', *Discourse and Society*, 10: 293–316.

Kramarae, C. 1981. *Women and Men Speaking*. Rowley, MA: Newbury.

Kuhn, T.S. 1970. *The Structure of Scientific Revolutions* (2nd edition). Chicago, IL: University of Chicago Press.

Kurtz, P. (ed.) 1985. *A Skeptic's Handbook of Parapsychology*. New York: Prometheus Books.

Laclau, E. and Mouffe, C. 1987. 'Post Marxism without apologies', *New Left Review*, 166: 79–106.

Lakoff, R. 1975. *Language and Woman's Place*. New York: HarperColophon.

Lawes, R. 1999. 'Marriage: an analysis of discourse', *British Journal of Social Psychology*, 38: 1–20.

Levinson, S. 1983. *Pragmatics*. Cambridge: Cambridge University Press.

Li, C.N. 1986. 'Direct and indirect speech: a functional study', in F. Coulmas (ed.) *Direct and Indirect Speech*. Berlin: Mouton de Gruyer, 29–46.

Locke, A. and Edwards, D. 2003. 'Bill and Monica: memory, emotion and normativity in Clinton's Grand Jury testimony', *British Journal of Social Psychology*, 42: 239–56.

Luff, P., Gilbert, G.N. and Frohlich, D. (eds) 1990. *Computers and Conversation*. London: Academic Press.

Lynch, M. and Bogen, D. 1996. *The Spectacle of History: Speech, Text and Memory at the Iran-Contra Hearings*. Durham, NC, and London: Duke University Press.

Lynch, M. and Bogen, D. 1994. 'Harvey Sacks' primitive science', *Theory, Culture and Society*, 11: 65–104.

McCloskey, M., Wible, C.G. and Cohen, N.J. 1988. 'Is there a special flashbulb memory mechanism?', *Journal of Experimental Psychology: General*, 117: 171–81.

McGuiniss, F. 1983. *Fatal Vision*. New York: McGraw-Hill.

McHoul, A. and Rapley, M. (eds) 2001. *How to Analyse Talk in Institutional Settings: A Casebook of Methods*. London and New York: Continuum.

McIlvenny, P. 2002. 'Researching talk, gender and sexuality', in P. McIlvenny (ed.) *Talking Gender and Sexuality*. Amsterdam and Philadelphia: John Benjamins, 1–48.

Manning, P. 1992. *Erving Goffman and Modern Sociology*. Cambridge: Polity Press.

Marin, L. 1983. 'Discourse of power – power of discourse: Pascalian notes', in A. Montefiore (ed.) *Philosophy in France Today*. Cambridge: Cambridge University Press.

Marks, D. 1993. 'Case-conference analysis and action research', in E. Burman and I. Parker (eds) *Discourse Analytic Research: Repertoires and Readings of Texts in Action*. London: Routledge, 135–54.

Marsh, P., Rosser, E. and Harré, R. 1978. *The Rules of Disorder*. London: Routledge and Kegan Paul.

Mauskopf, S.H. and McVaugh, M.R. 1980. *The Elusive Science: The Origins of Experimental Psychical Research*. Baltimore, MD and London: Johns Hopkins University Press.

Mayes, P. 1990. 'Quotation in Spoken English', *Studies in Language*, 14(2): 325–63.

Merton, R.K. 1973. *Sociology of Science: Theoretical and Empirical Investigations*. Chicago, IL: University of Chicago Press.

Meyer, M. 2001. 'Between theory, method, and politics: positioning of the approaches to CDA', in R. Wodak and M. Meyer (eds) *Methods of Critical Discourse Analysis*. London and Thousand Oaks, CA: Sage, 14–31.

Middleton, D. and Edwards, D. 1990. 'Introduction', in D. Middleton and D. Edwards (eds) *Collective Remembering*. London: Sage, 1–22.

Molotch, H.L. and Boden, D. 1985. 'Talking social structure: discourse domination and the Watergate hearings', *American Sociological Review*, 50: 273–88.

Mouffe, C. 1992. 'Feminism, citizenship and radical democratic politics', in J. Butler and J.W. Scott (eds) *Feminists Theorize the Political*. New York: Routledge, 369–85.

Mulkay, M.J. 1985. *The Word and World: Explorations in the Form of Sociological Analysis*. London: George Allen and Unwin.

Mulkay, M.J. 1991. *Sociology of Science: A Sociological Pilgrimage*. Milton Keynes and Philadelphia: Open University Press.

Mulkay, M. and Gilbert, G.N. 1982a. 'Joking apart: some recommendations concerning the analysis of scientific culture', *Social Studies of Science*, 12: 585–615.

Mulkay, M. and Gilbert, G.N. 1982b. 'Accounting for error: how scientists construct their social world when they account for error and incorrect belief', *Sociology*, 16: 165–83.

Mulkay, M. and Gilbert, G.N. 1983. 'Scientists' theory talk', *Canadian Journal of Sociology*, 8: 179–97.

Mulkay, M.J., Potter, J. and Yearley, S. 1982. 'Why an analysis of scientific discourse is needed', in K.D. Knorr-Cetina and M.J. Mulkay (eds) *Science Observed: Perspectives on the Social Study of Science*. London and Beverly Hills, CA: Sage, 171–203.

Neisser, U. 1981. 'John Dean's memory: a case study', *Cognition*, 9: 1–22.

Neisser, U. 1982. 'Snapshots or benchmarks?', in U. Neisser (ed.) *Memory Observed: Remembering in Natural Contexts*. San Francisco, CA: Freeman, 43–8.

Neisser, U. and Fivush, R. (eds) 1994. *The Remembering Self*. Cambridge and New York: Cambridge University Press.

Neisser, U. and Harsch, N. 1992. 'Phantom flashbulbs: false recollections of hearing the news about the Challenger', in E. Winograd and U. Neisser (eds) *Affect And Accuracy in Recall: Studies of 'Flashbulb Memories'*. Cambridge: Cambridge University Press, 9–31.

Neisser, U. and Winograd, E. (eds) 1988. *Remembering Reconsidered: Ecological and Traditional Approaches to the Study of Memory*. Cambridge and New York: Cambridge University Press.

Neisser, U., Bergman, E., Schreiber, C.A., Palmer, S.E. and Weldon, M.S. 1996. 'Remembering the earthquake', *Memory*, 4: 337–57.

Nelson, J.S., Megill, A. and McCloskey, B. 1987. *The Rhetoric of the Human Sciences*. Madison, WI: University of Wisconsin Press.

Nikander, P. 2002. *Age in Action: Membership Work and Stages of Life Categories in Talk*. Helsinki: Academia Scientiarum Fennica.

Palmer, D. 1997. *The Methods of Madness: Recognizing Delusional Talk*. Unpublished DPhil thesis, University of York.

Palmer, D. 2000. 'Identifying delusional discourse: issues of rationality, reality and power', *Sociology of Health and Illness*, 22(5): 661–78.

Parker, I. 1988. 'Deconstructing accounts', in C. Antaki (ed.) *Analysing Everyday Explanation: A Casebook of Methods*. London: Sage, 184–98.

Parker, I. 1989. *The Crisis in Modern Social Psychology – And How To End It*. London and New York: Routledge.

Parker, I. 1990. 'Discourse: definitions and contradictions', *Philosophical Psychology*, 3(2): 189–204.

Parker, I. 1992. *Discourse Dynamics: Critical Analysis for Social and Individual Psychology*. London: Routledge.

Parker, I. 1994. 'Discourse analysis', in P. Banister, E. Burman, I. Parker, M. Taylor and C. Tindall, *Qualitative Methods in Psychology*. Buckingham: Open University Press, 92–107.

Parker, I. 1997. 'Discursive psychology', in D. Fox and I. Prilleltensky (eds) *Critical Psychology: An Introduction*. London: Sage, 284–98.

Parker, I. 2001. Review of Billig's *Freudian Repression: Conversation Creating the Unconscious*, *Journal of Community and Applied Social Psychology*, 11(1): 69–73.

Pekala, R.J. and Cardena, E. 2000. 'Methodological issues in the study of altered states of consciousness and anomalous experiences', in E. Cardena, S.J. Lynn and S. Krippner (eds) *Varieties of Anomalous Experience: Examining the Scientific Evidence*. Washington, DC: American Psychological Association, 47–82.

Perelman, C. and Olbrechts-Tyteca, 1969. *The New Rhetoric: A Treatise on Argumentation*. Tr. J. Wilkinson and P. Weaver. Notre Dame, IL: University of Notre Dame Press.

Phillips, L. and Jørgensen, M.W. 2002. *Discourse Analysis As Theory and Method*. London and Thousand Oaks, CA: Sage.

Phillips, S.U. 1986. 'Reported speech as evidence in an American trial', in D. Tannen and J.E. Alatis (eds) *Languages and Linguistics: The Interdependence of Theory, Data and Application. Georgetown University Round Table on Languages and Linguistics 1985*. Washington, DC: Georgetown University Press, 154–70.

Pillemer, D.B. 1992. 'Remembering personal circumstances: a functional analysis', in E. Winograd and U. Neisser (eds) *Affect And Accuracy in Recall: Studies of 'Flashbulb Memories'*. Cambridge: Cambridge University Press, 236–64.

Pinch, T.J. and Clark, C. 1986. 'The hard sell: "patter merchanting" and the strategic (re)production and local management of economic reasoning in the sales routines of market pitchers', *Sociology*, 20(2): 169–91.

Pomerantz, A. 1984. 'Agreeing and disagreeing with assessments: some features of preferred/dispreferred turn-shapes', in J.M. Atkinson and J. Heritage (eds) *Structures of Social Action: Studies in Conversation Analysis*. Cambridge: Cambridge University Press, 79–112.

Pomerantz, A.M. 1986. 'Extreme case formulations: a way of legitimizing claims', in G. Button, P. Drew and J. Heritage (eds) *Human Studies*, 9 (Special Issue on Interaction and Language Use), 219–29.

Pomerantz, A. 2005. 'Studying understanding and misunderstanding: are cognitive and interactional approaches complementary?', in H. te Molder and J. Potter (eds) *Talk and Cognition: Discourse, Mind and Social Interaction*. Cambridge: Cambridge University Press, 93–113.

Potter, J. 1984. 'Testability, flexibility: Kuhnian values in scientists' discourse concerning theory choice', *Philosophy of the Social Sciences*, 14: 303–30.

Potter, J. 1996a. *Representing Reality*. London: Sage.

Potter, J. 1996b. 'Discourse analysis and constructionist approaches: theoretical background', in J.T.E. Richardson (ed.) *Handbook of Qualitative Research Methods for Psychology and the Social Sciences*. Hove: The British Psychological Society Books, 125–40.

Potter, J. 1997. 'Discourse analysis as a way of analysing naturally occurring talk', in D. Silverman (ed.) *Qualitative Analysis: Issues of Theory and Method*. London: Sage, 144–60.

Potter, J. 2000. 'Post-cognitive psychology', *Theory and Psychology*, 10(1): 31–7.

Potter, J. 2003a. 'Discursive psychology: between method and paradigm', *Discourse and Society*, 14(6): 783–94.

Potter, J. 2003b. 'Practical scepticism', *Discourse and Society*, 14(6): 799–801.

Potter, J. 2003c. 'Discourse analysis and discursive psychology', in P.M. Camic, J.E. Rhodes and L. Yardley (eds) *Qualitative Research in Psychology: Expanding Perspectives in Methodology and Design*. Washington, DC: American Psychological Association, 73–94.

Potter, J. 2004. 'Discourse analysis', in M. Hardy and A. Bryman (eds) *Handbook of Data Analysis*. London: Sage, 607–24.

Potter, J. and Edwards, D. 1990. 'Nigel Lawson's tent: discourse analysis, attribution theory and the social psychology of fact', *European Journal of Psychology*, 20: 405–24.

Potter, J. and Edwards, D. 2003. 'Rethinking cognition: on Coulter on discourse and mind', *Human Studies*, 26: 165–81.

Potter, J. and Hepburn, A. 2003. '"I'm a bit concerned": early actions and psychological constructions in a child protection helpline', *Research on Language and Social Interaction*, 36(3): 197–240.

Potter, J. and McKinley, A. 1989. 'Discourse – philosophy – reflexivity: comment on Halfpenny', *Social Studies of Science*, 19: 137–45.

Potter, J. and Mulkay, M. 1985. 'Scientists' interview talk: interviews as a technique for revealing participants' interpretative practices', in M. Brenner, J. Brown and D. Canter (eds) *The Research Interview: Uses and Approaches*. London: Academic Press, 247–69.

Potter, J. and Reicher, S. 1987. 'Discourses of community and conflict: the organization of social categories in accounts of a "riot"', *British Journal of Social Psychology*, 26: 25–40.

Potter, J. and Wetherell, M. 1987. *Discourse and Social Psychology: Beyond Attitudes and Behaviour*. London: Sage.

Potter, J. and Wetherell, M. 1995. 'Discourse analysis', in J.S. Smith, R. Harré and L. Van Langenhove (eds) *Rethinking Methods in Psychology*. London and Thousand Oaks, CA: Sage, 80–92.

Potter, J., Wetherell, M., Gill, R. and Edwards, D. 1990. 'Discourse: noun, verb or social practice?', *Philosophical Psychology*, 3(2): 205–17.

Psathas, G. 1990. *Interaction Competence*. Washington, DC: University Press of America.

Psathas, G. 1995. *Conversation Analysis: The Study of Talk-in-Interaction*. London: Sage.

Radin, D. 1997. *The Conscious Universe: The Scientific Truth of Psychic Phenomena*. New York: HarperEdge.

Rhine, J.B. 1948. 'The value of reports of spontaneous psi phenomena', *Journal of Parapsychology*, 12: 231–5.

Rhine, L.E. 1981. *The Invisible Picture: A Study of Psychic Experiences*. Jefferson, NC: McFarland.

Richardson, J.T.E. (ed.) 1996. *Handbook of Qualitative Research Methods for Psychology and the Social Sciences*. Leicester: British Psychological Society.

Rose, N. 1989. *Governing the Soul: The Shaping of the Private Self*. London: Routledge.

Sacks, H. 1979. 'Hotrodder: a revolutionary category', in G. Psathas (ed.) *Everyday Language: Studies In Ethnomethodology*. New York: Irvington, 7–14. (Edited by G. Jefferson from unpublished lectures: Spring 1966, lecture 18.)

Sacks, H. 1984a. 'Notes on methodology', in J.M. Atkinson and J. Heritage (eds) *Structures of Social Action: Studies in Conversation Analysis*. Cambridge: Cambridge University Press, 21–7. (Edited by G. Jefferson from unpublished lectures.)

Sacks, H. 1984b. 'On doing "Being Ordinary"', in J.M. Atkinson and J. Heritage (eds) *Structures of Social Action: Studies in Conversation Analysis*. Cambridge: Cambridge University Press, 413–29. (Edited by G. Jefferson from unpublished lectures.)

Sacks, H. 1992. *Lectures on Conversation*, Volumes I and II, edited by G. Jefferson and E.A. Schegloff, Oxford and Cambridge, MA: Basil Blackwell.

Sacks, H. and Schegloff, E.A. 1979. 'Two preferences in the organisation of reference to persons in conversation and their interaction', in G. Psathas (ed.) *Everyday Language: Studies in Ethnomethodology*. Hillsdale, NJ: Erlbaum, 15–21.

Sacks, H., Schegloff, E.A. and Jefferson, G. 1974. 'A simplest systematics for the organisation of turn-taking for conversation', *Language*, 50: 696–735.

Schegloff, E.A. 1972a. 'Sequencing in conversational openings', in J.J. Gumperz and D. Hymes (eds) *Directions in Sociolinguistics: the Ethnography of Communication*. New York: Holt, Rinehart and Winston, 346–380. (Originally published in *American Anthropologist*, Vol. 70, no. 6, 1968.)

Schegloff, E.A. 1972b. 'Notes on a conversational practice: formulating place', in D. Sudnow (ed.) *Studies in Social Interaction*. New York: Free Press, 75–119.

Schegloff, E.A. 1980. 'Preliminaries to preliminaries: "Can I ask you a question?"', *Sociological Inquiry*, 50: 104–52.

Schegloff, E.A. 1981. 'Discourse as an interactional achievement: some uses of "uh huh" and other things that come between sentences', in D. Tannen (ed.) *Analysing Discourse: Georgetown University Roundtable on Languages and Linguistics*. Washington, DC: Georgetown University Press, 71–93.

Schegloff, E.A. 1984. 'On some questions and ambiguities in conversation', in J.M. Atkinson and J. Heritage (eds) *Structures of Social Action: Studies in Conversation Analysis*. Cambridge: Cambridge University Press, 28–52.

Schegloff, E.A. 1986. 'The routine as achievement', *Human Studies*, 9: 111–52.

Schegloff, E.A. 1987a. 'Recycled turn beginnings: a precise repair mechanism in conversation's turn-taking organisation', in G. Button and J.R.E. Lee (eds) *Talk and Social Organisation*. Clevedon: Multilingual Matters, 70–85.

Schegloff, E.A. 1987b. 'Between micro and macro: contexts and other connections', in J.C. Alexander, B. Giesen, R. Munch and N.J. Smelser (eds) *The Micro–Macro Link*. Berkeley, CA: University of California Press, 207–36.

Schegloff, E.A. 1988a. 'Goffman and the analysis of conversation', in P. Drew and A.J. Wootton (eds) *Erving Goffman: Exploring the Interaction Order*. Cambridge: Polity Press, 89–135.

Schegloff, E.A. 1988b. 'Presequences and indirection: applying speech act theory to ordinary conversation', *Journal of Pragmatics*, 12: 55–62.

Schegloff, E.A. 1988/9. 'From interview to confrontation: observations on the Bush/Rather encounter', *Research on Language and Social Interaction*, 22: 215–40.

Schegloff, E.A. 1989. 'Reflection on language, development and the interactional character of talk-in-interaction', in M. Bornstein and J.S. Bruner (eds) *Interaction in Human Development*. Hillside, NJ: Erlbaum.

Schegloff, E.A. 1991. 'Reflections on talk and social structure', in D. Boden and D.H. Zimmerman (eds) *Talk and Social Structure: Studies in Ethnomethodology and Conversation Analysis*. Cambridge: Polity Press, 44–70.

Schegloff, E.A. 1992a. 'Introduction to Volume 1', in H. Sacks (1992) *Lectures on Conversation*, Volumes I and II, edited by G. Jefferson and E.A. Schegloff, Oxford and Cambridge, MA: Basil Blackwell, ix–xii.

Schegloff, E.A. 1992b. 'Repair after next turn: the last structurally provided defense of intersubjectivity in conversation', *American Journal of Sociology*, 97, 1295–1345.

Schegloff, E.A. 1992c. 'To Searle on conversation', in H. Parret and J. Verschueren (eds) *(On) Searle on Conversation*. Amsterdam: John Benjamins, 113–28.

Schegloff, E.A. 1997. 'Whose text? Whose context?', *Discourse and Society*, 8: 165–87.

Schegloff, E.A. 1998. 'Reply to Wetherell', *Discourse and Society*, 9(3): 457–60.

Schegloff, E.A. 1999a. '"Schegloff's texts" as "Billig's data": a critical reply', *Discourse and Society*, 10(4): 558–72.

Schegloff, E.A. 1999b. 'Naivete vs sophistication or discipline vs self indulgence', *Discourse and Society*, 10(4): 577–82.

Schegloff, E.A. and Sacks, H. 1973. 'Opening up closings', *Semiotica*, 7: 289–327.

Schegloff, E.A., Jefferson, G. and Sacks, H. 1977. 'The preference for self-correction in the organisation of repair in conversation', *Language*, 53: 361–82.

Schiffrin, D. 1994. *Approaches to Discourse*. Oxford and Cambridge, MA: Blackwell.

Searle, J. 1986. 'Introductory essay: notes on conversation', in D. Ellis and W. Donohue (eds) *Contemporary Issues in Language and Discourse Processes*. Hillsdale, NJ: Erlbaum, 7–19.

Silverman, D. 1998. *Harvey Sacks: Social Science and Conversation Analysis*. Oxford: Polity Press.

Simons, H.W. 1989. 'Introduction', in W.H. Simons (ed.) *Rhetoric in the Human Sciences*. London and Newbury Park, CA: Sage, 1–9.

Sklair, L. 1973. *Organized Knowledge: Sociological View of Science and Technology*. St. Albans: Hart-Davis MacGibbon.

Smith, D.E. 1978. '"K is mentally ill": the anatomy of a factual account', *Sociology*, 12: 23–53.

Smith, J.A. (ed.) 2003. *Qualitative Methods: A Practical Guide to Research Methods*. London and Thousand Oaks, CA: Sage.

Smith, J.A. and Osborn, M. 2003. 'Interpretative phenomenological analysis', in J.A. Smith (ed.) *Qualitative Methods: A Practical Guide to Research Methods*. London and Thousand Oaks, CA: Sage, 51–80.

Smith, J.A., Harré, R. and Van Langenhove, L. (eds) 1995a. *Rethinking Methods in Psychology*. London and Thousand Oaks, CA: Sage.

Smith, J.A., Harré, R. and Van Langenhove, L. (eds) 1995b. *Rethinking Psychology*. London and Thousand Oaks, CA: Sage.

Soyland, A.J. 1994. *Psychology As Metaphor*. London and Thousand Oaks, CA: Sage.

Speer, S. 2002. 'What can conversation analysis contribute to feminist methodology? Putting reflexivity into practice', *Discourse and Society*, 13: 783–803.

Speer, S. and Potter, J. 2000. 'The management of heterosexist talk: conversational resources and prejudiced claims', *Discourse and Society*, 11: 543–72.

Spender, D. 1980. *Man Made Language*. London: Routledge and Kegan Paul.

Stenner, P. 1993. 'Discoursing jealousy', in E. Burman and I. Parker (eds) *Discourse Analytic Research: Repertoires and Readings of Texts in Action*. London: Routledge, 114–32.

Stokoe, E.H. 2000. 'Towards a conversation analytic approach to gender and discourse', *Feminism and Psychology*, 10(4): 552–63.

Stokoe, E.H. and Smithson, J. 2001. 'Making gender relevant: conversation analysis and gender categories, in interaction', *Discourse and Society*, 12(2):243–69.

Stokoe, E.H. and Smithson, J. 2002. 'Gender and sexuality in talk-in-interaction: considering conversation analytic perspectives', in P. McIlvenny (ed.) *Talking Gender and Sexuality*. Amsterdam and Philadelphia: John Benjamins, 79–110.

Suchman, L. and Jordan, B. 1990. 'Interactional troubles in face-to-face survey interviews', *Journal of the American Statistical Association*, 85: 232–41.

Tainio, L. 2003. '"When shall we go for a ride?" A case of the sexual harassment of a young girl', *Discourse and Society*, 14: 173–90.

Tannen, D. 1991. *You Just Don't Understand: Women and Men in Conversation*. London: Virago.

Taylor, T. and Cameron, D. 1987. *Analysing Conversation: Rules and Units in the Structure of Talk*. Oxford: Pergamon Press.

Te Molder, H. and Potter, J. 2005. *Talk and Cognition: Discourse, Mind and Social Interaction*. Cambridge: Cambridge University Press.

Ten Have, P. 1999. *Doing Conversation Analysis: A Practical Guide*. London and Thousand Oaks, CA: Sage.

Tenney, Y.J. 1989. 'Predicting conversational reports of a personal event', *Cognitive Science*, 13: 213–33.

Thorne, B., Kramarae, C. and Henley, N. 1983. 'Language, gender and society: opening a second decade of research', in B. Thorne, C. Kramarae and N. Henley (eds) *Language, Gender and Society*. Rowley, MA: Newbury, 7–24.

Tracy, K. (ed.) 1991. *Understanding Face-to-Face Interaction: Linking Goals and Discourse*. Hillsdale, NJ: Lawrence Erlbaum.

Van Dijk, T.A. 1991. *Racism and the Press*. London: Routledge.

Van Dijk, T.A. 1993. 'Principles of critical discourse analysis', *Discourse and Society*, 4: 249–283.

Van Dijk, T.A. 1996. 'Editorial: discourse, cognition and society', *Discourse and Society*, 7: 5–6.

Van Dijk, T.A. 2001. 'Multidisciplinary CDA: a plea for diversity', in R. Wodak and M. Meyer (eds) *Methods of Critical Discourse Analysis*. London and Thousand Oaks, CA: Sage, 95–120.

Waismann, F. 1965. *The Principles of Linguistic Philosophy*. London: Macmillan. (Edited by R. Harré.)

Watson, G. and Seiler, R.M. (eds) 1992. *Text in Context: Contributions to Ethnomethodology*. Newbury Park, CA: Sage.

West, C. 1995. 'Women's competence in conversation', *Discourse and Society*, 6(1): 107–31.

West, C. and Zimmerman, D.H. 1983. 'Small insults: a study of interruptions in cross-sex conversations between unacquainted persons', in B. Thorne, C. Kramarae and N. Henley (eds) *Language, Gender and Society*. Rowley, MA: Newbury, 103–17.

West, D.J. 1948. 'The investigation of spontaneous cases', *Proceedings of the Society for Psychical Research*, 48: 264–300.

Wetherell, M. 1983. 'Socio-psychological and literary accounts of femininity', in P. Stringer (ed.) *Confronting Social Issues*, Volume 2. London: Academic Press.

Wetherell, M. 1986. 'Linguistic repertoires and literary criticism: new directions for a social psychology of gender', in S. Wilkinson (ed.) *Feminist Social Psychology*. Milton Keynes: Open University Press.

Wetherell, M. 1998. 'Positioning and interpretative repertoires: conversation analysis and post-structuralism in dialogue', *Discourse and Society*, 9(3): 387–412.

Wetherell, M. and Potter, J. 1988. 'Discourse analysis and the identification of interpretative repertoires', in C. Antaki (ed.) *Analysing Everyday Explanation: A Casebook of Methods*. London: Sage.

Wetherell, M. and Potter, J. 1992. *Mapping the Language of Racism: Discourse and the Legitimization of Exploitation*. Hemel Hempstead: Harvester Wheatsheaf.

Wetherell, M., Stiven, H. and Potter, J. 1987. 'Unequal egalitarianism: a preliminary study of discourse concerning gender and employment opportunities', *British Journal of Social Psychology*, 26: 59–71.

Wetherell, M., Taylor, S. and Yates, S. 2001a. *Discourse Theory and Practice: A Reader.* London and Thousand Oaks, CA: Sage.

Wetherell, M., Taylor, S. and Yates, S. 2001b. *Discourse As Data: A Guide For Analysis.* London and Thousand Oaks, CA: Sage.

Whalen, M.R. and Zimmerman, D.H. 1987. 'Sequential and institutional contexts in calls for help', *Social Psychology Quarterly*, 50: 172–85.

Whalen, J., Zimmerman, D. and Whalen, M.R. 1988. 'When words fail: a single case analysis', *Social Problems*, 35(4): 333–62.

White, R.A. 1985. 'The spontaneous, the imaginal, and psi: foundations for a depth psychology', in R.A. White and J. Solfvin (eds) *Research in Parapsychology 1984.* Metchuen, NJ: Scarecrow Press, 166–90.

White, R.A. 1990. 'An experience-centred approach to parapsychology', *Exceptional Human Experience*, 8: 7–36.

Widdicombe, S. 1993. 'Autobiography and change: rhetoric and authenticity of "gothic" style', in E. Burman and I. Parker (eds) *Discourse Analytic Research: Repertoires and Readings of Texts in Action.* London: Routledge.

Widdicombe, S. 1995. 'Identity, politics and talk: a case for the mundane and the every-day', in S. Wilkinson and C. Kitzinger (eds) *Feminism and Discourse: Psychological Perspectives.* London and Thousand Oaks, CA: Sage, 106–27.

Widdicombe, S. and Wooffitt, R. 1990. '"Being" versus "doing" punk: on achieving authenticity as a member', *Journal of Language and Social Psychology*, 9: 257–77.

Widdicombe, S. and Wooffitt, R. 1995. *The Language of Youth Subcultures: Social Identity in Action.* Hemel Hempstead: Harvester Wheatsheaf.

Wiggins, S. 2001. 'Construction and action in food evaluation: conversational data', *Journal of Language and Social Psychology*, 20(4): 445–63.

Wiggins, S. 2002. 'Talking with your mouth full: gustatory *Mmms* and the embodiment of pleasure', *Research on Language and Social Interaction*, 35(3): 311–36.

Wiggins, S., Potter, J. and Wildsmith, A. 2001. 'Eating your words: discursive psychology and the reconstruction of eating practices', *Journal of Health Psychology*, 6(1): 5–15.

Wilkinson, S. and Kitzinger, K. (eds) 1995. *Feminism and Discourse: Psychological Perspectives.* London and Thousand Oak, CA: Sage.

Willig, C. (ed.) 1999. *Applied Discourse Analysis: Social and Psychological Interventions.* Buckingham: Open University Press.

Willig, C. 2001a. 'Foucauldian discourse analysis', in *Introducing Qualitative Research in Psychology.* Buckingham and Philadelphia: Open University Press, 106–24.

Willig, C. 2001b. 'Discursive psychology', in *Introducing Qualitative Research in Psychology.* Buckingham and Philadelphia: Open University Press, 87–105.

Wilson, T.P., Wiemann, J.M. and Zimmerman, D.H. 1984. 'Models of conversational turn taking', *Journal of Language and Social Psychology*, 3(3): 159–83.

Wise, S. and Stanley, L. 1987. *Georgie Porgie: Sexual Harassment in Everyday Life.* London: Pandora.

Wittgenstein, L. 1953. *Philosophical Investigations.* Oxford: Basil Blackwell. (Edited by G. Anscombe.)

Wodak, R. 1997. 'Introduction: some important issues in the research on gender and discourse', in R. Wodak (ed.) *Gender and Discourse.* London and Thousand Oaks, CA: Sage, 1–20.

Wodak, R. 2001a. 'What CDA is about – a summary of its history, important concepts and development', in R. Wodak and M. Meyer (eds) *Methods of Critical Discourse Analysis.* London and Thousand Oaks, CA: Sage, 1–13.

Wodak, R. 2001b. 'The discourse-historical approach', in R. Wodak and M. Meyer (eds) *Methods of Critical Discourse Analysis.* London and Thousand Oaks, CA: Sage, 63–94.

Wodak, R. and Meyer, M. (eds) 2001. *Methods of Critical Discourse Analysis*. London and Thousand Oaks, CA: Sage.

Wood, L.A. and Kroger, R.O. 2000. *Doing Discourse Analysis: Methods for Studying Action in Talk and Texts*. Thousand Oaks, CA: Sage.

Wooffitt, R. 1988. 'On the analysis of accounts of paranormal phenomena', *Journal of the Society for Psychical Research*, 55: 139–49.

Wooffitt, R. 1992. *Telling Tales of the Unexpected: the Organisation of Factual Discourse*. Hemel Hempstead: Harvester Wheatsheaf.

Wooffitt, R. 1993. 'Analysing accounts of paranormal experiences', *Proceedings of the 36th Annual Convention of the Parapsychological Association*. New York: The Parapsychological Association, 317–33.

Wooffitt, R. 2000. 'Some properties of the interactional organisation of displays of paranormal cognition in psychic-sitter interaction', *Sociology*, 43(3): 457–79.

Wooffitt, R. 2001a. 'Raising the dead: reported speech in medium–sitter interaction', *Discourse Studies*, 3(3): 351–74.

Wooffitt, R. 2001b. 'A socially organised basis for displays of cognition: procedural orientation to evidential turns in psychic–sitter interaction', *British Journal of Social Psychology*, 40(4): 545–63.

Wooffitt, R. 2003. 'Conversation analysis and parapsychology: experimenter–subject interaction in ganzfeld experiments', *Journal of Parapsychology*, 67(2): 299–324.

Wooffitt, R. (forthcoming). 'Language and the study of parapsychological phenomena: sociology, communication and anomalous experiences' to appear in L. Storm and M. Thalbourne (eds) *Parapsychology in the 21st Century: The Future of Psychical Research*. Hatfield: University of Hertfordshire Press.

Wooffitt, R. and Widdicombe, S. (forthcoming). 'Interaction in interviews', in P. Drew and G. Raymond (eds) *Talking Subjects*. Cambridge: Cambridge University Press.

Wooffitt, R., Fraser, N., Gilbert, G.N. and McGlashan, S. 1997. *Humans, Computers and Wizards: Conversation Analysis and Human (Simulated) Computer Interaction*. London: Routledge.

Woolgar, S. 1980. 'Discovery, logic and sequence in a text', in K.D. Knorr, R. Krohn and R. Whitley (eds) *The Social Process of Scientific Investigation*. Dordrecht: Reidel, 239–68.

Woolgar, S. 1988. *Science: The Very Idea*. London: Tavistock.

Yamané, D. 2000. 'Narrative and religious experience', *Sociology of Religion*, 61: 171–90.

Zimmerman, D.H. and Boden, D. 1991. 'Structure-in-action: an introduction', in D. Boden and D.H. Zimmerman (eds) *Talk and Social Structure: Studies in Ethnomethodology and Conversation Analysis*. Cambridge: Polity Press, 3–21.

Zimmerman, D.H. and Pollner, M. 1970. 'The everyday world as phenomenon', in J. Douglas (ed.) *Understanding Everyday Life: Towards the Reconstruction of Sociological Knowledge*. Chicago, IL: Aldine, 80–103.

Zingrone, N.L. 2002. 'Controversy and the problems of parapsychology', *Journal of Parapsychology*, 66: 3–30.

Zusne, L. and Jones, W.H. 1989. *Anomalistic Psychology: a Study of Magical Thinking* (2nd edition). Hillsdale, NJ: Lawrence Erlbaum.

Web site

EMCA News (hosted by Paul ten Have) http://www.paultenhave.nl

Index